Philosophy 9/11

Philosophy 9/11

Thinking about the War on Terrorism

Edited by
TIMOTHY SHANAHAN

OPEN COURT
Chicago and LaSalle, Illinois

To order books from Open Court, call toll-free 1-800-815-2280, or visit our website at www.opencourtbooks.com.

Open Court Publishing Company is a division of Carus Publishing Company.

Library of Congress Cataloging-in-Publication Data

Philosophy 9/11 : thinking about the war on terrorism / edited by Timothy Shanahan.
     p. cm.
    Revisions of papers presented at a conference held at Loyola Marymount University, Sept. 11-13, 2003.
    Includes bibliographical references and index.
    ISBN-13: 978-0-8126-9582-3 (isbn 13 - trade pbk. : alk. paper)
    ISBN-10: 0-8126-9582-8 (isbn 10 - trade pbk. : alk. paper)
    1. Terrorism—Philosophy—Congresses. 2. War on Terrorism, 2001–Moral and ethical aspects—Congresses. I. Shanahan, Timothy, 1960-
    HV6431.P53 2005
    363.32'01—dc22

                       2005004947

To Robert H. Taylor, S.J.

Contents

Just War Theory and the War on Terrorism

Preemptive Strikes and Targeted Killing

Terrorists: Enemy Combatants or Criminals?

Counterterrorism: Torture

Acknowledgments

Completion of a project like this requires the assistance of many people and organizations. Earlier versions of the essays in this volume were presented at a conference on "Understanding Terrorism: Philosophical Issues" at Loyola Marymount University, September 11–13, 2003. I would like to thank the Bellarmine College of Liberal Arts and the Department of Philosophy at LMU for the Robert H. Taylor, S.J. Chair in Philosophy for 2002–2004, which made organization of the conference possible. Jason Baehr, Santiago Sia, Jennifer Lobo, and Zane Yi assisted in the running of the conference. A special thanks is due to Alexis Dolan, without whom the conference would not have been as successful as it was. Enthusiastic audiences at the conference helped to improve papers that were presented. I would like to thank the *International Journal of Applied Philosophy*, *Human Rights Review*, and *Theoretical Inquiries in Law*, respectively, for permission to include in this volume the essays by Fritz Allhoff, Simon Keller, and Daniel Statman. Thanks to Kathleen League for constructing the index. Finally, I would like to thank the editors at Open Court—David Ramsay Steele, Kerri Mommer, and Cindy Pineo—for their belief in and support for this project.

Introduction

On September 11, 2001, America and the world were shocked by the terrorist attacks in New York City and Washington, D.C. Terrorism was hardly new on the world stage, of course. From the Middle East, to Chechnya, to Africa, to Northern Ireland, terrorist acts have been a recurring feature of the modern world. America itself had firsthand experience of terrorism on several previous occasions—the bombing of the World Trade Center in 1993, the destruction of the Alfred P. Murrah Federal Building in Oklahoma City in 1995, and the attack on the U.S.S. Cole in 2000, to name the best known. Nonetheless, nothing on the scale of the attacks of 9/11 had been seen before. To many they seemed to herald a fundamental turning point. Even to those living outside of the cities directly attacked, the world seemed different after 9/11. The problem of terrorism suddenly assumed a new importance. For many, especially in the United States, responding to the threat of terrorism became the most urgent national imperative.

Enormous amounts of thought, energy, and money have been devoted to this task. Politicians, police, the military, and various governmental agencies swung into action. A new federal department (and along with it a new commercial sector of the economy) devoted to "Homeland Security" came into being. The President of the United States declared a "war on terrorism," and launched two military campaigns, ostensibly in order to disrupt bases of terrorist power (although critics claimed to detect other, less noble, motivations).[1]

In all this, there has been no shortage of action. Yet it is a truism that action follows from belief, and that beliefs are based on, and composed of, ideas. At the most fundamental level, the war on terrorism,

---

[1] The phrase "war on terrorism" (or "war on terror") appears here in quotation marks, both because this is the phrase used by the current U.S. administration to describe its ongoing efforts to combat terrorism, and because, as several of the contributions to this volume point out, the sense in which there *can* be a war on "terrorism," and the extent to which ongoing efforts to combat terrorist activities constitute such a war, are both problematic.

no less than terrorism itself, is a consequence of the *ideas* people embrace—ethical and religious ideas about justice and injustice, right and wrong, the holy and the profane, as well ideas about the consequences of actions—of flying planes into buildings, of martyrdom for one's god, of sending people and machines halfway around the world in order to depose regimes viewed as hostile. In every such instance, ideas drive action. Ideas matter. Ideas always matter.

On September 11–13, 2003, scholars met at Loyola Marymount University in Los Angeles to identify, discuss, and debate some of the central ideas connected with the war on terrorism. This book contains a selection of the papers presented at this conference, revised in light of the lively discussions that ensued over the three days of the meeting. Its aim is to assist the reader in rethinking some of her ideas about the war on terrorism, and to perhaps even provide her with a few new ideas that will deepen her grasp of this important issue.

At the most basic level, an understanding and evaluation of the "war on terrorism" presupposes an adequate understanding of what, exactly, constitutes terrorism itself. The first two essays address this primary issue. In "What Is Distinctive about Terrorism, and What Are the Philosophical Implications?" Michael Baur tackles the difficult problem of defining "terrorism" in a way that is neither too inclusive (i.e., including activities that few people would consider terroristic), nor too exclusive (i.e., excluding activities that most people would consider terroristic). After examining some of the difficulties of defining terrorism, and explaining why some of the most common "ordinary" understandings of terrorism are inadequate, he offers a working definition of terrorism that he believes overcomes these difficulties. According to Baur, terrorism involves the use of "systematically unsystematic" violence (whether directed at combatants or noncombatants), and suggests that recognizing the random or indiscriminate character of terroristic violence points us in the direction of seeing what is distinctively wrong with it. The fundamental problem, he argues, is that terrorism (unlike conventional war) is not committed to any rules of armed conflict or any principles that would make possible the eventual containment or termination of the violence it entails. This, in turn, puts modern, liberal society in a difficult bind: terrorism challenges civil society to defend itself; but since the modern terrorist cannot be deterred by more traditional (e.g., police or military) actions, civil society's war on terror must at times resort to invasions of privacy and to excessive force that cause intimidation and undermine trust—just what the terrorist also intends. The challenge, therefore, is to devise ways of responding to terrorism that do not themselves assist terrorists in their agendas.

According to a widespread perception, the terrorist attacks of September 11, 2001 were the most striking instances of what was essentially a "new" form of terrorism that emerged in the 1990s. Whereas there had been no dearth of terrorist attacks before then, there nonetheless seemed to be something fundamentally different about the sorts of terrorist attacks that were becoming more prevalent, especially the fanaticism of the terrorists and their willingness to use (if only they could acquire them) weapons of mass destruction. Some experts dubbed this phenomenon the "new terrorism." In "A Taxonomy of Terrorism," Liam Harte examines the concept of the "new terrorism" as exemplified in the work of Walter Laqueur. He argues that this concept is deeply flawed. In place of Laqueur's distinction between "traditional" and "new" terrorism, Harte proposes a more systematic "taxonomy of terrorism" which includes a distinction between "mythic" and "pro- or antimodern" terrorist activity. Such a distinction, he argues, allows us to usefully reduce the overwhelming complexity of the phenomena of terrorism without drawing an unnecessary, mystificatory distinction between new and traditional terrorism, enables us to better identify genuinely important differences in motivation between terrorists without making erroneous historical generalizations, and assists us in making better decisions regarding our responses to terrorism of all kinds.

Having examined "terrorism" itself in depth, the essays then turn to an analysis of the war on terror(ism). Shortly after the attacks of September 11, 2001, President George W. Bush declared a war on terror. In his essay "On What Is the War on Terror?" Simon Keller asks two questions: (1) Should there be a war on terror (or terrorism?); and (2) Can there even be such a thing as a war on terror (or terrorism)? In response to the first question, he argues that terrorism is not something on which there should be a war, because to proclaim a war on terrorism is to take an evaluative stance with regard to terrorism in all its forms, even though terrorism is not, in all its forms, something that ought to be opposed. When terrorism is employed in the service of a sufficiently worthy cause, and when other options are not available, terrorism can be justified for much the same reasons that all-out war can be justified. Additionally, in declaring a war on terrorism, we are committing ourselves to opposing terrorism wherever it is found, which in turn exposes us to the danger of taking a particular group to be a terrorist group on the mere grounds that the group's enemies have successfully painted it as terrorist. In the end, Keller argues, the "war on terror(ism)" is not really a war on terror(ism) at all. At best it is a war on particular terrorists or terrorist organizations (e.g., Al Qaeda). To describe ourselves as being engaged in a "war on terrorism" is to expose ourselves to various political dangers and to commit to a dubious claim.

Phillip McReynolds takes a very different approach to understanding terrorism and our responses to it. In "Terrorism as a Technological Concept: How Low versus High Technology Defines Terrorism and Dictates Our Responses," he makes two arguments. First, he argues that the concept of terrorism as it is typically understood is a technological way of defining a problem that is not really about technology; by conceptualizing terrorism in this way, we limit ourselves to responses that are almost exclusively technological. The so-called war on terror, for instance, is based almost exclusively on high-tech approaches to the problem (e.g., satellite imagery, laser-guided bombs, and computer databases) to the relative neglect of social, economic, and political responses. This is problematic, because a technological definition of the problem dictates a high-tech response, regardless of its effectiveness. Second, he argues that the almost exclusive focus on high-tech responses to terrorism is the result of the modalities of technology and terror in the context of an ideology of progress. We choose high-tech means to reinforce our sense of civility and pacifism and to distance ourselves from the brutal low-tech approaches of the terrorists. However, given that the war on terror is an ongoing campaign with no discrete end, a reliance on high-tech solutions wedded to an ideology of progress does not present a viable long-term strategy against low-tech aggressors. In the end, McReynolds argues, there is no technological fix to the problem of terrorism. But understanding the sources of our propensity to prefer high-tech solutions can help us to avoid costly, dangerous, and ineffectual responses and pave the way toward a more mature understanding of and response to terrorism.

The essays just discussed focus primarily on conceptual issues involved in thinking clearly about terrorism and the war on terrorism. But they also touch in passing on the deep and vexing *moral* issues involved in terrorism and our responses to it. One sort of moral issue, in particular, seems unavoidable. If terrorism is wrong, then it is wrong regardless of who practices it. And yet a number of "just" wars fought during the twentieth century have employed terror tactics to attain military and political objectives. This gives rise to a seemingly simple question whose answer is in fact anything but simple: "What is the difference between a (just) war and terrorism?" In "Defusing Fear: A Critical Response to the War on Terrorism," Andrew Fiala argues that, because the so-called war on terrorism is not a war between peoples or states, it should be understood not as a war at all, but instead as a law-enforcement concern. Consequently, it should be conducted within the limits established for law-enforcement actions, including restraint of force, due process, and respect for conventions about the burden of proof. If we are not to become terrorists ourselves, we must demand that the "war on terrorism" be conducted in a just manner, that terrorists be tried in open courts so that the truth might come out, and that our leaders honestly apprise us of the real risks of terrorism so that we are not seduced by fear to demand more than justice requires. Ultimately, we must be careful as we discuss the justification of violence, terrorism, and war not to be misled by the rhetoric and ideology that make these seem to be good things. At best, violence is a regrettable means of last resort. When we must use violence, this is a tragedy, not a triumph. In order to support these points, Fiala provides a critique of the post-9/11 rhetoric that has contributed to a widespread state of anxiety and panic. He argues that things are not as dire as many of us fear. By defusing fear, he suggests, we can begin to think more rationally about terrorism, war, and justice.

In acts of physical violence, agents apply external force so as to suddenly and intensely damage or destroy persons or other entities. In a political context, such violence can take the form of terrorism and war. In "Physical Violence in Political Conflicts: Grounds for a Strong Presumption against Violence," Trudy Govier explores the common presumption that those who resort to physical violence as a response to conflict bear a burden of justification and are acting wrongly unless they can show otherwise. Govier argues that, although this presumption is used selectively and inconsistently by those who wish to condemn violence by others yet engage in it themselves, it is worth retaining nonetheless. A presumptive case against physical violence emerges logically from any ethic in which one grants rights to persons and value to their interests and resources in the world. Consequently, the burden of proof lies on those who would use physical violence to show why they are entitled to do so. If so, then the arguments they proffer had better be good. Often, they are not good, because physical violence is not always or even usually the only or the best response to political conflict. In the context of political struggles, any country that would use physical violence as a means to its own ends owes to the rest of humanity some account of it, showing that it is legitimate because these goals are, in fact, achievable by violent methods, and are not achievable in any other way. Govier concludes that when the arguments are put forth, they should be subjected to intense scrutiny. Given the destructive nature of physical violence, its alienation from the best human capacities and its self-perpetuating and morally corrosive nature, the burden of proof is squarely on those who would propose to use it.

Virtually everyone would agree that some wars can be just. But what makes a war a just one? "Just war theory" originated in the writings of St. Augustine in the fifth century, was developed further by St. Thomas Aquinas in the thirteenth century, and continues to function as a set of standards for judging the morality of initiating and prosecuting wars. A basic tenet of just war theory is that wars can be fought only between legitimate authorities, for instance, states, not between a state and some abstract entity such as "terror." Nevertheless, the U.S.-led "war on terror" has been conducted for the most part *as* a conventional war, and many people have simply accepted it as a bona fide war. Does it follow that we must scrap traditional just war theory in light of the nature of war in the twenty-first century? Or should we question the belief that the war on terror really is a war? In "Just War Theory, Legitimate Authority, and the 'War' on Terror," Lorraine Besser-Jones tackles these and related questions. She explores what just war theory might have to say about the war on terror, focusing specifically on the requirement that wars must be fought between states. She argues that, ultimately, the war on terror fails to satisfy the conditions for a just war. She concludes that the so-called war on terror is not, in fact, a war at all, and if conducted as a war, will inevitably entail a violation of state rights.

It almost goes without saying that those who engage in terrorist acts believe that they are morally justified in so doing. Their victims, and many others, of course, disagree. Likewise, those who respond with violence to terrorist acts believe that they are morally justified in doing so, whereas their targets believe otherwise. Where is the measure of morality to be located in such actions and reactions? Can terrorism ever be morally justified? Can the victims of terrorism legitimately or "justly" respond, and if so, how do we measure the "justness" of that response? In "Moral Justification for Violent Responses to Terrorism," Brett Kessler attempts to answer such questions through an investigation into what terrorism fundamentally is, a reexamination of the rules of war articulated in just war theory and international law, and a determination concerning how these rules might render a violent response to terrorism "just" or "unjust." After defining "terrorism" as a particular sort of violent activity, he argues that modern just war theory's criteria of *jus ad bellum* (the conditions under which going to war is just), if understood in a "strong" sense, render a war on terrorism unjust. Unfortunately, understood in this sense such criteria would also render *all* wars unjust, even those which most people would consider just. To avoid this conclusion, Kessler proposes a revision of just war theory that captures the insights of the strong version of the theory, yet does so in a way that allows us to use the theory to make distinctions between what seem to be cases of genuinely justified uses of force, on the one hand, and unjustified naked aggression, on the other. Applied to the war on terrorism, this revision of just war theory yields the conclusion that violent responses to terrorism can be morally justified so long as they satisfy the criteria of this revised version of the theory.

According to traditional just war theory, the only legitimate cause for going to war is a defensive one. When attacked, a country is morally entitled to respond with force. Initiating a war when one's country has not been attacked is strictly forbidden. In an era of international terrorism and weapons of mass destruction (WMD), however, such a restriction might seem antiquated, if not suicidal. Why wait to be attacked when the consequences of doing so might be catastrophic, and the means are available for preempting a terrorist attack before it can be launched? Many would argue, for example, that a preemptive strike against Al Qaeda prior to the 9/11 attacks would have been morally justified. But if so, what becomes of the traditional just war theory's prohibition against preemptive strikes? Should the criterion for the justness of going to war be shifted from "imminent attack" to "sufficient threat"? And how can "sufficient threat" ever be adequately established? How big of a threat is "sufficient" to warrant initiating a war? In "The Moral Consequences of Preemptive Strikes and Preventive War," Richard C. Anderson tackles such questions by examining recent just war perspectives regarding preemptive strikes and preventive war. Despite assertions by some that twenty-first-century terrorism requires both a new type of war as well as new criteria for determining our moral warrant to engage in military action, Anderson suggests that the moral constraints resulting from our adherence to the just war doctrine should be strengthened rather than relaxed. Only if the U.S. conducts the war on terrorism within the constraints of just war theory, he argues, can the U.S. maintain its legitimacy as the standard-bearer of international law.

Terrorism may be considered either as an act of war waged by nonstate actors, or as a particularly brutal form of crime. Understood as an act of war, terrorism seems to require a military response. Yet the standard means of waging war seem irrelevant in the war on terrorism. Tanks, jet fighters, submarines, and other pieces of conventional military hardware are useful when arrayed against countries deploying similar weaponry, but useless when the threat comes from hijackers carrying knives, or terrorists wearing explosive belts. Understood as a form of crime, terrorism seems to require a police response. Yet the standard means of fighting ordinary crime—arrests, arraignments, trials—seem virtually useless in the fight against terrorism, in which terrorists are able to disperse across the globe and blend into local populations that may support their causes. The failure of conventional military and police responses to terrorism suggests that a quite different tactic might be necessary. In "Targeted Killing," Daniel Statman argues that the threat of terrorism merits consideration of the intentional killing of specific individuals who are identified as important in a terrorist organization or to a terrorist cause. According to the thesis Statman advances, one cannot accept the legitimacy of the killing and destruction in conventional wars while denying the legitimacy of targeted killing in the war against terror. A principled rejection of targeted killing would weigh equally heavily against the tactics of conventional war, and would entail pacifism—a conclusion many opponents of targeted killing would reject. Statman concludes that targeted killing must be accepted as a morally legitimate tactic in the fight against terrorism.

The longstanding question (e.g., in the British treatment of IRA volunteers) of whether terrorists should be considered as *criminals* or as *enemy combatants* has gained renewed significance in light of the ongoing war on terrorism. If terrorists are criminals, then they should be captured, tried in a court of law, and (if found guilty) sentenced in a way befitting their crime. If terrorists are enemy combatants, then they should be treated as enemy soldiers in a time of war who may claim immunity from criminal prosecution (e.g., their killings are not crimes), and who should be treated with all the respect and special rights granted in accordance with the Geneva Conventions (including the right to repatriation at the cessation of hostilities). The distinction between criminals and enemy combatants is crucial for determining the just treatment of captured terrorists (and indeed, whether they should be captured alive at all). Unfortunately, in practice the distinction is not always clear, leading to inconsistent and capricious policies. In "Legitimate Combatancy, POW Status, and Terrorism," Michael W. Brough attempts to resolve this problem by articulating criteria that distinguish combatants from criminals. He argues that individuals take on legitimate combatancy as a function of membership in an organization with legitimate combatancy. He then proposes three criteria for an organization to have legitimate combatancy—military command structure, observance of the war convention, and representativeness—that together permit us to determine the legitimate combatancy of organizations. Unless an organization satisfies all three criteria, he concludes, then it is a group of criminals rather than soldiers, and its members should be treated as criminals rather than as enemy combatants.

One result of the U.S.-led war in Afghanistan was the detention of Taliban and Al Qaeda prisoners at the U.S. military base in Guantanamo Bay, Cuba. The Bush administration made it clear that they were not to be regarded as prisoners of war and were therefore not able to claim protections under the Geneva Conventions relating to Treatment of Prisoners of War. That decision was and remains controversial, leading many to reexamine international statutes concerning the rules of war and how they might apply in this case. In "Nothing New Under the Sun at Guantanamo Bay: Precedent and Prisoners of War," Pauline M. Kaurin takes a somewhat different approach by focusing on how the U.S. has dealt with similar situations in the past. She argues that an examination of U.S. precedent in relation to the treatment of prisoners in previous times of armed conflict (the American Revolutionary War, the Civil War, and the Vietnam conflict) raises serious questions about the Bush administration's position, because even in cases where there was no international statute or where the statute was unclear, it has been the consistent practice of the United States to accord prisoner of war status to such detainees. She maintains that precedent ought to be considered in relation to the status of the detainees at Guantanamo Bay, and that if it is to be rejected, then a clear and unequivocal rationale must be given as to why such a long tradition of according prisoner of war status no longer applies.

Consideration of the status of captured terrorists leads to the final issue to be considered in this volume. Successful major terrorist activities require the cooperation of a number of people and a good deal of advance planning. In the fight against terrorism, obtaining reliable "intelligence" about terrorist organizations and their plans is crucial. Unfortunately, terrorists are typically unwilling to voluntarily share such information with their enemies, even when they are being held in custody with the threat of indefinite imprisonment, or even death. Given the imperative to disrupt terrorist networks and to thwart planned terrorist actions, some counterterrorist strategists have recommended torture interrogation of captured terrorists as a means of obtaining information that can be used to save innumerable innocent lives. To others, however, the very suggestion that torture be used on anyone is proof of moral bankruptcy. Nonetheless, the critical questions remain: Is torture ever morally justified as a means of extracting information from terrorists being held in custody? If not, why not? If it is sometimes morally justified, is it possible to spell out the conditions under which (and only under which) torture may be used?

In "Terrorism and Torture," Fritz Allhoff argues that torture is morally justified in certain limited cases. Setting aside questions of the legality of torture in various political states (restrictions that are often breached in fact if not in principle), he explores the central moral issues involved, examining utilitarian, deontological, and rights-based perspectives on torture. Whereas on a utilitarian basis torture interrogation of terrorists might sometimes be morally justified, on a deontological moral theory it would never be. Turning to a rights-based ethical perspective, he argues that a strong case can be made for the claim that torture can be justified, even if it entails rights violations, so long as we find ourselves in a dilemma in which rights will end up being violated whether torture occurs or not. He then proposes four conditions, all of which must be satisfied, if torture is to be morally justified. Allhoff's conclusion, if correct, has obvious and important implications for policies concerning the treatment of captured terrorists and the fight against terrorism.

As Allhoff's essay demonstrates, one way to assess the morality of torture interrogation of captured terrorists is to apply basic moral theories (utilitarian, deontological, and rights-based perspectives) and to ask for each whether, or under what conditions, torture interrogation could be morally justified. Reflecting on Michael Walzer's "supreme emergency" test, William D. Casebeer in "Torture Interrogation of Terrorists: A Theory of Exceptions (With Notes, Cautions, and Warnings)" attempts to meld utilitarian and deontic moral approaches into a coherent system to formulate a "theory of exceptions" that tells us when it is morally permissible to engage in torture interrogation.

He is careful to note, however, there are vanishingly few circumstances wherein torture interrogation of terrorists would *actually* be justified. He focuses in particular on "virtue ethical" factors involved in the institutional use of torture interrogation, and cautions against the morally corrosive effects that the practice of sanctioned torture interrogation would have both on the character of individuals and on their institutions. He concludes that torture interrogation *is* permissible in tightly constrained circumstances, and therefore that it should not be ruled out in principle. Nonetheless, the use of such a tactic in the fight against terrorism is fraught with perils, and in practice it will be practically impossible to justify any particular decision to act on an exception to the prohibition of torture interrogation of terrorists.

The astute reader will note that the essays comprising this volume, summarized above, form a continuous philosophical investigation into fundamental issues concerning the war on terrorism. From the very conception of terrorism to the moral permissibility of torture interrogation of terrorists, deep philosophical issues abound. It is my hope that this volume will assist the reader in thinking more clearly, and more deeply, about these vitally important matters.

Timothy Shanahan
Los Angeles, California, USA

Conceptualizing Terrorism

| 1 |

What Is Distinctive about Terrorism, and What Are the Philosophical Implications?

MICHAEL BAUR

On September 11, 2001, Americans were painfully reminded of a truth that for years had been easy to overlook, namely, that terrorism can affect every person in the world—regardless of location, nationality, political conviction, or occupation—and that, in principle, nobody is beyond terrorism's reach. However, our renewed awareness of the ubiquity of the terrorist threat has been accompanied by wide disagreement and confusion about the moral status of terrorism and how terrorism ought to be confronted. Much of the disagreement and confusion, I contend, is rooted in an inadequate understanding of just what it is that constitutes terrorism. In this paper, I offer the beginnings of a response to the challenge of terrorism by providing an account of what terrorism is and of some of the philosophical issues involved.

My account is divided into two sections. In the first section I examine some of the difficulties involved in defining terrorism, and show that some of the most common "ordinary" understandings of terrorism are inadequate. In the second section I offer a working definition of terrorism that overcomes many of the difficulties outlined in the first section. I argue that terrorism consists in the use of "systematically unsystematic" violence (whether directed at combatants or noncombatants), and that the random or indiscriminate character of terroristic violence points us in the direction of seeing what is distinctively wrong with it. The fundamental problem is that terrorism is not committed to any rules of armed conflict or any principles that would facilitate the eventual containment or termination of the conflict.

I. The Difficulty of Defining Terrorism

All terrorism involves violence or the threat of violence, and yet not all forms of violence are terroristic. What, then, is distinctive about the violence that characterizes terrorism? In seeking to answer this question, theorists have typically focused on issues such as the political or ideological goals pursued by the terrorist; the illegality or immorality of the terrorist's method of pursuing those goals; or the innocent or noncombatant status of those who are harmed by terroristic violence. The focus on such features, however, typically leads to definitions that are underinclusive, overinclusive, or simply question-begging. My aim in this section of the paper is to examine some of the difficulties of defining terrorism. Once we have analyzed some of the problems involved, we might be in a better position to see our way out of the difficulties.

Let us begin with one of the most obvious difficulties. A definition of terrorism is *under*-inclusive if it would fail to include within its scope instances of violent activity that are, in fact, genuinely terroristic, even if they may not seem so at first glance. For example, one common understanding of terrorism tends to focus on the revolutionary or subversive intent of the terrorist's actions. However, it is plain that not all terroristic activity has to be directed against existing systems or subversive of existing political orders. Terrorists can also be functionaries or heads of governments (we might call them "proestablishment terrorists") who seek to maintain the existing political order or status quo through their terrorism. Indeed, some of the earliest innovators of modern terrorism—those who carried out the Reign of Terror during the French revolution, and from whom we in fact derive the word "terrorism"—were government officials; and their goal was not to undermine any existing government (for the *ancien regime* had already fallen), but rather to maintain and ensure the stability of the newly established government. Since the time of those first modern terrorists, the world has seen many instantiations of proestablishment terrorism, represented by figures such as Hitler, Stalin, Mussolini, Pol Pot, Idi Amin, certain military leaders of Central and South America, the government officials of Taliban-controlled Afghanistan, and—last but not least—Iraq's Saddam Hussein and sons.

Another way in which a definition of terrorism can be underinclusive is if it would focus primarily on the "neutral" or "noncombatant" status of the terrorist's victims. Such a definition would be underinclusive, since the victims of terrorism can be combatants as well as noncombatants. For example, a proestablishment terrorist can terrorize not only his own citizens (who are noncombatants), but also his own government underlings and even personnel within his own military. Furthermore, a terrorist can perpetrate terroristic activity even against the military personnel of an opposing regime or power. Consider, for example, the attack on the U.S.S. Cole in Yemen's Aden Harbor on October 12, 2000, in which seventeen American soldiers were killed, and another thirty-nine wounded. Even though all the intended and actual victims of that attack were combatants, it is still the case that that attack can accurately be described as terroristic in nature. If one focuses primarily on the noncombatant status of the terrorist's victims, however, then such an attack could not be regarded as genuinely terroristic.

The point can be illustrated by reference to even more recent events. Consider the suicide bombings that took the lives of American soldiers in March and April of 2003, near the conclusion of the combat phase of Operation Iraqi Freedom. In one such attack (on March 29), a suicide bomber killed four U.S. 3rd Infantry Division soldiers at a road checkpoint near the city of Najaf in central Iraq. In a second attack (on April 4), two Iraqi women (one of them pregnant) killed five people, including three U.S. soldiers, when their vehicle exploded shortly after one of the women appeared to scream for help, at a checkpoint southwest of the Haditha Dam, northwest of Baghdad. At the time of these attacks, the U.S. Central Command, as well as independent commentators and the news media, referred to these as terrorist actions, and not regular military operations.[1] But if one seeks to define terrorism by focusing on the noncombatant status of the victims, then these attacks would not be terroristic in nature. Later in this paper, I shall offer a definition of terrorism that might help explain just why such attacks can be considered terroristic in nature, even though the victims were combatants. As I shall suggest, what makes these actions terroristic is not just the use of disguises or deception by the perpetrators (for disguise and deception can also be legitimate techniques employed in regular military operations), but rather the specific *nature* of the deception used in these attacks.

---

[1] Consider the statement from Brig. Gen. Vincent Brooks, Central Command Deputy Director of Operations: "These are not military actions. These are terrorist actions." "Vehicle Explosion at Military Checkpoint Kills Five," Online NewsHour, pbs.org, April 4, 2003, http://www.pbs.org/newshour/updates/checkpoint_04-04-03.html.

Yet another way in which some of the traditional definitions of terrorism can be underinclusive is if they focus exclusively on the use or the threat of violence done to persons, and thus overlook the use or threat of violence that can be done to the property or other vital interests of persons. Accordingly, some traditional definitions of terrorism would exclude increasingly important subsets of terrorism such as "industrial terrorism," "electronic terrorism," "digital terrorism," "information terrorism," and "cyberterrorism" (these types of terrorism can target urban power grids, natural gas and oil pipelines, governmental records, stock markets and bank accounts, air traffic control centers, etc.). One of my aims in this paper will be to offer an account of terrorism that would not be underinclusive in this, or in any, of the above-mentioned ways.

Let us now turn to the opposite problem that can arise when one tries to define terrorism: a definition of terrorism is *over*-inclusive if it would include within its scope instances of violent activity that are not genuinely terroristic, even if they might resemble terroristic activities in certain respects. One of the ways in which a definition of terrorism can be overinclusive, ironically enough, is if it focuses inordinately on one of the characteristics that can also render the definition underinclusive. We saw above that a misguided focus on the noncombatant status of the terrorist's victims can render a definition underinclusive; but focusing inordinately on the noncombatant status of the terrorist's victims can also render a definition of terrorism overinclusive as well. For as we know all too well, even regular and nonterroristic military operations can have noncombatants or innocent persons as their victims.

Of course, one can make the further argument that terroristic actions *deliberately* target noncombatants, while nonterroristic military actions do not. But there is a threefold problem with this approach to defining terrorism. First of all, it is often very difficult (especially during times of conflict, when information, resources, and patience may be more or less in short supply) to distinguish meaningfully between deliberate and nondeliberate attacks upon noncombatants. Second, it is becoming increasingly difficult to distinguish meaningfully between combatants and noncombatants. Consider the case of computer engineers at the IBM research lab in upstate New York, whose job is to produce the world's largest supercomputer, which will be used to model and thereby to "test" nuclear weapons; or consider the case of civilian oil engineers who were called upon during Operation Iraqi Freedom to provide crucial informational and logistical support in the securing of Iraqi oil fields; or consider even the case of average American citizens, whose tax dollars are used to feed a growing military budget, and thus—indirectly—to help underwrite American military operations overseas. Because of the ever-tightening networks of social and economic interdependence in our modern societies, those who play an indirect role in supporting military endeavors can no longer be so easily distinguished from those who play a more direct role. Third, it is quite possible for regular military actions deliberately to target noncombatants, yet without necessarily being qualified as terroristic in nature. For example, some military actions might involve the deliberate targeting of urban areas, where it is known that noncombatants may suffer and die; and such areas are targeted, not so much because of their immediate military value, but because such targeting carries greater "shock value" and can help demoralize and break the will of the noncombatant citizens who might otherwise support a dying regime. Consider Hiroshima in 1945, or Baghdad in 2003, as examples of such deliberate targeting. Such targeting of civilian centers may be immoral or unjustified for a wide variety of reasons, but it is not obvious that such actions are terroristic in nature.

With the above observations, I am certainly not saying that it is altogether impossible to draw a valid distinction between combatants and noncombatants, or between deliberate and nondeliberate attacks upon certain persons or certain areas. Rather, my point is simply that—all things considered—a more helpful and less contentious definition of terrorism would be one whose content did not *depend* on the making and justifying of these very difficult distinctions. Besides, a definition of terrorism that did not necessarily depend for its content on the making and justifying of these distinctions would also be harder to dismiss by terrorists or terrorist-sympathizers as being "question-begging." After all, when terrorists are condemned for their deliberate targeting of noncombatants, their infuriatingly plausible response (a response that one cannot simply dismiss without appearing hypocritical) is to point out that: (a) even those who appear to be the noncombatant victims of terrorism are not entirely neutral or innocent, since they do, in fact, provide indirect and necessary support to those who are directly involved in combat; and (b) even regular military actions undertaken by counterterrorist agencies involve attacks upon noncombatants, and such attacks do at times seem to be deliberate (or at least avoidable, if just a bit more care had been taken).

This now brings me to my final topic in this section, namely the topic of how a definition of terrorism can fail by being question-begging. A definition of terrorism is question-begging if it depends for its content on a particular distinguishing feature that is supposed to illuminate the nature or essence of terrorism, but instead only postpones a satisfactory determination of what terrorism really is. For example, there is a common tendency to think about the nature of terrorism by linking it with particular persons or groups who are now famous for being terroristic, such as Osama bin Laden, Al Qaeda, Islamic Jihad, Hamas, Hezbollah, Saddam Hussein, the Red Army Faction, the Ku Klux Klan, Unabomber Theodore Kaczynski, and Oklahoma City bomber Timothy McVeigh. But if it is only the identity of certain persons or groups that makes particular types of activity terroristic, then we are left with an important, unanswered question: why is it that these people or these groups are terroristic, and not others? And more importantly, is it the case that the actions are called terroristic because of the people that perpetrate them; or is it rather the case that such people are called terrorists because there is something distinctive about the actions that they perpetrate? If the latter is the case, then we have to focus once again on what is distinctive about terroristic actions as such, and no longer think of terrorism just in terms of the persons or groups that we associate with it. This point may seem painfully obvious, but it is worthy of mention here, since it has become all too common (especially since September 11) for even the best commentators and analysts to identify terrorism simply by referring to the people who perpetrate it, and not by referring to some intrinsic feature that distinguishes it as such.

Another way in which a definition of terrorism can be question-begging is if it seeks to illustrate what is distinctive about terrorism by relying on the claim that terrorism consists essentially in the "unjustified" or "immoral" use of violence. Even if this is a true claim (and I believe that it is), it is not the kind of claim that can underwrite an illuminating definition of terrorism. First of all, such a definition would be overinclusive, since there are many unjustified or immoral uses of violence that nevertheless do not qualify as terroristic in nature. Secondly, and most importantly, a definition that focuses on the immoral or unjustified character of terroristic violence would be question-begging. For we can once again ask—following the question suggested above—whether the violence at issue is said to be terroristic because it is unjustified, or whether it is unjustified because it is terroristic. The former option (that it is terroristic because it is unjustified) would yield an overly inclusive definition of terrorism; therefore, we must accept the latter option (that it is unjustified because it is terroristic). However, the latter option leaves us with an important, unanswered question. If terroristic violence is said to be unjustified because it is terroristic, then what is *distinctive* about terroristic violence that makes it unjustified (for surely not all forms of violence are unjustified)? In order to answer this question adequately, we must identify some additional characteristic or characteristics (something different from the fact that it is immoral or unjustified) that will tell us just what terrorism is. So, what is it that makes terroristic violence specifically terroristic? Once we have answered that question, we can then go on to ask whether and why specifically terroristic violence—unlike other forms of violence—is unjustified or immoral.

With this framing of the issues, we have begun to see why the topic of terrorism as such is ripe for philosophical analysis. When confronted with a similar set of problems regarding the definition of terms, Plato asked (in the *Euthyphro*) whether pious activity is said to be pious because it is pleasing to the gods; or conversely, whether it is pleasing to the gods because it is pious, in which case it would possess some intrinsic characteristic that makes it pious, and that also happens to make it (derivatively) pleasing to the gods. In a similar vein, we have asked whether terroristic activity is said to be terroristic simply because it is immoral or unjustified; or whether it is immoral or unjustified because it is terroristic, in which case it would possess some intrinsic characteristic that makes it terroristic, and that also happens to make it (derivatively) immoral or unjustified as well. But what is this distinguishing characteristic (or set of characteristics) that qualifies terroristic violence as specifically terroristic?

Plato tells us that there must be some intrinsic characteristic about pious activity that makes it pious, apart from the further question of whether or why that activity is pleasing to the gods. In a similar vein, I want to suggest that there is some intrinsic characteristic about terroristic activity that makes it terroristic, apart from the further question of whether or why that activity is immoral or unjustified. But this way of approaching the issue leads us to yet another difficulty, a difficulty that Plato also saw. In the *Meno*, Plato asks with characteristic incisiveness: "How can you begin searching for the defining characteristic of a thing, if you do not already know what you are looking for and thus if you do not *already* possess the definition being sought (for if you don't already know what you're looking for, you'll be unable to recognize it when you find it)? Furthermore, if you already *do* possess the definition being sought, then isn't the search unnecessary and superfluous?" In short, it would seem that any search for the defining characteristics of a thing is either impossible or superfluous.

Plato's answer to the dilemma of defining was to hold that the search for the defining characteristics of a thing was not impossible, since we do, in a sense, already know what it is that we are seeking when we try to define things. On the other hand, the search is also not superfluous, since our knowledge of what we are looking for is not fully clear, comprehensive, or well developed in the first instance. For Plato, the whole purpose of defining is not really to arrive at altogether new and different information, but rather to expand, clarify, and deepen our "ordinary" understanding of things. In a similar vein, I offer in the second section of this paper a definition of terrorism that will resound with some of our ordinary intuitions about terrorism. But as I've suggested above, some of our ordinary intuitions about terrorism are not entirely adequate, and—if left unexamined—are apt to mislead us when we are called upon to make difficult judgments and implement important decisions on how to deal with it. In everyday discourse, it might well be sufficient to say of terrorism that "we know it when we see it." But in a world that has been made infinitely more complicated and confusing with the onset of globalized terror, we cannot just claim to "know it when we see it." Instead, it is necessary to supplement our ordinary understandings of terrorism with a more careful and rigorous conceptual analysis, one that will withstand critical scrutiny and begin to illuminate the many difficult issues that are raised by the threat of terrorism.

II. A Working Definition of Terrorism

One recent philosopher who has dedicated significant mental energy to the issue of terrorism, Haig Khatchadourian, argues that terrorism is essentially "bifocal," insofar as it is aimed at two different foci or targets.[2] First of all, terrorism is aimed at its "direct" victims or targets (those who directly or immediately suffer the violence done by the terrorist); these are the victims who are killed, wounded, and maimed in terrorists attacks, and/or whose vital interests are directly harmed by other forms of terrorism such as industrial terrorism, elec-

---

[2] Haig Khatchadourian, *The Morality of Terrorism* (New York: Peter Lang, 1998), 6.

tronic terrorism, or cyberterrorism. Secondly, terrorism is also aimed at a set of "indirect" victims or targets. These indirect victims of terrorism do not suffer the terrorist's violence directly, but instead are observers of the violence done to the terrorist's direct targets. As a result, they are the recipients of a generalized threat or "message of fear" conveyed by the terrorist's violent actions.

The bifocal character of terrorism points to a crucial distinguishing characteristic of terroristic violence. The aim of terroristic violence is not only to achieve ends directly through the use of force or violence (e.g., the direct killing of certain persons, or the direct destruction of particular material assets or infrastructural goods). Above and beyond achieving its direct ends (death and destruction), terroristic violence also aims at sending an accompanying message, a message of fear, or intimidation, or—as the name itself suggests—a message of terror. This description of what is distinctive about terroristic violence is not only etymologically sound (for the word "terrorism" is etymologically derived from the notion of terror), but also agrees with our common understandings of what terrorism is. In cases where the violence or the threat of violence terminates entirely with a particular act of violence, it is not accurate to refer to the particular act of violence as terroristic in nature. In order for a particular act of violence to be specifically terroristic, it is not enough that the violence be done; in order to be terroristic, the violence also has to be accompanied by a message of fear or intimidation, no matter how oblique or implicit that message may be.

The preceding consideration points us to yet another feature of terroristic violence: in order to be effective, terrorism needs an audience, and this audience is what we have called the terrorist's "indirect target" group. If members of the terrorist's indirect target group did not observe the terrorist's acts of violence or if they had no sense that they were members of the indirect target group, then the terrorist will not have succeeded in causing fear or terror among his indirect target group, in which case he will have failed as a terrorist. The terrorist's need for an audience points us to the role that publicity plays in the terrorist enterprise, and suggests that modern media outlets may themselves be the unwitting—though perhaps inevitable—instruments of the terrorist. This fact about terrorism points to a fundamental irony: because the terrorist needs publicity, it is often the case that "antitechnology" terrorists such as the Unabomber must rely on modern media technologies in order to be fully effective; or similarly, "antidemocracy" terrorists such as Islamic fundamentalists rely on modern journalistic coverage and the free exchange of information in order to be fully effective. In some respects, then, the terrorist can be most effective by working precisely within the modern, technologically advanced, free-market society that he or she might aim to destroy. In other words, the terrorist's effectiveness as a terrorist is often parasitic upon the very features that characterize the host society being terrorized; one of the terrorist's strategies may be to use certain features of modern society in order to turn modern society against itself and make it a party to its own destruction.

As we have seen, the terrorist uses violence, not only to cause actual harm to the individual persons or vital interests that are directly targeted, but also to cause wider fear and panic among members of the terrorist's indirect target group. Because of this, terroristic violence can yield more "bang for the buck" in comparison with other, nonterroristic uses of violence, whose aim is restricted to what is immediately or directly achieved by the violence itself. For example, a regular computer hacker might aim to hack into a target system and bring that system down; but the effect of terroristic computer hacking is to bring about fear and anxiety that goes well beyond the direct target of the hacking. Terroristic violence aims to make effective use of limited resources, and thus—not surprisingly—has been called the "poor man's answer" to modern warfare. Thus it took only one computer hacker in the Philippines to devise the "I love you" virus and cause panic among hundreds of institutions and businesses (the virus was first encountered at the University of Oregon on May 4, 2000). It took only two individuals (perhaps with a few yet-unknown accomplices) to bomb the Murrah Federal Building in Oklahoma City (April 19, 1995) and terrorize an entire country. And finally, it took only nineteen hijackers and a fairly tight circle of financial and logistical support to bring down the twin towers on September 11 and spread terror throughout the entire world.[3] In the terrorist's hands, even a single act of violence—if sufficiently spectacular and well publicized—can go a long way in spreading fear.

We have considered the bifocal character of terrorism and some of the immediate implications, but what exactly is the message that the terrorist seeks to convey to his or her indirect victims or to the target audience? It is clear, of course, that different terrorists have different motivations, and so different terrorists seek to convey different types

---

[3] Four flights were hijacked on September 11: there were five hijackers on each of three flights, and four hijackers on a fourth flight.

of messages. One message might have to do with the dangers of modern technology (consider the Unabomber). Another message might have to do with the evils of modern secularism (consider Islamic fundamentalist groups). Still another message might have to do with the supremacy of a particular race or of a particular ruling authority (consider the Ku Klux Klan, the Nazi party in Germany under Hitler, or the Baathist party in Iraq under Hussein). Finally, the terrorist's message might be temporally localized or territorially specific; for example, the message might have to do with the undesirability of the Russian presence in Chechnya, the Spanish presence in the Basque region, or the Israeli presence in Palestine. Terrorists can have widely divergent goals and ideological commitments: religious, secularist, rightist, leftist, proestablishment, antiestablishment, and so forth.

If we look to the explicit beliefs or aims of the terrorist, then it is not likely that we will arrive at any common ideological denominator or any fundamental ground of agreement. But there is indeed something common to the message that the terrorist seeks to convey. This message has nothing to do with the terrorist's explicit aims or beliefs, but is connected rather to the terrorist's *modus operandi*, that is, to the *manner* in which the terrorist pursues his or her particular aims. The terrorist may have any number of possible messages about politics, religion, territory, and so forth; but the message that belongs generically to terroristic violence as such has to do with the random or indiscriminate character of the violence being done. Even if not deliberately formulated or self-consciously acknowledged by the terrorist, the message conveyed by the terrorist—regardless of the terrorist's particular aims—is that the direct victims of terroristic violence are to be targeted in a manner characterized by randomness and indiscriminateness. As I shall show later, this message of randomness or indiscriminateness entails yet a further, more far-reaching message about terrorism.

Before going further, it would be helpful now to formulate a basic working definition of terrorism, one that incorporates various elements touched upon thus far. Terrorism is (1) the systematic use (2) of actual or threatened violence (3) against persons or against the vital interests of persons (i.e., against the terrorist's direct target) (4) in the pursuit of political, ideological, religious, social, economic, financial, and/or territorial objectives, (5) whereby the violence is sufficiently random or indiscriminate (6) so as to cause fear among members of the terrorist's indirect target group, (7) thus creating a generalized climate of fear, distrust, or instability within certain sectors of society or within society at large, (8) the ultimate aim of which is to influence popular opinion or governmental policy in a manner that serves the terrorist's objectives.

According to this definition, terrorism is akin to extortion or hostage-taking, since these two types of criminal activity create and exploit fear and intimidation for the purpose of causing another party to act or forbear from acting. However, terrorism is unlike simple extortion or hostage-taking, since the terrorist's actual or threatened use of violence is sufficiently random (i.e., indiscriminate, uncontained, unpredictable, or nonindividualized), so as to cause fear not only in a particular person or family, but in broader sectors of society or in society as a whole. In a sense, then, terrorism is a form of extortive hostage-taking, where the general, indeterminate, nonindividualized "hostage" of the terrorist is some sector of society or society at large.

It is worth pausing for a moment to reflect further on two essential features of terroristic violence, namely that it is randomized or indiscriminate, and yet also systematic. Because terroristic violence is indiscriminate, random, unpredictable, or nonindividualized, it causes fear in certain sectors of society or in society as a whole. This is because such violence conveys to observers (i.e., to the terrorist's indirect target group) that there is in principle nothing preventing such violence from being visited upon them as well. But while random and indiscriminate, terroristic violence is different from "ordinary" uses of random violence. This is because terrorism involves a systematic policy, and does not achieve its goal immediately and directly through the individual and randomized acts of violence themselves. Rather, terrorism achieves its goal precisely through the subsequent fear engendered by the target audience's awareness that such acts of violence—while randomized—are part of a systematic policy and not merely accidental. Thus a petty thief who achieves his goal immediately and directly by robbing people—even if such acts of robbery are indiscriminate and random—is an ordinary criminal and not a terrorist. By contrast, a local gang leader is acting as a terrorist if he achieves his aim (e.g., preventing people from reporting to the police) by intimidating inhabitants in an entire neighborhood through a systematic policy of randomized violence. We can thus say, paradoxically, that terrorism involves the "systematically random" or "systematically unsystematic" use of violence for the purpose of creating and exploiting a climate of fear in certain sectors of society or in society as a whole.

The randomness or indiscriminateness that characterizes terroristic violence applies not only to the selection of those who become the victims of terrorism. It applies also to the choice of venue in which the terroristic violence occurs, and to the self-presentations or guises used by those who perpetrate the violence. In other words, to say that terroristic violence is characteristically random or indiscriminate is to say not only that all persons within society or within a particular sector of society might be targeted as the random or indiscriminate victims of violence. It is to say, furthermore, that the violence can occur at any random time, place, or context, and can be perpetrated by those who might effect the appearance of being neutral, innocent civilians or random strangers. In short, terroristic violence can be random or indiscriminate in at least three significant ways: with respect to the selection of the victims; with respect to the venue (time, place, or context) of the violence; and with respect to the self-presentation or ostensible identity of those who perpetrate the violence.

What is crucial here is not just that terroristic violence occurs in a way that involves three possible kinds of randomness or indiscriminateness. For it is obvious that the world as we know it is full of unexpected and random occurrences; violence often does befall certain people in random fashion, and can take place in unexpected contexts, and can be perpetrated by those who might at first appear to be random strangers. But what is crucial and unique about the randomness characterizing terroristic violence is that the terrorist employs such randomness in a systematic fashion. The terrorist makes systematic use of this threefold potential for randomness precisely in order to maximize the effectiveness and fearfulness of his or her violence. Because of such randomness, the terrorist can gain easy access to victims in unexpected contexts (e.g., busses, trains, airplanes, roadways, and shopping malls) and can sow seeds of fear across very broad sectors of society.

If we focus on this threefold potential for randomness, we can begin to see just why it is that terrorism can be perpetrated not only by antiestablishment revolutionaries, but also by proestablishment operatives. Consider, for example, Nazi thugs or Baathist party operatives whose reign of terror in Germany and Iraq depended in large measure on the doings of randomly placed informants in civilian dress, and on the infliction of indiscriminate, arbitrary punishments. By focusing on this threefold potential for randomness, we can also begin to see why terrorism can be perpetrated not only against noncombatants within civilian settings, but also against military personnel in the midst of military operations. Consider, for example, the terroristic tactics of the Iraqi soldiers who waved white flags of surrender during Operation Iraqi Freedom, only to open fire when their American counterparts moved to accept their surrender. That is a form of terrorism, even though the victims were combatants. Furthermore, this focus on the threefold potential for randomness allows us to understand what is distinctive about terrorism, yet without reliance on the problematic distinction between combatant and noncombatant, or on the question-begging distinction between justified and unjustified uses of violence. Finally, this account of terrorism allows us to explain in an illuminating and non-question-begging way just why it is that terroristic violence is immoral and unjustified. For the operative claim I want to make is not just that the terrorist makes use of this threefold potential for randomness; I also want to suggest that it is the systematic use of randomness or indiscriminateness that, in turn, makes terroristic violence immoral or unjustified.

What is crucial here is what is implied by the threefold potential for randomness: it implies that the terrorist in principle does not recognize any rules of armed conflict. But is this really distinctive about terrorism? Doesn't this way of characterizing terrorism run the risk of being overinclusive? After all, it would seem that any conflict—especially any conflict involving violence—between human beings involves disagreement about which rules or laws are to be recognized. And so by focusing on the terrorist's refusal to recognize rules of armed conflict, do we not run the risk of defining terrorism in terms that might legitimately characterize other, nonterroristic instances of conflict? Even if it is true that other conflicts—especially armed conflicts—involve the refusal of one party to recognize rules or laws whose recognition is insisted on by the other party, there is still something distinctive about the terrorist's refusal to recognize any rules of armed conflict.

On the most obvious level, the terrorist's refusal to recognize any rules of armed conflict means that for the terrorist there are in principle no contexts, no conditions, no times or places, and no persons that fall under the basic rules of armed conflict. Accordingly, the terrorist may target anyone at any time (in bus stations, shopping malls, office buildings, or even hospitals), and may do so under the guise of being anyone at all (an ambulance driver, a security guard, a police officer, or a simply a nondescript stranger). But the terrorist's refusal to recognize any rules of armed conflict also means something deeper than this. It means that the terrorist in principle refuses to recognize any rule that—in spite of the parties' obvious disagreement—governs the parties' conduct during the time of conflict. This means, in turn, that the terrorist in principle recognizes no rules that effectively remain "above the conflict," and that can govern the terms of an eventual transition by the parties from a state of conflict to a state of peace.

In effect, the terrorist's refusal to recognize any rules of armed conflict is an implicit commitment to a state of perpetual conflict or war, for it is only through some basic rules of armed conflict that the conflicting parties can have at their disposal some protocols for reaching an eventual truce. Because of this, the terrorist is implicitly committed to a perpetual state of war (either an antiestablishment or a proestablishment state of war). This does not mean, of course, that the terrorist can never be led to forsake violence and opt for peace. But it does mean that the terrorist—insofar as he or she remains a terrorist and refuses to recognize any rules of armed conflict—systematically refuses to recognize what conflicting parties need in order to move together from a state of conflict to a state of peace. Even if individual terrorists themselves might be led to choose peace, the terrorist *qua* terrorist is committed to a *modus operandi* that implicitly denies that any rules remain "above the conflict"; and thus the terrorist's *modus operandi* involves an implicit refusal to recognize those rules that are needed for reaching an eventual truce.

We can better understand what is at issue here if we take a brief look at how the rules of armed conflict are meant to function during times of actual conflict. The rules of armed conflict are certainly not intended to give military advantage to one side or another; otherwise, no disadvantaged party could ever be expected to recognize rules of armed conflict. Nor are rules of armed conflict intended to make any claims about which party to a conflict is in the right; if the rules of armed conflict were content-specific in this way, then only one party could be expected to recognize rules of armed conflict. Rather, one of the fundamental—and content-neutral—purposes of rules of armed conflict is to ensure that the warring parties will recognize and be bound by certain norms throughout the conflict, so that a truce can be agreed to and relied upon by both parties at the end of the conflict. Without such rules of armed conflict already in place and already accepted by both warring parties, it is systematically impossible for the warring parties ever to agree to a principled truce or state of peaceful coexistence.

Let us flesh this out by reference to the often overlooked "principle of chivalry" within the law of armed conflict. Among other things, the principle of chivalry prohibits the use of treachery during times of armed conflict; for example, it prohibits the misuse of enemy flags or flags of truce or surrender (e.g., the traditional white flag). Without such a principle, a conflict between two parties could, in principle, go on forever. For without such a principle in place, any expression of surrender or truce could be used, not in order to signal the conflict's end, but for the purpose of deceiving and gaining a military advantage over one's adversary. Instead of aiming to bring the conflict to a close, the showing of a white flag could be used precisely in order to perpetuate the conflict. Without some principle of chivalry at work, no expression of surrender could ever be trusted, and so no principled truce could ever be reached. As Aristotle rightly says, the purpose of war is to secure the peace. But the terrorist's activities (whether aimed at combatant or noncombatant victims) make such a transition from a state of war to a state of principled peace systematically impossible. In refusing to recognize any rules of armed conflict, the terrorist refuses to recognize any rules or protocols by means of which the conflicting parties might trust each other and agree together to end the state of conflict.

This, then, is what is fundamentally wrong with the terrorist's refusal to recognize any rules of armed conflict: this refusal amounts to a refusal to conduct armed conflict in a way that aims at and allows for the deliberate and principled termination of the conflict. And with this, we have arrived at what we have been looking for in our attempt to define terrorism. The animating spirit of terrorism is the spirit of systematically unsystematic violence, which—as we have seen—involves a threefold potential for randomness. And such randomness, in turn, betokens the terrorist's refusal in principle to recognize any rules of armed conflict. And this refusal, in turn, reveals that the terrorist *qua* terrorist is implicitly committed to the principle of uncontained and perpetual war, that is, to the kind of war that can never end through mutual recognition or a negotiated truce, but only through the ongoing suppression or complete obliteration of the adversary. And this, in a word, is what is distinctively wrong with terrorism.

An important elaboration might be in order here. On one level, it might seem that some groups that are traditionally labeled "terroristic" are not really committed to perpetual or uncontained war, since such groups have rather limited and well-defined objectives. Because of the limited or circumscribed character of their objectives (e.g., the expulsion of a particular group from a particular region), it might seem that some terrorist groups are not really committed to perpetual war, after all. But it is important to be mindful of two crucial distinctions. First of all, there is a difference between (i) a particular group's stated objectives, and (ii) the means by which the group pursues those objectives. Even if a particular group claims to have rather limited objectives and thus denies that it is committed to the principle of perpetual war, it might nevertheless be the case that the group's *means* or *methods* of pursuing those objectives actually contradict the stated objectives themselves. So even if a particular group claims to desire only territorial autonomy and peaceful coexistence with its neighbor(s), that group undermines its own message when it refuses to recognize rules of armed conflict and thus when it shows that it cannot be trusted to be bound by rules (including those contained in its own promises) that are supposed to transcend particular conflicts or disagreements as they arise. Even if a particular group claims to have only limited objectives, its terroristic *modus operandi* shows that it really cannot be trusted to recognize any limits if there is actual (or future) disagreement or conflict.

This brings us to the second crucial distinction, which is a distinction between the two ways in which open hostilities between conflicting parties might be suspended. The suspension of open hostilities might amount to (i) a genuine state of peace based on mutual agreement or recognition between the parties; or (ii) a mere state of stability based on the morally arbitrary fact that circumstances have led to a stalemate or impasse in the conflict between the parties. While the former condition constitutes a state of genuine peace, the latter condition is perfectly consistent with the persistence of a state of war. If a shift in circumstances (such as a shift in the relative balance of power between two warring parties) happens to lead to the suspension of open hostilities, it does not automatically follow that a state of peace has been achieved. In the absence of any mutual recognition or agreement, the mere suspension of open hostilities between conflicting parties is arbitrary from a moral point of view; and the open hostilities will reignite just as soon as a new (and also morally arbitrary) shift occurs in the prevailing circumstances (e.g., a shift in the relative balance of power between the parties). The point here is that a genuine state of peace cannot arise simply through morally arbitrary changes in circumstance or shifts in the balance of power between parties. Rather, as Kant argues, genuine peace can only be the result of mutual recognition or agreement.[4] But meaning-ful agreement—in turn—is possible only if the two parties can be trusted to be bound by rules (including those contained in their own agreements) that are supposed to transcend particular (future) con-flicts or disagreements that might arise. By adopting a terroristic *modus operandi* (and thus by refusing to be bound by rules which remain "above the conflict"), terror groups show that they cannot, in fact, be trusted in the requisite way. And a state in which the suspen-sion of open hostilities always depends on morally arbitrary circum-stances and balances of power (rather than on mutual recognition or agreement) is nothing other than a state of perpetual war.

By way of conclusion, I would like to formulate two final theses about terrorism and why it is apt to become an increasingly difficult problem for liberal democracies in the years to come. These two the-ses are meant to be more suggestive than conclusive:

1) *Terrorism systematically undermines trust in a context of increasing mutual dependence.* As systematically unsystematic vio-lence, terrorism undermines trust on two levels: (a) it undermines the citizens' trust in their government's ability or will to protect them, and (b) it undermines the citizens' trust in one another as individuals. Terrorism thus has the effect of delegitimizing and destabilizing social institutions and relationships that are based on trust, and sup-planting such institutions and relationships with ones that are based on fear or coercion. Thus in a civil society facing the threat of terror-ism, citizens find it harder to trust that their government will protect them and to trust that strangers with whom they come in contact (e.g., in shared public spaces, on roads, in the skies, and on the information superhighway) will not cause them harm or harassment. In effect, ter-rorism makes it more difficult to trust in the effectiveness of govern-ment and in the good will of strangers, precisely at a time when our modern economies and technologies are engendering increasingly wide networks of mutual dependence, thereby making such trust all the more necessary.

2) *The ultimate effect of terrorism is to put modern, liberal soci-ety into conflict with itself.* To the extent that the terrorism tends to undermine trust and lawfulness and replace it with fear, it marks a serious challenge to civil society's fundamental commitment to the

---

[4] See Immanuel Kant, "To Perpetual Peace: A Philosophical Sketch," in *Perpetual Peace and Other Essays*, trans. Ted Humphrey (Indianapolis: Hackett Publishing Company), 111.

view that justice is something more than just the will of the strongest or the will of the most intimidating. The recent trend in suicide bombings indicates just how difficult the problem is. For suicide bombing is not just a more effective way of delivering explosives. More importantly, suicide bombing embodies a terrifying new message, namely the message that there may be persons among us who—in principle—cannot be trusted to care about our lives, since they cannot be trusted to care about their own lives, and thus whose terroristic actions cannot be deterred even by the threat of force or death. But if one cannot deter the terrorist by appealing to his or her self-interest, then terrorism seems altogether unstoppable, unless the "war on terrorism" aims at the complete eradication—and not just the deterrence—of the terrorist. But this fact, finally, shows just why the problem of terrorism is so intractable. Terrorism is a challenge to modern liberal civil society not only "from the outside," but also "from the inside." This is because civil society's attempt at preserving itself through the "war on terrorism" requires the increasing surveillance of possibly innocent transactions, and the use of overwhelming force against the perceived perpetrators and sponsors of terrorism (consider, for example, the recent privacy concerns raised in the United States, and the sometimes indiscriminate bulldozing of Palestinian houses in the West Bank). But such methods in the war on terrorism are precisely the kinds of methods that can cause widespread intimidation and destroy trust. Thus the more we execute the war on terror (a war that we cannot fail to engage in some fashion), the more we run the risk of using means that are difficult to distinguish from those used by the terrorists themselves. And this, I contend, is precisely the terrorist's purpose. Terrorism puts civil society in a difficult bind: terrorism challenges civil society to defend itself; but since the modern terrorist cannot be deterred by more traditional, less extreme methods, civil society's war on terror must at times resort to invasions of privacy and to preemptive and excessive force—precisely the kinds of techniques that cause intimidation and undermine trust—and that is just what the terrorist also aims at doing.

| 2 |

A Taxonomy of Terrorism

LIAM HARTE

September 11, it is said, changed everything. Whether this dictum is completely true or not, the event certainly served to focus most people's attention on what many experts assert to be an unprecedented breed of terrorist: the fanatic, often religiously motivated, who is willing to inflict huge casualties with weapons of mass destruction, if possible. The earliest serious operation by such "new terrorists" was a nerve-gas attack on the Tokyo subway, carried out in 1995 by the millenarian cult called Aum Shinri Kyo, which killed eleven people and injured over five thousand. Currently, the most notorious new terrorists are probably Osama bin Laden, the leader of Al Qaeda, and Timothy McVeigh, who blew up the Murrah Federal Building in Oklahoma City. I share the intuition that men like these seem different from members of, say, the Irish Republican Army or the Red Army Faction, and that their activities seem to likewise differ in some way. The questions I am raising here, however, are whether these differences are mere seeming and, if not, whether they are genuinely important.

To answer these questions, I shall do three things in this essay. First, I shall explicate the concept of terrorism that I take for granted throughout; then, second, and on that conceptual basis, I shall critically analyze the concept of the "new terrorism." Third, I shall propose some new concepts as a collective replacement for that of new terrorism. The first of these tasks is necessary since, while the concept of a "new" terrorism implies that of an "old" terrorism, both imply a general concept of terrorism that subsumes them both. I shall then contend that the most widely accepted analysis of the concept of new terrorism is faulty, on three grounds. For a start, it mistakes quantitative differences in the destructiveness of the operations carried out by discrete terrorist organizations for qualitative differences between kinds of terrorism. Next, its notion of fanaticism is so narrow that it mistakes the most intense commitment to a cause for a new kind of motivation, which is really another way of mistaking quantity for quality. On both these matters, I shall argue also that emphasis on means and motivation is misplaced. Last, the concept of new terrorism fails to cover any clear cases in the real world. The new concepts I shall propose—namely, those of *mythic* terrorism (in strong and weak senses of the term) and *pro-* and *antimodern* terrorism—rectify these shortcomings, and therefore have greater analytical power than that of new terrorism.

Having said that the concept of new terrorism is inapplicable to real world cases, I must stress that my main claims are conceptual, not empirical. Work in fact already exists that casts doubt on the claim that any acts of new terrorism have ever yet taken place[1]; but, even if that claim is incorrect, this is no reason to infer that acts of new terrorism will never occur. For my part, I shall venture the suggestion that acts of new terrorism *cannot* occur precisely because the very concept is ill formed. Indeed, although I accept that something is happening in the universe of terrorism that existing categories somehow fail to capture adequately, I also believe that trying to articulate the idea of an entirely new kind of terrorism overstates its novelty and is therefore unnecessary and misleading. Part of my intention, consequently, is to show that such well-established concepts as those of state and nonstate terrorism are still applicable to the phenomena in question if my new categories are used alongside them. The resultant taxonomy reduces the complexity of the phenomena of terrorism in a way that renders intelligible not only the puzzling new phenomena but many familiar old ones, too.

I. Kinds of Terrorism

Though I begin with some preliminary thoughts on the general concept of terrorism, I shall sidestep the controversy that usually accom-

---

[1] I would refer the reader to Ariel Merari, "Terrorism as a Strategy of Struggle: Past and Future," *Terrorism and Political Violence* 11 (Fall 1999): 52–65; and David Tucker, "What is New about the New Terrorism and How Dangerous is It?" *Terrorism and Political Violence* 13 (Autumn 2001): 1–14.

panies the issue of defining the term *terrorism*, which seems to me philosophically uninteresting. For what it is worth, I agree that one person's terrorist is another's freedom fighter, but do not see that this necessarily makes the freedom fighter less of a terrorist, nor the terrorist more of a freedom fighter. What, then, is the concept of terrorism that leads me to this view? Paul Wilkinson asserts that no explication can have much substance unless it explicitly relates the putative phenomenon to the emotion of terror.[2] I would contest his insistence that terrorism must always be linked to terror, partly because he notes further that terror can be only more or less reliably induced relative to the given person's temperament and the given situation.[3] A bomb exploding in a café will probably terrify all bystanders to some degree, while those who hear about the explosion at second hand, however, may experience quite other emotions, or even none at all. The latter group, however, is being terror*ized* without having to be terrified. Contrary to Wilkinson, then, I take the main work of an explication of the concept of terrorism to be linking it not to the experience of being *terrified*, which has a necessary connection with an actual emotion of terror, but to that of being *terrorized*, which has none.

In the light of the foregoing, I explicate my concept of terrorism in the following way. With respect to ends, an agent terrorizes some given individual or group (the *target*) when the agent tries to produce fear in the target in order to affect the target's conduct in some way that the terrorist finds desirable. So, under my analysis, a terrorist must have both a proximate end (i.e., producing fear in the target) and an ultimate one (i.e., changing the target's conduct). A wide variety of means can be used to attain each. Where there are ends in view, there must be an allied intention, with respect to which the agent must be resolved to keep trying to produce fear until it affects the target's conduct in the desired way. As a consequence, one cannot be said to terrorize a target in whom one tries to produce fear only once; but one

---

[2] From this point of view, one of the most influential definitions, the RAND Corporation's, is rather lacking. Terrorism, it states, comprises a range of politically motivated crimes that are intended to produce some "psychological effect" in a target audience. Presumably, this effect is terror; but it would be helpful if the definition said so. See Brian Jenkins, foreword to *Countering the New Terrorism*, ed. Ian O. Lesser (Santa Monica, CA: RAND, 1999), v.

[3] Paul Wilkinson, *Political Terrorism* (New York: John Wiley/Halsted Press, 1974), 11–12.

could still be said to terrorize a target in whom one only ever had one chance to try to produce fear. This is to say that terrorism is a *practice*; and, since the attempt to produce conduct-altering fear is intrinsic to it, terrorism is an *intimidatory* practice. It goes without saying that the terrorist must be motivated (and remain motivated) to engage in this practice, but motivations are by their nature so heterogeneous that they too often have only the most contingent connection to intended ends, and so I leave them aside.

There are three things to note about this analysis. First, I do not claim that actually producing any kind of fear is a necessary condition for it to be true to say of any agent that he is terrorizing a target. Like many (perhaps most) activities, terrorism is subject to the law of unintended consequences, including that of failure to achieve the intended ends. Second, I claim that even persons actually put in fear are not being terrorized if that fear has not been caused purposefully. Third, I make no reference to either the use or threat of violence, not because I think that terrorism is never violent, or not usually, but because my analysis is designed to exclude all mention of means. Together, these points mean that the term "terrorism," in the strictest sense of my analysis, is a striving-noun rather than a success-noun denoting an intimidatory practice. Notwithstanding the narrowness of this analysis, I am aware that it covers a great range of phenomena, some of which (e.g., conventional warfare, blackmail, extortion rackets, wife-beating, or legal punishment) it may strike some readers as counterintuitive to call terrorism. For the time being, I am not disturbed by these wide implications, since they do not seem to be so wide as to indicate that the analysis is incorrect. It may reduce the counterintuitivity somewhat to point out that I do not claim that every practice covered by my analysis must be *nothing but* terrorism, but that is all I have space to say about the matter here.

With the extension of the general term "terrorism" thus delimited, it is necessary to subdivide that extension in several ways before considering new terrorism. Counterterrorism literature usually assumes terrorists to be motivated by political commitments: that is, that they want either to alter the conduct of those who operate public institutions or to use such institutions to alter the conduct of those subject to them (or both). Walter Laqueur, for instance, says that, as

> . . . the use of covert violence by a group for political ends, [terrorism]
> is usually directed against a government, but it is also used against other
> ethnic groups, classes or parties. The aims may vary from the redress of

specific grievances to the overthrow of a government and the seizure of power, or to the liberation of a country from foreign rule. Terrorists seek to cause political, social and economic destruction, and for this purpose frequently engage in planned or indiscriminate murder.[4]

Even in terms of ends and intentions, it seems to me clear that Laqueur is here describing only one species of the genus "terrorism." That species I shall term "political terrorism," which I define much as Laqueur does above. Since, however, it is just as possible that an agent's end in terrorizing a target may be gaining some personal advantage (and because any interest he has in altering the conduct of those who operate public institutions may be quite incidental to this end), I need to coin a term complementary to "political terrorism" for the sake of completeness. Let this term be *social terrorism*. It happens, though, that political terrorism is my primary concern here, so I shall have little occasion to use this new term.

Saying that political terrorism is terrorism that serves political ends may seem rather unsatisfactory, because it is undoubtedly a circular definition if one is looking for sets of necessary and sufficient conditions for a given agent to be correctly described as a political terrorist. This is because political terrorism is a family-resemblance concept. It is therefore best to understand the political nature of such terrorism by drawing the following distinctions, upon which there is broad consensus among experts, and with which I have no significant disagreement. Acts of political terrorism are classifiable according to both their geographical scope and the identity of the agents. With regard to scope, political terrorism comes in two basic varieties: *domestic* and *international*. Domestic terrorism[5] is conducted within a single country, while the international variety is conducted without regard to borders. These categories are cross-divided by two classes of agent: *state* and *nonstate* terrorists. State terrorists are governments (de facto, if not de jure), while any other kind of agent can be only a nonstate terrorist. State terrorists use some nation's public institutions to terrorize a target, while the targets of nonstate terrorists are those who operate some state's public institutions. State ter-

---

[4] Walter Laqueur, *The Age of Terrorism* (Boston: Little, Brown, 1987), 72.
[5] Since these are all distinctions within the category of political terrorism, I shall not say things such as "domestic *political* terrorism," and so on. When I say "domestic terrorism" instead, the political character of that kind of terrorism is always understood.

rorists are divisible between *regime-* and *state-sponsored* terrorists, according to the instruments used and the identity of the target. Regime terrorists employ a state's public institutions directly to terrorize all or part of some people, though not necessarily its own— domestic regime terrorists terrorize their own people. International regime terrorists terrorize the people of another state that the first state controls. State-sponsored terrorists, on the other hand, are nonstate terrorists employed or supported by some state, and can carry out operations either domestically or internationally. On this understanding, then, all state terrorism is a form of rule, whereas all nonstate terrorism is a challenge to rule. State-sponsored terrorism is a phenomenon produced by the overlapping of state and nonstate terrorism.[6]

While there is broad consensus on the definitions above, any taxonomy encounters borderline cases and outright exceptions. This is to be expected, because all kinds of theories tend to be articulated *ceteris paribus*, and usually have to be modified by actual circumstances. Without any typology at all, however, one is confronted with an irreducible confusion of unintelligible contingencies. The important question is whether any part of a given typology has to be modified so much to accommodate the alleged instantiations of its categories that it fails to make anything intelligible. In the case of the typology given above, I think the answer to that question is no. In the next section, I shall examine the concept of "new" terrorism.

II. A New Kind of Terrorism?

In the early 1990s, analysts noticed that nonstate terrorism seemed to be changing. Most of its prior exponents had been ethnic nationalists or leftist radicals (or both) who made fairly clear if not always realistic demands of their targets and used small firearms and high explosives as their main weapons. After about 1990, however, nonstate terrorists seemed more and more often to be motivated by religious or right-wing ideologies and to be uninterested in wringing specific con-

---

[6] The notion of regime terrorism, in fact, comports well with Montesquieu's diagnosis of the principle of despotic government as being fear. See Baron de Montesquieu, *The Spirit of the Laws*, trans. Thomas Nugent (New York: Macmillan/Hafner Press, 1949), book 3, chap. 9. State-sponsored terrorism is a form of rule insofar as it is a way of pursuing either some aspect of foreign policy (it is often referred to as "war by proxy") or some aspect of domestic policy on foreign soil.

cessions from their targets. Moreover, they seemed happy to take violence to deadlier extremes than previous terrorists—who were constrained by strategic and even moral considerations—had been.[7] In short, the main aims of the religious or rightist terrorists appeared to be destroying their targets in order to replace the existing order with something new.

To cover such cases, the concept of "new terrorism" had been pretty fully articulated by about 1997. I shall take Laqueur's prominent analysis of the concept as exemplary. Its protagonists' fanaticism and the greater destructiveness of their activities, he claims, distinguish "new" from "traditional" terrorism (by which term he means what I call nonstate terrorism). Traditional terrorism is, as he puts it, "nuisance" terrorism, which, in absolute terms, has never caused very great casualties or property damage. He even concedes that regime terrorism in almost any of its forms has killed, maimed, or made destitute far more people than traditional terrorism has ever contrived or attempted to.[8] New terrorists, however, are both willing and able to cause very great harm, to the extent of having no objection in principle to using weapons of mass destruction (WMD).[9] The enormous casualties caused on September 11, or in Oklahoma City and the Tokyo subway, are clear examples of what Laqueur has in mind here.

Although Laqueur attributes new terrorists' unprecedented bloodthirstiness to the difference between their motivations and those of traditional terrorists, he finds it hard to explain what that difference is. He notes that traditional terrorists "had political and social aims, such as gaining independence, getting rid of foreigners, or establishing a new social order," and "aimed at forcing concessions . . . from their antagonists." The new terrorists, to the contrary, aim "not at clearly defined political demands but at the destruction of society and the elimination of large sections of the population. In its most extreme form, this new terrorism intends to liquidate all satanic

---

[7] The *locus classicus* of this view is probably Bruce Hoffman, "Terrorism and WMD: Some Preliminary Hypotheses," *The Nonproliferation Review* (Spring/Summer 1997): 45–53, wherein he argues (on 47–48) that religiously motivated international terrorism is proving to be more lethal than other kinds. See also Bruce Hoffman, "Terrorism Trends and Prospects," in Lesser, *Countering the New Terrorism*, 7–38. Tucker does an interesting job of reinterpreting such figures ("What is New about the New Terrorism?" 5–7).

[8] Walter Laqueur, *The New Terrorism: Fanaticism and the Arms of Mass Destruction* (New York: Oxford University Press, 1997), 9.

[9] See also Hoffman, "Terrorism and WMD," 47–48.

forces, which may include the majority of a country or of mankind, as a precondition for the growth of another, better, and in any case different breed of human. In its maddest, most extreme form it may aim at the destruction of all life on earth, as the ultimate punishment for mankind's crimes."[10]

If the difference between these two orientations seems so subtle as to be invisible, this is because Laqueur is not really talking about the new terrorists' motivations, but their intentions. Luckily, he is not alone in propounding an analysis of new terrorism. In a now-classic article, Jose Vegar interviews famous names including Brian Jenkins, Bruce Hoffman, Ron Purver, Brad Roberts, Amy Smithson, and Kyle Olsen, whose analyses are mostly in striking accord with Laqueur's and serve to describe what the distinctive motivations of new terrorists are usually taken to be. Terrorists of the "new breed," all these experts agree, are subject to various "nontraditional" motivations (that is, neither leftist nor nationalist causes) that lead them to try to either subjugate or destroy those who stand outside their communities of belief. As a result, they take themselves to be absolved from all limits on the use of force, including that which prohibits the use of WMD. Traditional terrorists, with their traditional motivations, see the strategic folly of alienating their constituencies through unlimited violence, or else have their own moral scruples about causing death and suffering on such a scale.[11]

Apart from this infelicity on the matter of motivation, Laqueur's work captures the essentials of all the other analyses succinctly.[12] I

---

[10] Laqueur, *The New Terrorism*, 81.

[11] Jose Vegar, "Terrorism's New Breed," *Bulletin of the Atomic Scientists* 54 (March/April 1998): 50–55. See also Jonathan B. Tucker and Amy Sands, "An Unlikely Threat," *Bulletin of the Atomic Scientists* 55 (July/August 1999): 47–52; and Steven Simon and Daniel Benjamin, "America and the New Terrorism," *Survival* 42 (spring 2000): 59–75.

[12] Because Laqueur does not make them a part of his analysis, I am leaving aside other more or less oft-mentioned contrasts between new and traditional terrorists. The organization of new terrorists is a fluid network, that of traditional terrorists a rigid hierarchy; new terrorists are more likely to be amateurs, and traditional, professionals; new are more likely to utilize new, and especially digital technologies, whereas traditional seem to be stuck in the analog era; new terrorists rarely claim responsibility for their actions, traditional always do. The piece that most comprehensively employs this approach is Michael Whine, "The New Terrorism," from the annual report of the Stephen Roth Institute for the Study of Contemporary Anti-Semitism and Racism (Tel Aviv: Antisemitism Worldwide 2000-2001), http://www.ict.org.il/articles/articledet.cfm?articled=427 (accessed May 18, 2003).

shall therefore refer to the most common analysis of the concept of new terrorism as the "Laqueurian" analysis, with apologies to all the other thinkers who have contributed to the effort, though there are other reasons for taking it as canonical. For one thing, an analysis very like Laqueur's has been widely adopted by opinion-forming journalists, where it can have a much greater influence on the academic and policy establishments.[13] Where practice were concerned, new terrorism would require (and suggest) new response strategies, as different from existing ones as new terrorism is supposed to be different from traditional. We might wish, then, the Laqueurian analysis to be complete and correct. If it is not, we would need to reconsider the new phenomena in a way that does justice to our intuitions that there is a profound difference between the likes of Al Qaeda and the Irish Republican Army (IRA), even if it is not what Laqueur and the others say it is.

How convincing is the Laqueurian analysis? Let us look at its structure. The willingness to use all degrees of force up to and including the deployment of WMD and "new fanaticism" are posited as necessary and jointly sufficient for an agent to be a new terrorist. *Ex hypothesi*, traditional terrorism is conducted with conventional weapons and tactics in the name of specific political ends. The analysis is clearly intended to elucidate a *qualitative* difference between traditional and new terrorism—that is, to show that they are quite different in kind from each other, quite apart from their many minor differences. I am going to argue that the definition cannot establish this qualitative difference, for two reasons. On the one

---

[13] Consider, for instance, the following passage:

> . . . al-Qaeda's terrorism is different in kind from the sort practiced by traditional terrorists. Well before September 11th, expert opinion started to worry that terrorists would turn to chemical, biological, radiological or nuclear weapons, and so threaten millions of victims, not just hundreds or thousands. In the late 1990s a succession of warnings were sounded that this would soon become America's chief security threat. The warnings were ignored, not only because the cost of fending off such threats looked prohibitive, but also because of a lingering calculation that even terrorists were rational, deterrable political actors, with a strong interests in keeping their violent actions within some limits if they were to achieve their political ends.
>
> Everything that is known now about al-Qaeda indicates that it does not fit this template. Its aims are mystical, not rational. It does its violence in the name of Allah and so accepts no worldly obligation to moderate it. It is rich, and it is capable. Mr bin Laden and his men have made it plain that they are out to inflict maximum punishment on the infidel nations, and that they want unconventional weapons. "Preparing for Terror," *The Economist*, November 30, 2002, 11.

hand, the first necessary condition can establish only a certain kind of *quantitative* difference. On the other, the second condition's stipulation of a "new fanaticism" is, for one thing, a more figurative way of mistaking quantity for quality, but, even were that not the case, it could not differentiate any form of terrorism from another. I look at the individually necessary conditions of the analysis in that order.

Since Laqueur takes it that new terrorism is always deadlier than traditional, for the moment I shall set aside the mere willingness to use WMD (which he considers enough for any agent to satisfy this condition), and treat the matter as if new terrorists used WMD always, traditional terrorists, never. This poses the difference Laqueur sees between the two kinds of terrorism as starkly as possible. Under those circumstances, I submit, the difference would be only quantitative: to be precise, it would be no more than the relative destructiveness of the techniques used by new and traditional terrorists to produce fear in their targets. In other words, it would not distinguish one kind of terrorism from another, precisely because they would have in common the aim of terrorizing those targets regardless of the means to that end. True, different traditional nonstate terrorists in fact use different techniques; but such differences do not and cannot indicate any qualitative difference between them, so long as their aim in using them is to produce fear in and thereby alter the conduct of their targets. Irish nonstate terrorists, for instance, have scarcely ever engaged in suicide bombing, whereas Palestinian ones often have. Can one thereby conclude that Irish nonstate terrorism, as terrorism, is intrinsically different from Palestinian? I do not see how. By parity of reasoning, I do not see how using WMD could contribute to making terrorism qualitatively "new," rather than just more deadly, if one assumes that all terrorists, as terrorists, want to change their targets' conduct by producing fear in them, irrespective of the means by which they seek to produce fear. As far as I can see, new terrorists who actually used WMD would simply be capable of wreaking greater destruction in pursuit of their aims than traditional terrorists are.

Refuting this narrow point does not, of course, automatically refute Laqueur's broader one. But even if I consider the mere willingness to use all degrees of force up to and including the deployment of WMD, I still do not see how this establishes any qualitative difference. The basic question here is whether it is literally inconceivable that traditional terrorists might be willing to use all degrees of force if they believed that doing so might further their cause. They may have so far shrunk from using certain means for strategic or moral reasons, but there are two obvious rejoinders. First, this empirical point has no conceptual value. If Laqueur's inference were correct, it would be impossible to imagine that traditional terrorists would ever consider using any kind of highly destructive violence, whereas it is all too imaginable. After all, any traditional terrorists who use any kind of violence have conquered whatever scruples they may once have had about doing so, and it is therefore unclear why at least some of them should not be able to conquer all their remaining scruples and use (or at least advocate the use of) all manner of violence so long as their goals remained unachieved. Some counterterrorism experts who accept the Laqueurian analysis have proffered similar speculations. As Kyle Olsen asks: "If, for a nuclear nation, it is rational sometimes to use a nuclear weapon, they why isn't it for a terrorist group when what is at stake is their survival or a very important goal?"[14] Both Amy Smithson and Jessica Stern imaginatively note that using WMD may well gain greater attention for a terrorist action, since everyone is now so desensitized to traditional methods of terrorism.[15]

Even Laqueur himself admits that the sensibilities of traditional terrorists have coarsened, since "evidence . . . tends to show that Western terrorist groups, including the IRA and ETA, and various factions in the former Yugoslavia, have shown greater cruelty in their attacks than European terrorist groups did in an earlier age."[16] Without actually predicting that any traditional terrorists will ever turn to WMD, one can reasonably ask why Laqueur considers it a foregone conclusion that they would never so much as consider it. Moreover, he notes, unquestionably correctly, that armaments and strategies are in as continual an evolution for terrorists as they are for

---

[14] Quoted in Vegar, "Terrorism's New Breed," 53.

[15] Smithson, quoted in Vegar, "Terrorism's New Breed," 52; Jessica Stern, *The Ultimate Terrorists* (Cambridge, MA: Harvard University Press, 1999), 70. An interesting case for analysis would be traditional terrorists who, despairing of attaining their goals, threaten to use WMD that they neither have nor truly intend to use. Do they still count as traditional terrorists, or have they thus become new terrorists?

[16] Laqueur, *The New Terrorism*, 266. This irresistibly calls to mind the story that Michael Walzer tells in *Just and Unjust Wars* about the IRA's attempt to bomb a water plant in Coventry in 1936. The operation was bungled and led to the deaths of five passers-by, an eventuality which reportedly distressed the terrorists. Compare this to the cruelty of, say, the Birmingham and Guildford pub bombings that the provisional IRA carried out in 1974, and it becomes clear that even the scruples characteristic of traditional terrorism do not stay static. See Michael Walzer, *Just and Unjust Wars* (New York: Basic Books, 1977), 199.

any armed force. Laqueur's text suggests why even traditional terrorists may become willing to entertain the use of WMD.

> When terrorism has been effective in the past, it has usually been in the framework of a wider political strategy. In most cases, the political results of terrorism have been insignificant or even the opposite of what the terrorists intended, and its lasting impact has usually been in inverse proportion to the attention it got in the media. But these observations are true only with regard to the past; they do not offer a clue for the future. In the past, terrorists have not had access to means of mass destruction; technology has changed this state of affairs, and the consequences could be beyond our imagination.[17]

In short, for all terrorists, WMD are, in the jargon of the field, very effective force multipliers. Since the power of nonstate terrorists is usually—in the jargon again—asymmetrical to that of their targets, it could surely be tempting to traditional terrorists to make the terms more symmetrical—especially if the struggle were against a nonnuclear state that could not respond in kind.

The reader may not find it convincing to argue that any use of violence is the thin end of the wedge. My second refutation of the first necessary condition, then, begins with the question: Why are new terrorists not subject to the strategic constraints that, we are told, make traditional terrorists think at least twice about using extreme violence? Laqueur inadvertently concedes that they are. Writing about the potential for using biological weapons, he says that since "[w]eapons of mass destruction will not appeal to terrorists pursuing clear political aims, especially if friends might be among the victims," it is the case that "[o]nly the most extreme and least rational terrorist groups, or those motivated not by distinct political aims but by apocalyptic visions or by some pan-destructionist belief, are likely to employ weapons of this kind."[18] It seems, then, that new terrorists, insofar as they are likely to use WMD, necessarily lack distinct political aims. Must one not ask, in the light of my general analysis of terrorism, whether depriving political terrorists of such aims simultaneously removes all intention to terrify any target in order to reach those aims; which leads to the question of whether Laqueur is describing terrorism of any sort. I am inclined to say not, and shall explain why later, when I look at the second necessary condition of the Laqueurian analysis.

---

[17] Laqueur, *The New Terrorism*, 48.
[18] Laqueur, *The New Terrorism*, 71.

On the grounds given so far, I reject the first condition of the Laqueurian analysis as being incapable of establishing any qualitative difference between kinds of terrorism, although it does identify quantitative differences in the destructive potential of different terrorists. As such, though, it is at most an empirical and not a conceptual distinction. Assuming I am right on this point, only the success of the second necessary condition—"new fanaticism"—can prevent the complete inoperativeness of the whole analysis. Sad to say, then, I once more find it impossible to see what qualitative difference this new fanaticism makes; for, surely, engaging in terrorism absolutely requires some motivating enthusiasm, subscription to which it is never any abuse of the term to call "fanaticism." Besides, Laqueur cannot seem to stop himself from qualifying his own condition out of existence. For example, he states that, whereas the motivations of such traditional terrorists are socialist or nationalist ideologies, new fanaticism is basically religious ideology. The origin of such ideology he traces to a violent minority of eschatological sectarians.[19] Such new fanatics, it seems, appear at the fringes of mainstream religious traditions, or "among madmen."[20] But then Laqueur claims that the roots of *all* terrorism are "quasireligious," and cites, among others, the case of members of the provisional IRA—paradigmatic traditional terrorists—martyring themselves by hunger strikes.[21] Surely he is right that this self-immolation (not directly part of a terrorist operation but intended to secure the men the status of political prisoners) bespeaks a devotion to a traditional cause no weaker than that displayed by any new terrorist. All the same, it is clear that the aim of the provisional IRA is *not* to fulfill the prophecies of some sectarian eschatology. If that is the case, however, it is hard to see what the difference between new and traditional fanaticism is in Laqueur's own terms. Moreover, the insistence on at least quasi-religious motivations does not make obvious sense of the actions of some members of the other great class of new terrorists: right-wing ideologues like Timothy McVeigh. Laqueur hardly becomes more convincing when he artlessly notes that, despite the etymology of the term, fanaticism is not the exclusive preserve of the religious, and cites not only the

---

[19] Laqueur, *The New Terrorism*, 79–80. Laqueur (84) stresses that this is a minority of religious people.

[20] Laqueur, *The New Terrorism*, 92.

[21] Laqueur, *The New Terrorism*, 83.

IRA martyrs again, but also the great regime terrorists of the twentieth century, including Stalin, as evidence.[22]

Perhaps I am being unfair to Laqueur. Even if the actions of traditional terrorists can be described as "fanatical," is this not a rather pale sense of the term? Laqueur draws attention to fanaticism in the strongest sense, terminating in the apocalyptic mania that motivates groups like Aum Shinri Kyo. His stipulation seems arbitrary, however, because it is so hard to find any relatively clear qualitative boundary between the motivations of new and traditional terrorists. What is easy to find is a difference in the specific ends served by fanaticism in different cases; but such differences show again that Laqueur mistakes quantity for quality. New fanaticism he takes to be quantitative in the sense that the ends for which new terrorists strive are larger in scale than those for which traditional terrorists do. The provisional IRA wants a united Ireland and therefore wages war against the British in Ulster, whereas Al Qaeda wants to purify Islam's holy lands by waging a worldwide *jihad* against the infidels who have corrupted them. Aum Shinri Kyo, for its part, covets the destruction of the whole world. Certainly, each ambition is quite different from all the others, but each group's dedication to its aims— its motivating enthusiasm, its fanaticism—is indistinguishable from that of each of the others. Fanaticism is fanaticism, regardless of what a given fanatic is fanatical for. Once more, I cannot see what qualitative difference such an essentially quantitative factor makes in Laqueur's eyes.

This concludes the bulk of my case against the Laqueurian analysis, but I would add two final criticisms. First, it has only one clear instantiation in the real world: Aum Shinri Kyo. Those members of this group who carried out the Tokyo subway attack certainly subscribed to its apocalyptic outlook; and the fact that they actually used sarin, even if not truly "weaponized," makes it undebatable that they would have used true WMD, had they been able to. That said, all other supposedly paradigmatic new terrorists such as Al Qaeda and Timothy McVeigh are unclear cases precisely because one can at best speculate about their willingness to use WMD, and they do have some specific demands.[23] Furthermore, I am inclined to question the

---

[22] Laqueur, *The New Terrorism*, 97–99.

[23] The anthrax attacks in the USA in late 2001 may seem to offer a clear instantiation, and again it is reasonable to suppose that whoever uses crude biological weapons would use better ones if they were available. Since no one but whoever sent the tainted

description of even Aum Shinri Kyo as new terrorists, not because they fail to satisfy either condition of the Laqueurian analysis but because, on my definition, they are not terrorists! Shoko Asahara and his cohorts wished to purify the world by destroying humankind, not to produce fear in order to affect conduct of any target. Under my analysis of terrorism, then, Aum Shinri Kyo members do not even count as social terrorists, let alone political ones. If I am correct about that, then the one clear case of new terrorism is not a member of the class of terrorists.

III. Terrorism, *Mythos*, and *Logos*

My conclusions about the Laqueurian analysis, then, are quite negative. Leaving aside its paucity of clear cases, Laqueur's crucial conceptual mistake is that of taking quantitative differences in means and motivation to be differences in the very natures of different kinds of terrorism, when the irreducible heterogeneity within these realms must fail to make any putative phenomena theoretically intelligible. Can anything be said for the Laqueurian analysis? Despite the fact that its first necessary condition strikes me as quite unsalvageable, I think so. Where Laqueur discusses new fanaticism, he has put his finger on something that sets the likes of Al Qaeda apart from any of the IRA's incarnations—even though it is not what he thinks has put his finger on. Given how unsatisfactory the concept of new fanaticism is, I shall propose some new ideas, which, I believe, afford greater analytical insight into truly qualitative differences between types of political terrorism. These ideas do not ground such differences in means and motivations but, like my general concept of terrorism, in broad classes of intentions and ends.

These new ideas are historical. Saying this may seem to undermine my insistence, heretofore, that I am making conceptual rather than empirical claims. I would demur to such an objection, since analytically useful concepts come in two varieties. There are those which adequately describe actual phenomena and those which describe potential ones—that is, phenomena either logically but not practically possible or both logically and practically possible but, in either case, not actual. One point on which Laqueur is indisputably correct is that political terrorism is a subject with a history, because *any* actual phenomenon

---

letters has any idea what the demands—if any—are, however, we must suspend judgment on the question of whether that individual or group is new-fanatical.

has a history and, to that extent, an analytically useful concept of an actual phenomenon must make some very general reference to historical circumstances. Take, for instance, the useful distinction between the concepts of state and nonstate terrorism. In a world in which there were no states, this distinction would be otiose but not meaningless as long as the difference were conceivable between that world and another in which states existed. That is, under those circumstances state terrorism would be a potential, though not actual, phenomenon. (Were the difference between the two worlds inconceivable, the distinction would be meaningless, and state terrorism therefore not even a potential phenomenon.) In a world in which only one state existed, however, the distinction would be both useful and meaningful, but in itself no different from how it would be in a world in which there were more than one state. The Laqueurian analysis is like the second kind of case, and I have argued that it describes neither an actual nor a potential phenomenon but one which, though conceivable, cannot be actualized in its own right. The components of the analysis are logically or practically possible either individually or together, but are at most the *ne plus ultra* of existing concepts. There is as little difference between his concepts of new and traditional terrorism as there is in the concept of regime terrorism in a world with ten states rather than one.

If I am right about this, then it should be possible to analyze the phenomenon that Laqueur calls new terrorism to at least some extent in terms of the categories that he takes to apply only to traditional terrorism. I intend now to sketch a way of analyzing what the existing categories do not, and the Laqueurian analysis cannot, capture. So, taking the basic categories I outlined earlier—the general concept of terrorism and the family of political terrorisms—as something like fixed points, I shall set alongside them two new categories. First, there is the double category of *promodern* and *antimodern* terrorism. Second, there is that of terrorism that is *mythic* and in either a strong or a weak sense of the term. The very names *pro-* and *antimodern* terrorism indicate the essential historicity of this brace of categories, which I can define very briefly in terms of their ends: promodern terrorists seek to extend the reach of modernity, antimodern terrorists to inhibit it. The aim of mythic terrorism, in either the strong or weak sense, is to establish the temporal ascendancy of some given *mythos* (a difficult term that I shall define later). These classes cut across each other, so that one can talk about strongly or weakly mythic pro- or antimodern terrorism. These notions thus supply a scheme of analysis at once finer grained and wider in scope than the rather crude dichotomy of traditional and new terrorism. I would contend that every political terrorist or political terrorist organization falls under one of the four categories thus defined. It is also my view that the combination of these concepts explains the puzzling phenomena of latter-day political terrorism far better than the Laqueurian analysis can, or than the standard analysis can without them.

Why do we need these new categories? I have to answer this question at some length and somewhat indirectly, by focusing on a conflict between the Laqueurian analysis and the actual world-views of paradigmatically traditional terrorists.[24] Robert A. Friedlander conceives of political terrorism as a response to as a reaction to "perceived injustice."[25] This coheres with Laqueur's notion of traditional terrorism, which is a response to what the agent believes to be injustice brought about by modern society (which is to say, usually, liberal democracy). So, the activities of the provisional IRA, for instance, are justified as a response to British colonialism, those of the RAF to the domination of the bourgeoisie, and so on.[26] Understandings of modernity, however, are by no means a unitary phenomenon, and those who accept the Laqueurian analysis of traditional terrorism take the terrorist to be motivated by either of the distinctively modern ideologies of nationalism (as in the case of the IRA) and socialism (as in that of the RAF), or by combinations of them (as in that of ETA). Ideologues like this are old-fanatical: fully committed to the cause of establishing the ascendancy, in some given place, of some interpretation of the *logos* of modernity (of which, more later), but

---

[24] Even though I reject Laqueur's categories of new and traditional terrorism, I shall frequently have recourse to his terminology. So, wherever I use them, his terms should be understood in contrast to my own.

[25] Robert A. Friedlander, ed., introduction to *Terrorism, Documents of International and Local Control*, vol. 1 (Dobbs Ferry, NY: Oceana, 1979–1999), 61.

[26] To avoid possible confusion, I should point out that the abbreviation "RAF" refers not to the United Kingdom's Royal Air Force (which, indeed, has been accused of terrorizing civilians), but to the Red Army Faction. This ultra-left group, led by Andreas Baader and Ulrike Meinhof, operated in West Germany from the late 1960s until it formally disbanded itself in 1998. Its methods were those of what experts usually take to be classic urban terrorism: bombings, shootings, kidnappings. The most usual motivation of its rather few hardcore members appear to have been visceral disgust with capitalism.

possessing scruples, whether moral or strategic, that will serve to limit the means they will employ.

When one predicates old fanaticism of extreme left-wing groups, however, the contradiction that I have mentioned above arises. As examples, one may take any of the any of the groups prominent in Europe and the Americas from the mid-1960s to the present day: the RAF, the Weather Underground, the Shining Path, and so on. In Laqueurian terms, each is a traditional terrorist group because it has political or social goals, in each case identical with realizing that very modern vision of justice, a socialist utopia. Since inaugurating the workers' paradise requires the complete eradication of bourgeois society, however, such groups just as surely satisfy Laqueur's second necessary condition for being new terrorists, since they aim "at the destruction of society and the elimination of large sections of the population . . . as a precondition for the growth of another, better, and in any case different breed of human." The difference between new fanaticism and old fanaticism thus disappears—especially when one bears in mind that Stalin and Mao, those avatars of communist regime terrorism, killed more people between them than all new terrorists put together will perhaps ever have the chance to. Nonetheless, it is also quite clear that there is some qualitative difference between such socialist groups and the radical Islamicism of, Hamas, Hezbollah, and Al Qaeda—or, for that matter, between such right-wing but promodern nonstate terrorists as Timothy McVeigh and such nonsocialist but promodern ones as the provisional IRA. Saying that they are "extremists" explains nothing, since this is just a different way of saying that they are somehow fanatical, without even invoking the difference between the old and new varieties.

This, then, is the reason for my proposal of the new categories I have defined: because, while the standard analyses of political terrorism fail to capture something important, the Laqueurian analysis does not only fails to do better but also makes a retroactive mystery of the motivations of traditional terrorists. Approaching the matter from the new angle I am suggesting can resolve these problems. The first matter to consider is the notion of subscribing to some interpretation of the *logos* of modernity. I borrow the relevant sense of the term *logos* from the work of Karen Armstrong, who borrows it from Johannes Sloek and defines it by contrast with the term *mythos*. Even though both, as she tells us, are "ways of thinking, speaking, and acquiring knowledge," *mythos*, as one would expect, is founded on myth, which "looks back to the origins of life, to the foundations of culture, and to the deepest levels of the human mind."[27] *Logos*, on the other hand, is "the rational, pragmatic, and scientific thought that enable[s] men and women to function well in the world," and which, Armstrong notes, "is the basis of our society," by which she means Western modernity.[28] Similarly, Jürgen Habermas notes that "[w]hat we find most astonishing" about *mythos* ". . . is the peculiar leveling of the different domains of reality: nature and culture are projected onto the same plane. From this reciprocal assimilation of nature to culture and conversely culture to nature, there results, on the one hand, a nature that is outfitted with anthropomorphic features, drawn into the communicative network of social subjects, and in this sense humanized, and on the other hand, a culture that is to a certain extent naturalized and reified and absorbed into the objective nexus of operations of anonymous powers. . . ."[29]

Such leveling of domains, Habermas notes, "makes possible not only a theory that explains the world narratively and renders it plausible, but also a practice through which the world can be controlled in an imaginary way."[30] The "we" who are astonished by this operation are, of course, moderns who are at home with complexity. The fault line between *mythos* and *logos*, then, is usually taken to be the same as that between modernity and the world of tradition.

How do these issues relate to political terrorism? To put the point as simply as I can: when the prestige and worldly power of *mythos* is undermined by forces promoting some *logos*, adherents to the displaced *mythos* may attempt, perhaps violently, to rehabilitate the traditional way of life associated with it (or, more or less wittingly, to assert new ones). Terrorists in the grip of *mythoi* thus will certainly attempt to control the world, but, *pace* Habermas, do so in a far from imaginary way. Several things may seem to follow from this notion of *mythic* terrorism, any of which would be confusions. First, my reader may think either that I intend the notion to be identical with Laqueur's traditional terrorism, or else the counterpart to my own notion of promodern terrorism. In both cases, this would be a confusion, though an understandable one given the profusion of the antithetical terms "traditional" and "modern" in my own and Laqueur's analyses.

---

[27] Karen Armstrong, *The Battle for God* (New York: Alfred A. Knopf, 2000), xiii.

[28] Armstrong, *The Battle for God*, xiv–xv.

[29] Jürgen Habermas, *The Theory of Communicative Action,* vol. 1, *Reason and the Rationalization of Society* (Boston: Beacon Press, 1984), 47.

[30] Habermas, *Theory of Communicative Action*, vol. 1, 48.

Alternatively, it might seem that I intend the idea to map directly onto that of new terrorism and, correlatively, that I intend Laqueur's traditional terrorism to answer to some as-yet-undefined idea of non-mythicism. I shall do my best to briefly forestall such possible mistakes about my meaning.

On the first point, recall how Laqueur defines both new and traditional terrorism in terms of means and motivations. The traditionality of terrorism hence bears no necessary relation to the any traditional ways of life. Rather, Laqueur has in mind a somewhat figurative "traditionality" in means and motivations themselves: "conventional weapons" and "ideologies," respectively. If we once again contemplate the activities of, say, the RAF, we can see that their socialist beliefs were, if anything, opposed to the traditions of German culture, and sought their destruction. Recall also that I defined promodern political terrorism as seeking to rectify injustices perpetrated in the name of some understanding of the *logos* of modernity, by extending the reach of another, more just one. Plainly, one need not subscribe to a modern ideology to combat perceived injustices perpetrated by the dominant interpretation. One could instead seek to destroy all manifestations of all and any *logoi*, and reinstate a traditional *mythos*. Once more, though, the activities of the RAF give the lie to this view, since their aim was to break the domination of the capitalistic *logos* and institute the socialist. The RAF's *logos*, though, had all the motivating power that any traditional *mythos* can have, even though the aims sought under its aegis were self-consciously antitraditional. Had the Baader-Meinhof Gang triumphed, the beliefs and practices that they would have made hegemonic in German society would eventually have come to have the status of traditions, which is the kind of situation that I had in mind earlier, when I referred in passing to "more or less wittingly" seeking to institute new traditions in place of some modern *logos*.

On the second possible point of confusion, it is pretty clear that, since I consider the Laqueurian analysis fundamentally flawed, I am hardly going to propose that my concept of mythic terrorism should simply replace it. Furthermore, I do not intend mythic terrorism to be the counterpart of promodern terrorism—that honor goes to *anti*-modern terrorism. Bear in mind that I intend this idea, along with those of promodern and antimodern terrorism, to do necessary work that neither the standard analysis nor the Laqueurian analysis can. Consequently, all my concepts embrace both the standard and Laqueurian analyses. On top of that, as I have already mentioned, the concept of mythic terrorism cuts across those of pro- and antimodern terrorism so that, far from being counterparts, promodern and mythic terrorism can be used to modify each other. Apart from that, the argument I made in the previous paragraph—that a *mythos* need not be traditional, but can indeed be antitraditional—applies to this matter, too.

As I have said, my new concepts are intended to be analytically useful in ways that the standard and Laqueurian analyses cannot be. I have remarked also that Laqueur's notion of new fanaticism has some virtue. Combining these assertions might lead to a third misunderstanding of my position, such that mythic terrorism is taken to be identical not with the whole Laqueurian analysis, but with new fanaticism alone. Saying once more that it is again hardly likely that I would want my idea to occupy exactly the same ground as one which I have rejected is not sufficient to make the difference between my own position and Laqueur's clear, nor to make sense of my limited approval for the concept of new fanaticism. To do that, I must explain and justify one last distinction, which I drew earlier but did not expand on: that between terrorists who are mythic in strong and weak senses of the term. I criticized the idea of new fanaticism on the grounds that it does not properly accommodate the fact that commitment to a cause can show itself in various intensities. Laqueur takes it that, because members of one terrorist organization can seem to display so much greater intensity of commitment than the members of another, the former class is different in kind from the latter. Clearly, though, such differences can in principle appear not only between entire organizations but also between either different members of the same organization or in the same organization (or any given member of it) at different times. Empirically speaking, moreover, the greatest intensity of commitment, supposedly unique to new terrorists, can easily be discerned in traditional terrorists as well. As before, then, my objection is that the Laqueurian analysis lies at the mercy of the inevitable heterogeneity, both theoretical and practical, of motivation; and my distinction between strong and weak mythicism relies, as my other concepts do, on the necessary intentions and ends of terrorist activity.

Every terrorist group is mythic in the sense of having some motivating narrative. In the weakest sense of the term, however, any human action is mythic in that agents act in accordance with some narrative that enables them to interpret the world coherently, though incompletely to a greater or lesser degree. This fact is innocuous enough. To walk down the street, one must take it for granted that the

street will not collapse under one's feet, even though the logical possibility of the street collapsing shows the incompleteness of such
essential quotidian mythicism. The fact is, though, that this *mythos* is
more often correct than incorrect. One whose actions are mythic in
the strong sense, however, disregards everything standing outside his
mythos—except, maybe, whatever helps establish its temporal
supremacy. Were a given person's *mythos* founded on the possibility
of the street collapsing, he would never set foot on it, despite the
fairly impressive disconfirmation by the street's integrity.

A mythic terrorist's aims (or, perhaps I should say, any terrorist's
mythic aims) can be understood in the same way. Weakly mythic aims
can be adequately met by some kind of compromise with other *mythoi*,
or with *logoi*. Strongly mythic aims can be met only when everyone
within some defined population accepts the terrorist's *mythos*. In other
words, weakly mythic terrorists demand only concessions from those
who do not share their *mythoi*, whereas strongly mythic terrorists
demand either conversion to their *mythoi*, or death.[31] Strongly mythic
terrorists, then, are not necessarily religious or right-wing fanatics, nor
fanatical in any unprecedented way. Rather, they simply will brook no
compromise on their demands—which, it must be said, is a long way
from saying that these demands must be somehow unrealistic.
Similarly, weakly mythic terrorists are not necessarily left-wingers or
ethnic nationalists, and their limited demands are not necessarily realistic. Laqueur's new fanaticism is in important respects the same thing
as strong mythicism. Furthermore, since I am not concerned with the
motivations behind political terrorism but its aims, being strongly
mythic in my sense of the term means being committed to the sole
ascendancy of one's own *mythos* (including some *logos*) in a public
realm whose only necessary limit is the entire sentient creation.[32]

---

[31] This would explain why "new" terrorists never claim responsibility for their operations or issue clear demands connected to them—would, that is, if there were much
to explain. Once again, I think that this characteristic is a matter of degree rather than
kind. True, "traditional" terrorists often (though by no means always) make the connection between their actions and demands quite explicit—the provisional IRA even
used to call press conferences after many of theirs. But Osama bin Laden has issued
a long *fatwa* as a standing iteration of Al Qaeda's demands, among which are the
removal of infidels from the holy places, and the destruction of Israel. In other words,
Al Qaeda's only demand is that everyone accept its *mythos*, or die.

[32] In the light of what I say here, it does not require much reflection to see that terrorism is not the only phenomenon that can be described mythic, whether strongly or
weakly. I shall leave it to the reader to try applying it elsewhere.

Because mythicism of any sort is not "new" in any important sense, my analysis does not fall prey to the uninviting dilemma of classing traditional left-wing terrorists such as the RAF either contradictorily as traditional terrorists but new fanatics, or anachronistically as "new" terrorists. On the grounds that they are strongly mythic, my position allows us to easily distinguish them from, say, the provisional IRA, who are weakly mythic. The fact that the provisional IRA has almost completely suspended terrorist operations for eight years at the time of this writing indicates that it is at least open to negotiations, and therefore to some kind of compromise with the injustices that its members believe Britain to have perpetrated in the name of the colonialist *logos*. Violence might, of course, continue in some way—after all, there are irreconcilables in every movement (many of whom, in the IRA's case, have joined such "splinter groups" as the INLA or the Real IRA). By contrast, however, there would be little hope of finding the point at which an organization such as Al Qaeda or the RAF would be prepared to enter a peace process, because strongly mythic terrorism *is* the terrorism of irreconcilables. Notice, though, that this means that at least one traditional terrorist outfit (the RAF) has more in common with a paradigm of new terrorism (Al Qaeda) than with the others of its supposed type, while neither has much in common with Aum Shinri Kyo.

Even if one accepts my argument so far, one thing that may still be unclear is how the concept of mythicism relates to those of pro- or antimodernism. To explain this, I shall examine how combining them can illuminate the difference between Al Qaeda and the RAF. I repeat that I do not consider the distinction between *mythos* and *logos* to be a straightforward distinction between traditionality and modernity, conceived of as mutually exclusive categories. As Armstrong points out, *mythos* and *logos*, given their different functions, need not be at odds with each other. Neither she nor Habermas, however, notes that the borderline between the two is so blurred that any given *logos* can be or become a *mythos*. Scientists, for instance, accept the scientific *logos* in very much the same spirit as the Egyptians accepted the idea of Ma'at. This, indeed, is the sense in which any *logos* can itself become traditional, when tradition is understood as unreflective engagement in practices rooted in certain propositions that are accepted uncritically. Such a phenomenon is characteristic, particularly, of groups like the RAF, whose promodern socialist *logos* takes on the all-encompassing character of a strong but (as yet) nontraditional *mythos*. Needless to say, a strong traditional *mythos* can displace a *logos* in a similar way, as is usually the case with religious groups such as Al Qaeda.

The distinction between such cases is accentuated by the fact that adherents to the views of religious terrorist groups see themselves as standing foursquare against all modern *logoi*, a tendency that Edward M. Shils calls *traditionalism*. He asserts that traditional practices and beliefs "recommend themselves by their appropriateness to the present situation confronted by their recipients and especially by a certain measure of authoritativeness which they possess by virtue of their provenience from the past."[33] *Traditionalism*, on the other hand, is an intransigent adherence to traditions.

> Traditionalism is the self-conscious, deliberate affirmation of traditional norms, in full awareness of their traditional nature and alleging that their merit derives from that traditional transmission from a sacred origin. This is a revivalist, enthusiastic attitude. It is always dogmatic and doctrinaire and insists on uniformity. It insists on thoroughgoing adherence; it does not discriminate between the workable and the unworkable and it regards all elements of the tradition it praises as equally essential. Traditionalism, which is a form of heightened sensibility to the sacred, demands exclusiveness. It is content with nothing less than totality. Traditionalism is not content with the observance of a tradition in a particular sphere, such as in family or religious life. It is satisfied only if the traditionalist outlook permeates all spheres—political, economic, cultural, and religious—and unifies them in a common subordination to the sacred as it is received from the past.[34]

On this reading of the phenomenon, Laqueur's new fanatics are more traditionalist than many of his traditional terrorists. Given that my own argument has the consequence that "traditional" terrorists are in many cases no less fanatical than "new" (or, that the former cannot be assumed to be any more so than the latter), I might coin the term "modernism" to denote the tendency to reject all traditional categories and make some *logos* one's *mythos*. This mirror image of Shilsian traditionalism is in fact the case with the left-wing groups of whom the RAF is a paradigm. As modernist terrorists, the RAF wants to correct the injustice of modern capitalism by replacing it with a socialism that is a child of the *logos* as interpreted by Marx and that

---

[33] Edward M. Shils, "Tradition and Liberty: Antimony and Interdependence," *Ethics* 68 (April 1958): 154.

[34] Shils, "Tradition and Liberty," 160.

discards almost all traditional and modern *mythoi* and *logoi*. Traditionalist terrorists like Al Qaeda, on the other hand, desire socialism no more than capitalism if it fails to accord with the revelation of the Qur'an, and as such espouse just the kind of traditional *mythos* and *logos* that modernists reject. So, while the RAF is as strongly mythic as Al Qaeda, the qualitative difference between them becomes easily comprehensible once we understand the differing orientations of their attitudes toward modernity.

The notions of traditionalism and modernism need to be both delimited and further refined. As to their delimitation, each concept covers only one of two types of strong mythicism and has no application to weak mythicism, which usually comprises some combination of subscription to both *mythos* and *logos*. The aim of both the provisional IRA and ETA, for instance, is to have a people, defined by ethnic traditions, take up its rightful place among the nations of the modern world. Obviously, weak mythicism comes in different strengths, according to the relative emphasis on modernity and traditionality, and the greater the importance of either, the closer the group or individual approaches strong mythicism. In theory, as I have noted, strong mythicism excludes any trace of subscription to either modernity or traditionality, but in practice there probably can never be such purity of commitment. Thus, the real boundary between strong and weak mythicism will fall at points in a continuum where the commitment to either modernism or traditionalism is so feeble as to effectively be overwhelmed by the other.

The necessary refinement of the two concepts can be achieved by distinguishing, within the domain of modernism, *technical* modernism from *moral* modernism—or, by parity of reasoning, technical from moral traditionalism within the realm of traditionalism. The first variety is a commitment to what most people probably have in mind when they speak casually of modernity itself: the nearly complete replacement of natural powers by artificial ones, as the horsepower of the internal combustion engine replaced that of the horse. Moral modernism is most simply defined as a pluralism brought about by anthropological awareness and underwritten by the virtue of tolerance. Because commitment to one strand of modernism does not automatically imply commitment to the other, one can approve of what one might call moral modernity and disapprove of technical, disapprove of moral modernity in its entirety but of only a part of technical (e.g., the media that purvey images of moral modernity), disapprove of both, and so on.

Taken together, these last two points should clear up the apparent contradiction of traditionalist terrorists such as the members of Al Qaeda or the Taliban using modern technology to undertake their antimodern (and antitraditional, to the extent that each movement opposes non-Islamic traditions) jihads. For there is, in fact, no contradiction in the adherents of a traditionalist *mythos* calling on the resources of technical modernity to suppress moral modernity. Everything in the modern world stands outside their strong *mythos*, but their members use motor vehicles, digital technology, and even the mass media to further their cause of ending modernity. In the case of Al Qaeda, the notion of *jihad* as a literal holy war against an un-Islamic modernity personified by the United States did not deter Mohammed Atta and his associates from using jet airliners, that symbol of the modern transcendence of our earthboundedness, to destroy the World Trade Center while the most all-pervasive and technically advanced mass media in the world recorded and almost obsessively replayed the event from every available angle.

Such an orientation, defined in opposition to modernity, always includes an appeal to values that are conceived to be traditional in the sense of being premodern, and therefore purer than modern values. This very fact obviously implies that this appeal takes place during modernity, a point which at once makes it impossible for those values to be literally *pre*-modern, and difficult for them to be truly nonmodern, either. Armstrong's synthetic work on religious fundamentalism suggests that participants in such reactions to modernity have usually lost contact with a great part of the traditional past that they lionize, and therefore that the reactions themselves cannot truly be either premodern or nonmodern. And, as Samuel P. Huntington notes, religious fundamentalism is only part, if an important one, of a wider traditionalist reaction to modernization in (usually) the non-Western world.[35] As with all such reactions, antimodern terrorism cannot exist without modernity itself. Its frequent use of high modern technology and institutions serves as an ironic comment on this fact. As Shils might put it, although traditionalist terrorism is a form of traditionalism that fails to tell the workable from the unworkable aspects of the traditions it reveres, it cannot be indifferent to the means of implementing its moral traditionalism and thus to discerning what the arsenal of technical modernity may supply it with.

---

[35] Samuel P. Huntington, *The Clash of Civilizations and the Remaking of World Order* (New York: Touchstone, 1997), 95–96.

I have now generated a brace of categories—strongly and weakly mythic, and pro- and antimodern—to enrich the taxonomy of terrorism. It hardly needs saying that any of these types of terrorism can come in domestic or international varieties and be carried out by state or nonstate agents. This expansion of our diagnostic powers clears up the confusions that Laqueur's notion of new terrorism is prone to and opens up analysis to new possibilities—for instance, there is no reason why the willingness to use WMD, or their actual use, need be the exclusive domain of strongly mythic terrorists, whether traditionalist or modernist. My new categories allow us to define the hitherto puzzling qualitative difference (and the hitherto concealed similarity) between strongly mythic groups like the RAF and Al Qaeda, and their common difference from weakly mythic ones such as the IRA. As it happens, this schema at once reveals and resolves another merely apparent contradiction, considering which allows me to say a few words about the application of these categories to state terrorism. If left-wing terrorists tend to be modernists, what can we make of the regime terrorism of the Khmer Rouge in Cambodia between 1975 and 1979? There, people were herded out of the cities and made to work in the countryside, while the attempt was made to execute everyone with a college education. A communist terror this certainly was; a promodern one it was certainly not. My taxonomy now allows us to categorize the Khmer Rouge not simply as domestic regime terrorists, but as strongly mythic against both moral and a great part of technical modernity (that is, fully traditionalist) ones—communist terror via Rousseau as much as Marx. Whereas the Khmer Rouge was antimodern and strongly mythic, the strongly mythic regime terrorism of Stalin, Mao, Castro, and other communist dictators is anti–moral modernity but pro–technical modernity, as was the communist nonstate terrorism of the RAF and others. Thus, my new typology refines not only the class of nonstate terrorism (which is all that the Laqueurian analysis, even if successful, could have done), but those of state terrorism, too.

It should hardly need saying that, where terrorism is concerned, both strongly and weakly mythic terrorism, whether pro- or antimodern, can be domestic or international and be carried out by state or nonstate agents. This expansion of the diagnostic powers of the standard analysis clears up the confusions that the Laqueurian analysis is prone to while explaining the same range of phenomena and more. I would not argue, though, that my new categories are more fundamental to understanding terrorism than any others, and this fact I believe to be largely a function of their historicity. For example, the idea of antimodern terrorism (whether anti–moral modernity or anti–technical modernity, or both) is neither more nor less basic than that of, say, nonstate terrorism; and the idea of strongly mythic terrorism is neither more nor less abstract than those of domestic or international terrorism. For that reason, the categories can be arranged with the more general categories in any way that proves productive, except insofar as each of them is subordinate to the overall concept of terrorism. In deciding how to respond to terrorism that is anti–technical modernity, for instance, it may not be necessary to specify whether it is state or nonstate terrorism (and, in the case of state-sponsored terrorism, it would in a sense be both).

I do not intend to say more about the actual application of the concepts in responding to particular cases of terrorism, but I do want to pass on a final thought related to that concern. I noted earlier how ironic, though comprehensible, it is that traditionalist terrorists often employ modern technology to serve the purpose of destroying moral modernity. Just as ironic is the consequence that the aims of an effective response to traditionalist terrorism of any sort must, it seems, be modernist—that is, strongly mythic but promodern. Otherwise, the defenders of modernity will have no clear ends to aim at in their response, beyond the most pragmatically literal. We are therefore left with a paradoxical aftertaste. Traditionalist terrorism often must use technical modernity's *logos* to be effective; and responses to it must draw on a *mythos* of moral modernity that will elicit sincere tropes regarding the desirability of rationality, tolerance, progress, and so on. The outpouring of patriotism in the U.S. following September 11 is, it seems to me, but one manifestation of such a modern *mythos*. Whether it can become hardened into a narrow traditionalism—as all *mythoi* may, regardless of whether they originated in *logos* or not—is one of the more unsettling long-term questions for those of us who identify with modernity of all kinds. The dehumanizing pseudo-scientific military blather that denotes civilian deaths during war as "collateral damage" is, perhaps, just the tip of the iceberg.

Conceptualizing the War on Terrorism

| 3 |

On What Is the War on Terror?

SIMON KELLER

After Japan attacked Pearl Harbor, America declared war on Japan. After members of Al Qaeda attacked the World Trade Center and the Pentagon, America declared war on terror. But the War on Terror is not literally a war on terror, because terror is a feeling and the War on Terror is not a war on a feeling. It is sometimes called a war on terrorism; is that what it really is? Or is it rather a war on *a* terror—perhaps in the sense in which a person can be a terror, or in the sense in which there was a terror in France in the 1790s? Or is it a war on terrorists (and those who harbor them), or on *some* terrorists, or simply on Al Qaeda? I'll try to make some progress towards an answer to this question, not by examining in any detail the ways in which the war is being conducted, but rather by asking which of the things just mentioned are things on which it makes sense to have a war. I should admit at the outset that I take this question in its normative sense; I'll be saying something not just about what the war is on, but what it should be on, and what we should call it.

1. Wars On and Wars Between

Talk of having a war *on* something is interestingly different from talk of having a war *against* or *with* something, and of having a war *between* two things, because it's possible to have a war on something that is not the sort of thing that can have a war on you. On the one

Previously published in *Human Rights Review* 5, no. 2 (2004). Copyright 2004 by Transaction Publishers. Reprinted by permission of the publisher.

hand, there are wars like America's war on Japan. When America fought a war on Japan, Japan fought a war on America, there was a war between America and Japan, and America and Japan were at war with each other.[1] On the other hand, there are wars like the War on Poverty and the War on Drugs. While Lyndon Johnson's government fought a war on poverty, poverty did not fight a war on the Johnson government, the Johnson government and poverty were not at war with each other, and there was not a war between the Johnson government and poverty; and this isn't because poverty declined to participate in the war, but because it isn't the sort of thing that could.

When a war is described using the first kind of talk—as a war on a country, an organization, or something else that can conceivably wage a war itself—there need not be the suggestion that the thing on which the war is being fought is, just in virtue of its being that thing, something on which a war should be fought. The Second World War could be described, from the Allies' point of view, as a war on Germany (amongst other countries), without its being thereby understood that for as long as there is such a thing as Germany it will be something on which the Allies will, or ought to, be fighting a war. The bare fact that Germany is Germany constitutes no reason to go to war against it.

Things are different if we describe the Second World War using the second kind of talk—as, for example, a war on fascism. (While the Allied Powers might have fought a war on fascism, fascism did not fight a war on the allied powers, and the war was not a war between the Allies and fascism.) When we describe ourselves as fighting a war on fascism, we are to be understood as suggesting that fascism is by its very nature something that ought to be eradicated— that fascism's being fascism constitutes a reason to fight it. It would not make sense to say, "At the moment, we're fighting a war on fascism (or poverty or drugs), but we hope that at a future time we'll be on better terms with fascism (or poverty or drugs) and the reason for fighting it will have gone away."

To declare war on something that could not conceivably go to war itself—something like drugs or poverty or fascism—is to offer a strong negative evaluation of that thing, considered in itself and under

---

[1] The same locutions can be used with regard to wars whose protagonists are not countries but, for example, organizations or tribes; think of the wars between Israel and the PLO, and between the Chinese Communists and the Kuomintang.

the operative name or description.[2] The negative evaluation need not be so strong as to imply that no instance of the thing in question could ever merit approval. You can in good faith declare war on fascism while thinking that there may be extremely odd hypothetical situations—situations that might arise in a science fiction story if not in the actual world—under which fascism would be justified. But such a declaration at a minimum suggests that the thing on which the war is being fought is an evil, and one whose existence could not be justified under conditions that do or are likely to obtain.

Let me turn now to the question that will occupy my attention for the bulk of this paper: should the War on Terror be regarded as a war on terrorism? In the relevant respect, terrorism is like poverty and fascism and unlike Germany and Japan, because it's not the sort of thing that can, literally, wage a war. So, if we're to be comfortable with a declaration of a war on terrorism, then we'd better be comfortable with a declaration that terrorism always deserves condemnation, and with a campaign to stamp it out. This raises two questions. Would such a declaration be true? And, regardless of its truth, what effects would it have?

2. Is "Terrorism" Thick?

Perhaps terrorism can safely be regarded as a bad thing because the very concept of terrorism is evaluative. Perhaps, that is to say, the possibility of a morally commendable terrorist or act of terrorism is conceptually ruled out; if something truly falls under the concept "terrorism," then that's enough for us to know that it deserves condemnation. If this is right, then "terrorism" is a thick moral concept, one whose application implies both a nonnormative description and an evaluation.[3]

---

[2] Something similar is going on when you describe your opponents as fighting a war on something that cannot itself fight a war. You might say that your adversaries are fighting a war on freedom or a war on democracy; the suggestion is that the thing against which your opponents are fighting is something that, just because of its being that thing, ought to be defended.

[3] Talk of thick moral concepts appears to originate with the anthropologist Clifford Geertz. See, for example, his "Thick Description: Toward an Interpretative Theory of Culture," in Geertz, *The Interpretation of Cultures: Selected Essays* (New York: Basic Books, 1973), 3–30. Bernard Williams puts it to philosophical use in *Ethics and the Limits of Philosophy* (Harvard University Press, 1986).

It is useful to think of the thickness of moral concepts as coming in degrees. The thickness of a moral concept is a matter of how much nonevaluative information we get about something upon learning that it falls under the concept in question; the more information, the thicker the concept. So, "right" and "wrong" are very thin moral concepts, because the bare knowledge that something is right or wrong involves very little more than knowledge of its moral status; things meeting all sorts of different nonnormative descriptions can share the properties of rightness or wrongness.[4] "Evil" is thicker; to learn that something is evil is to learn that it has a negative moral status, as we might put it, but also that it involves certain sorts of malicious intentions or other attitudes. Still thicker are the familiar examples of thick moral concepts—concepts of character traits like courage, kindness, cowardice, and untrustworthiness. To call someone courageous, for example, is to say something about her psychological profile and about what sorts of acts she can be expected to perform under various circumstances, as well as saying something about her that is, as we might put it, morally positive.

As such concepts become thicker, it can become controversial whether we are still dealing with *moral* concepts. Consider the question of whether or not "patriotism" is a moral concept. If it is, it's a thick one; to learn that someone is patriotic is to learn something quite specific about how she regards her own country. Popular debate about the nature of patriotism generally proceeds as it would be expected to proceed if patriotism were a moral concept. Most people seem to take the charge "unpatriotic" as an insult, and arguments about what is morally permissible or commendable are often presented as arguments about what is truly patriotic. It's common at the moment, for example, to see buttons that say Dissent Is Patriotic, the message being that dissent is okay.

Nevertheless, there exists an interesting philosophical debate over whether or not patriotism is a good thing, and those who disapprove of patriotism do not appear to be making the sort of conceptual mistake that they would be making if they tried to argue that goodness or rightness is bad, or that evil is good.[5] So, it appears that someone can

---

[4] I think that knowledge that something is right or wrong involves *some* knowledge of its nonmoral properties, and hence that the concepts "right" and "wrong" contain some small nonnormative element. If I know that something is morally right, for example, then I know that it's not a washing machine or a color.

[5] For the philosophical debate about patriotism, see the papers collected in *Patriotism*,

have complete mastery of the concept "patriotism" while believing that patriotic things are not thereby good, which suggests that patriotism is not a moral concept after all.

One strategy for resolving the question of whether or not "patriotism" is a moral concept is to say that it isn't, but that there are reasons to see why it sometimes acts like one. "Patriotism," runs the thought, is a nonmoral concept that picks out a particular set of attitudes and behaviors. Those are attitudes and behaviors of which many people, as it happens, approve; many think that it's good to love and admire your own country. It's not always clear, however, exactly when those attitudes and behaviors are being manifested, and disagreements about this are linked to disagreements about wider ethical and political matters; if, for example, patriotism includes a commitment to the flourishing of your own country, then people who disagree about what it takes for a country to flourish can be expected to disagree about where real or right-minded patriotism is to be found. So it's no surprise that disagreements about what is patriotic can come down to disagreements about what is commendable. Yet, because patriotism is not a moral concept, there's also room for people to disapprove of the attitudes and behaviors to which "patriotism" refers—to say, for example, that it's not all desirable to have the kind of love for country that patriotism involves—and hence to say that patriotism is a bad thing.[6]

(Thinking along these lines may yield good reasons to draw the same conclusions about, for example, the concepts of compassion and cowardice. Most of us think compassion good and cowardice bad, but someone—like Ayn Rand—can know exactly what compassion is without thinking it commendable, and someone—like John Cleese in his somewhat serious defense of cowardice as a way of life—can know exactly what cowardice is while thinking it to be thoroughly commendable.[7] This suggests that the evaluative judgments typically associated with ascriptions of compassion and cowardice are not built into the concepts themselves, and hence that "compassion" and "cowardice" are not, in the relevant sense, moral concepts.[8])

---

ed. Igor Primoratz (Amherst, NY: Humanity Books, 2002), and in Martha C. Nussbaum and Joshua Cohen, *For Love of Country?* (Boston: Beacon Press, 2002).

[6] I explore these issues in my "Patriotism As Bad Faith," forthcoming in *Ethics*.

[7] I believe that John Cleese's defense of cowardice was originally given as a lecture to the Oxford University Debating Society in 1971. It can sometimes but not always be found at www.pythonline.com.

[8] I take my line of thought here to have something in common with that expressed by

Whether or not this is the right story to tell about patriotism, it's grounded in concerns that are also present when it comes to determining the status of the concept "terrorism." Most people take it that anything properly called a terrorist act must automatically be deserving of condemnation. This way of thinking often leads people to decide whether something is an act of terrorism based on an independent judgment about whether it deserves approval. To take a hackneyed example, it feels awkward to wonder whether Nelson Mandela was a terrorist, not because we don't know enough about the exact nature of the military activities with which he was involved, but because we're so sure that, whatever they were, they were on the whole justified. From the opposite direction, antiwar protesters have recently been distributing stickers that read War Is Terrorism, the message being that war is bad.

Nevertheless, someone who says that she doesn't disapprove of terrorism in all instances—that something's being an act of terrorism is not enough to establish its wrongness—need not, it appears, be suffering from a conceptual confusion. We know well enough what she means. Does this mean that "terrorism" is not a moral concept, but merely denotes something of which most of us usually disapprove? Before answering this question, it will be helpful to concentrate for a moment on the nonnormative aspect of the concept of terrorism. Evaluative questions aside, what makes a terrorist?

3. The Purpose of Terrorism is to Terrorize

Evaluative questions aside, and with clarifications and qualifications to come, let me suggest this as a roughly correct definition (close enough to the truth to support the main points that I wish to make in this paper). An act of terrorism is one whose primary purpose is to incite terror amongst the members of a particular community in order to achieve a political goal, and a terrorist is a person who performs such acts.[9] Consider some ways in which someone who wants to achieve a political goal may think it useful to terrorize a community.

Simon Blackburn in "Through Thick and Thin," *Proceedings of the Aristotelian Society*, supplement 66 (1992): 285–99.

[9] I won't describe the relations between my account of terrorism and those provided elsewhere. A classic definition of terrorism is given in C. A. J. Coady, "The Morality of Terrorism," *Philosophy* 60 (1985): 47–70, and a good argumentative survey of some philosophical work on the question is given in Virginia Held, "Terrorism,

First, he may want that community or its government to perform some act or to adopt some policy—to release some prisoners, for example, or to withdraw from an occupied land. The terrorist does not try to influence the target community by changing its members' minds about what is the best or proper thing to do, nor does he try in the straightforward sense to *force* the community to do what he wants. Rather, he sets out to create a situation in which members of the community believe that until and unless they do as the terrorist desires, they will live in fear. An example of this brand of terrorism is provided by the IRA bombings in Britain in the seventies and eighties. The IRA wished the British to withdraw from Northern Ireland, but it did not have the capacity to defeat the British army, and it was not—not through the bombings anyway—trying to convince the British that leaving Northern Ireland was the just thing to do. Instead, the purpose of the bombings was to leave particular British people terrified that an IRA bomb could cause harm to them or to those they care about, and to make them believe that the only way to get rid of the terror was to accede to IRA demands.

A second use that the terrorist may find for terror is that of gaining attention for his political cause. Where this is the goal, the terrorist may see reason to terrorize a community different from, or not limited to, the community whose actions or policies he is trying to affect. If people are terrified of a particular terrorist group, then they are likely to become aware of the existence and goals of that group. Hence, the terrorist might expect, those terrorized people will become aware of the justness of the terrorist's cause—at the least, the issue will be more widely discussed. Such, it seems, was a goal of the Palestinians who abducted and eventually killed eleven Israeli athletes at the Munich Olympics. One of the surviving terrorists was interviewed for the documentary "One Day in September," and his comments suggest that the terrorists did not expect to have any direct influence on the Israeli government, but rather wanted to bring the Palestinian cause to the world's attention.[10]

Rights and Political Goals," in *Violence, Terrorism and Justice*, ed. R. G. Frey and Christopher W. Morris (New York: Cambridge University Press, 1991), 59–85. For a vigorous attack upon goal-directed analyses of the type that I offer, see Loren E. Lomasky, "The Political Significance of Terrorism," in *Violence, Terrorism and Justice*, ed. Frey and Morris, 86–115.

[10] "One Day in September," directed by Kevin MacDonald, 1997, BBC.

Third, the terrorist may try to cause terror amongst one group of people in order to galvanize or otherwise influence another. By provoking an aggressive response from the terrorized community, the terrorist may succeed in creating resentment against it; by terrorizing a community that is seen as invincible, the terrorist may inspire others to take up the fight. In the sorts of cases discussed earlier, there are clear reasons why the terrorist will likely want to publicly claim responsibility for his act; he wants the terror of the terrorized to be associated with *his* political cause, rather than any other. When the terrorist's goal is of this third sort, however, the point is just to bring terror into existence, and so he may see no need for the terrorized to know why or by whom their terror is caused. The attacks of September 11, 2001, appear to fall into this category. The attacks were not associated with any explicit demands, so it's not clear what exactly the U.S. could do to appease the terrorists and take away their motivation for future attacks. And although it has since become clear that it was behind the hijackings, Al Qaeda did not announce to the world that it was responsible. To the extent that the political motive of the attackers is clear, it seems that it was to prove a point to, or incite further attacks from, people who were not themselves part of the terrorized community.

It seems to me, then, that my proposed definition captures the central cases of terrorism. Still, there are several points at which it might be thought that the definition could benefit from modification. One is to do with the question of the terrorist's motives. I've said that terrorists act to achieve political goals, but there are those who set out to terrorize a community not for a political purpose, but for revenge, or money, or self-aggrandizement, or just for its own sake, or whatever; examples might be the snipers who recently killed several people around Washington, D.C., and perhaps those of the James Bond villains who aim to get rich but not powerful. To the extent that these people lack political goals, I say, they fail to be terrorists. This is in one way an odd result, because such people do after all intentionally cause terror, but it seems to accord with our ways of speaking. Once the police determined that the Washington-area snipers were probably working alone and for their own sakes, media outlets announced that "the sniper shootings are not the work of terrorists." But I admit that this is a point on which intuitions can go either way.

My proposed definition does not say that the targets of properly called terrorism must be civilians or noncombatants. Someone could count as a terrorist, on my view, in virtue of their trying to terrorize members of opposing military forces. While it's certainly true that terrorism is most closely associated with attacks upon civilians, I think that it would be a mistake to stipulate that terrorism can only involve such targets; the attack on the U.S.S. Cole in 2000, for example, is commonly and naturally described as an act of terrorism, even though its victims were not civilians. Still, I accept that many will favor some more nuanced modification along these lines.

A terrorist might cause people to become terrified without doing anything violent. Without actually carrying out any violent deeds, she might convince people that she will if she doesn't get her way. Or, the terror that she incites may not be terror of violence. In a suitably neurotic community, a threat to interfere with the broadcast of popular sitcoms might be enough to incite terror, and to win political concessions. On the approach that I suggest, these types of acts *do* count as terrorist, which is, once more, perhaps a counterintuitive result.

I think that the proposed definition of terrorism is about right, while accepting that there are reasons to think that it doesn't perfectly capture our ordinary concept. For the purposes of this chapter, we could go either way on the worries about the definition that I've mentioned. The following is at any rate true, and will be enough: if you carry out violent acts that are intended to cause deep and widespread terror, are likely to involve the harming of innocents, and are performed with a political goal in mind—then you are a terrorist.

4. Bad Terrorism

Terrorism, as I've painted it so far, is, characteristically, a political tactic. My description of the tactic has been evaluatively neutral; there's nothing in the description that makes it automatically the case that terrorism will always deserve condemnation. "Terrorism" is not an evaluative concept. Nevertheless, there are clear reasons why terrorism, as I have described it, will not be something towards which most people take a neutral attitude.

Terrorism involves the intention to carry out acts of the sort that are likely to incite terror, and it's important to remember just what a powerfully destructive thing that is. Terror is not mere fear; it is the vivid, visceral fear of something that you regard as truly awful.[11]

---

[11] This is why it's silly to say (and why analyses like mine do not imply) that you're a terrorist if you try to make your students fearful of the consequences of failing to hand in their papers on time. See footnote 9 in Lomasky, "Political Significance of Terrorism."

When you are in the grip of terror, you feel, as we might put it, under attack from within, and often find yourself unable to think clearly or to fully exercise your powers of rationality. To deliberately subject someone to sustained terror is to deprive him of any possibility of contentment, and—it's not going too far to say—to assault his capacity to deliberate and act in light of his most considered values and priorities. If you are terrified of mice, then that's what it's like to be in the presence of a mouse. A successful terrorist takes a terrifying possibility and makes it a part of the backdrop to everyday life, making it more likely that people will fall, and make decisions, under the grip of terror.

Terror is all the worse when it is terror of something unpredictable. One who wants to incite terror of violence within a community will be motivated to make the members of that community believe that violence could come at any time, and with any target. It is therefore in keeping with the terrorist's aims that his violent attacks should have the appearance of randomness, and hence that their victims should include the innocent and the especially vulnerable.

To incite terror, you need not be especially strong militarily, and you certainly need not be popular. While terrorism may be used by powerful governments and armies, it is the natural, distinctive tool of the marginalized, of those who could not hope to make an impact through straightforward military might or persuasion. Rightly or wrongly, terrorism is often imagined as involving a small and resented group of people making life horribly unpleasant for a large group of people.

For all of these reasons, it should be no surprise that terrorism is widely despised. Within a reasonably homogeneous, reasonably empowered community, and certainly within a reasonably content community, people will see themselves as potential victims, rather than beneficiaries, of terrorism.

There is also a clear moral case to be made against terrorism. In the forms in which it can be expected to (and does) manifest itself in the real world, the use of terror as a political tactic almost always involves the creation of terrible misery, and the violation of some of the most treasured of human rights. Terrorism almost always involves threats to the lives of people who do not deserve to die, and interferes with rights to genuine autonomy and self-determination.

In light of these considerations, there are those who will, in virtue of their broader moral commitments, think that terrorism is wrong under any circumstances. I have in mind a broadly Kantian perspective according to which it is always wrong to make an attack upon an individual's autonomy, and a more broadly nonconsequentialist perspective according to which it's always wrong—regardless of consequences—to threaten innocent life.[12] In taking fundamental rights as rigid side constraints, such views will not allow terrorism (in its typical manifestations at least) to be a justified tactic in the service of any goal, no matter how laudable.

It hence turns out, in my view, that an evaluatively neutral account of the nature of terrorism can give us all we want from an account of the nature of terrorism. "Terrorism" is not a moral concept, but after making certain fairly obvious observations we can tell a plausible story about why no one much approves of it as a general proposal, and why calling someone a terrorist is in general taken to be an affront. And we can leave room for someone to say, without falling into conceptual error, that terrorism is, in some cases, commendable.

5. Good Terrorism

There is a clear argument towards the conclusion that terrorism, just in virtue of its being the sort of thing that it is, is never justified and ought to be opposed wherever it arises. That argument appears, however, to be an equally clear argument for the conclusion that the waging of a certain sort of war—what we might call "all-out war"—is never justified. If this is right, then it would be disingenuous to accept the argument that terrorism is always deserving of condemnation without drawing the same conclusion about all-out war.

By an all-out war, I mean the kinds of wars that involve invasion, civilian casualties, and so on; I mean wars like the American Civil War, both World Wars, and the wars in Vietnam, Afghanistan, and Iraq. Almost always, all-out war involves all the awful things that terrorism involves, including the creation of widespread terror and all the associated phenomena. All-out war involves the foreseeable and deliberate killing of people who don't deserve to be killed, the ruining of lives, and the loss by many of the capacity to choose and act in light of their most deeply held values. Communities that are under the attack of terrorists are generally in situations far preferable to those

---

[12] I'm imagining that a Kantian approach to the intentional incitement of terror might be similar to the approach to torture taken in David Sussman's excellent essay "What's Wrong with Torture?" *Philosophy and Public Affairs* 31, no. 3 (2005): 1–33. (I should note, though, that Sussman doesn't conclude that torture is *never* justified.) See also pp. 6–9 of Frey and Morris, "Violence, Terrorism and Justice."

of communities that are caught up in an all-out war. Yet, most of us think that there are cases, probably actual and certainly not too difficult to imagine, in which all-out war is justified.[13]

Is there any good reason to think that all-out war is sometimes justified, but terrorism is not? There are some relevant differences that might be brought into play. All-out war, unlike terrorism, needn't involve the deliberate, strategic creation of terror. All-out war might be thought justified only when waged by legitimately elected national governments, but the perpetrators of terrorism do not characteristically have that status. Rather than confront such issues directly, think of the following example, which represents an unapologetic return to the domain of the hackneyed.

Suppose that, in the months before the outbreak of World War II, a group of Germans decided to try to make the Nazis change their racist and expansionist policies. Suppose further that the dissidents thought, quite reasonably, that their only chance of succeeding was to damage the ability of the Nazi leadership to unite and keep safe the German population, and that the only way to do that was through a campaign of violence. Such a group might have launched attacks upon military facilities, carried out assassinations, and blown up government buildings; it may have tried to destabilize and demoralize the country by planting bombs in schools, shopping centers, and other public places. It is reasonable to think that, for this imaginary group, only such tactics would have been likely to have the desired impact, and it's surely the case that it would have been a terrorist organization. And surely—assuming that it's possible to justify the carnage that was actually visited upon Germany during the war—the use of such tactics would have been justified.

Once this point is granted, it can easily be extended to several other cases very close to us in history. It takes very little effort to come up with regimes and organizations that would be the legitimate objects of certain sorts of terrorism.

I said earlier that terrorism can by its nature be expected to involve violations of some of the most cherished of human rights. What's suggested by cases like those just mentioned, however, is that there also exists the right to fight against certain sorts of regimes and organizations, using violence if necessary—and that this right sometimes fails

---

[13] The parallels between terrorism and various widespread and condoned uses of violence are more thoroughly explored in Annette C. Baier, "Violent Demonstrations," in Frey and Morris, *Violence, Terrorism and Justice*, 33–58.

to be outweighed by rights that have to be infringed for such resistance to be effective. This translates into the permissibility of the use of terror as a political tool, in the service of certain types of goals and under certain sorts of circumstances. A principled pacifist, as I say, could deny the existence or scope of such a right, but it is very difficult to see how anyone else could. To put things provocatively, it is very difficult to see how someone could think *both* that the acts carried out so far in the prosecution of the so-called War on Terror (like the invasion of Afghanistan) are justified, *and* that terrorism is by its very nature something that ought to be stamped out.

There remains, of course, the very large question of exactly what are the conditions under which acts of terrorism are justified, and of how we can know with sufficient certainty that they obtain. I won't pursue this issue, except to say that it seems to me to be a good example of a debate that cannot proceed far so long as it is expressed only in the language of rights. Sometimes, the right to damage an obnoxious force or government makes the infringements of other rights permissible, but sometimes it doesn't. Perhaps an informative account of which cases are which can come from a consideration of even more fundamental rights, or something like that, but I suspect that our intuitions about such matters incorporate a strong consequentialist element, one that the language of rights is ill equipped to capture.[14]

A proper understanding of the nature of the concept "terrorism" does not yield a guarantee that anything falling under the concept is evil. And if the argument of this section is correct, then there will be few who can in good faith resist the claim that there have arisen, and are likely to arise in the future, circumstances under which terrorism would be justified.

6. Terrorists and Freedom Fighters

On the story that I have provided, whether or not something is an act of terrorism depends in part upon the strategy being pursued by its perpetrators; are they setting out to incite terror or not? In many cases, those who are in fact trying to use terror as a political tactic will claim that they are not. They'll say that they are simply trying to defend their people, or making deliberate strikes against particular guilty parties—that any terror produced is but an unfortunate consequence. There are other reasons why the truth about whether or not

---

[14] See R. M. Hare, "What is Wrong with Slavery," *Philosophy and Public Affairs* 8, no. 2 (1979): 103–21.

someone is a terrorist might be obscured. It is often difficult, in real life, to say exactly which groups have exactly which political goals, and exactly how they are trying to achieve them. The issue of whether or not the PLO is presently a terrorist organization, for example, is very messy, involving questions about what the true goals of the PLO are, what connections it has to various other groups, whether or not it encourages suicide bombings, what those controlling the suicide bombers are trying to achieve, and so on. Things are similarly complicated with regard, for example, to rebel groups in Chechnya, Kurdish separatists in Turkey and Iraq, various governments around the world, and—historically—to Greek partisans, the Black Panthers, and the apartheid-era ANC.

Not only is it often difficult to tell whether or not a particular political group is trying to achieve its goals through the incitement of terror, but also we can expect that people's opinions on the matter will sometimes be influenced by their independent appraisals of the group in question.[15] If you are in sympathy with its goals, you're more likely to see it as a group that acts in self-defense, or that is party to a straightforward war, or that is otherwise producing terror (if it is) only as an unfortunate byproduct of its activities; you're more likely to be impressed by the nastiness of the target and by the strength of the right to attack it. If you are not in sympathy with the group's goals, you're more likely to see it as trying to get what it wants just by making people frightened; your focus is more likely to be upon the rights of the victims of the group's activities.

Imagine, for example, a group of prodemocracy North Koreans that takes the present regime as its enemy. And imagine that members of the group assassinate government figures, plant bombs at political rallies, and deliberately contaminate food and water supplies used by the North Korean military. Were such a group to arise, I doubt that those who presently take themselves to be waging a war on terrorism would describe it as "terrorist"—and that's because they see North Koreans as having good reason to resist their government, even if not in order to incite terror.

7. Should We Have a War on Terrorism?

I am now, at last, equipped to return to the paper's main line of thought. Is terrorism something on which there ought to be a war?

---

[15] See the opening pages of Held, "Terrorism, Rights and Political Goals."

No, it isn't, for two reasons. The first reason is this. To proclaim a war on terrorism is to take an evaluative stance with regard to terrorism in all its forms; it's to say that terrorism, just because it's terrorism, should be wiped out. But terrorism is not, in all its forms, something that ought to be opposed. When the incitement of terror is in service of a sufficiently worthy cause, and when other options are not available, terrorism can be justified—justified for much the same reasons that all-out war can be justified—and relevant cases are close to hand.

The second reason why there shouldn't be a war on terrorism is that there are too many hazards associated with real-world judgments about who is and who is not a terrorist. It is often difficult to say whether or not a particular group is engaged in terrorism, and often easy to make people believe that a particular group is engaged in terrorism, even if it isn't—or that a particular group is not engaged in terrorism, even if it is. In declaring a war on terrorism, we are committing ourselves to opposing terrorism wherever it is found. This opens us to the danger of being convinced that a particular group is a terrorist group, and of hence taking it to be an enemy, but only because the group's enemies have successfully painted it as terrorist. The War on Terror has already furnished illustrations. Russia has, with some success, attempted to quiet international support for Chechen rebel groups by representing such groups as terrorist; the Russian war in Chechnya, runs the message, is a branch of the war on terrorism. Some in the Israeli government have said the same of Israel's battle with Palestinian resistance movements. But the question of whether the relevant groups in Chechnya and Palestine deserve outright condemnation is far more complicated than such arguments admit.

Imagine a government that announces a campaign for patriotism. The campaign would merit suspicion, partly because it's not clear that patriotism is ever (let alone always) a good thing, and partly because there is something very distasteful about a political body making official judgments about who is and who is not patriotic; we'd worry that such judgments would be infected with political maneuverings, personal grudges and—if things go really badly—hysteria. I think that we ought to worry about a purported war on terrorism for the same reasons that we would worry about a campaign for patriotism. Both projects would ride roughshod over some subtle moral and conceptual issues, with potentially disastrous results.

8. On What Is the War?

If not a war on terrorism, then a war on what? I suggest Al Qaeda. It is, after all, the organization whose attacks provoked the war, and whose destruction would most likely indicate that the war had been won. Al Qaeda is aggressively setting out to damage the U.S. and other countries in an effort to achieve detestable political goals; it is just the sort of thing against which it makes sense for the U.S. and its allies to go to war. Are there any drawbacks to my suggested redescription?

A label like "War on Terror" might be thought preferable to "War on Al Qaeda" because it more vividly captures the truth that this is a new sort of war; one against a dispersed and loosely organized force that does not hold territory or employ conventional military methods. But Al Qaeda is a dispersed and loosely organized force that does not hold territory or employ conventional military methods, and in the present setting, those are exactly the associations that mention of Al Qaeda elicits.

It might be protested that the war is not just a war on Al Qaeda, but also on all of the individuals, countries, and organizations from which Al Qaeda garners support. But the war on Japan was not just a war on Japan, but also on individuals, countries, and organizations from which Japan garnered support; that doesn't mean that it wasn't really a war on Japan. To declare war on something is to suggest that you'll take a hostile attitude towards whatever supports that thing. And if it turns out that there are other organizations that deserve to be fought just as much as Al Qaeda—well, we can have a war on them too. The one war can be a war on more than one country, or on more than one obnoxious organization.

The War on Terror is not a war on terror. Whether or not it is really a war on terrorism, I have argued, it shouldn't be; to describe ourselves as having a war on terrorism is to expose ourselves to various political dangers and to make a commitment to a claim to which we shouldn't be committed. The war is, I suppose, a war on a terror—namely, Al Qaeda—and a war on some terrorists—namely, those who are working for Al Qaeda. And it's by construing and describing ourselves as waging a war on Al Qaeda that we are best able to capture these facts.[16]

---

[16] For helpful comments and suggestions, thanks to Aaron Garrett, Gary Herbert, David Lyons, Amélie Rorty, and Casey O'Callaghan. The thoughts in this paper were also greatly influenced by discussions with the participants in the "Understanding Terrorism: Philosophical Issues" conference held at Loyola Marymount University in September 2003.

| 4 |

Terrorism as a Technological Concept: How Low versus High Technology Defines Terrorism and Dictates Our Responses

PHILLIP McREYNOLDS

In the wake of the terrorist attacks on the Pentagon and the World Trade Center on September 11, 2001, the United States has embarked upon an international "War on Terror" that is based largely on high-tech approaches to the problem. Remarkably, for example, the September 11 attacks, which were conducted with technologies no more sophisticated than pocket knives and duct tape, have been cited as evidence that we need to revive the Space Defense Initiative.[1] Moreover, the initial response to the terrorist attacks has been almost exclusively technological in nature, rather than social, economic, or political, and has relied overwhelmingly upon high technology such as satellite imagery, laser guided bombs, computer databases, and explosive scanning devices. How might we explain the apparent incongruity between the technological levels of threat and response? In this essay I make two principal points. First, the problem we have come to define as "terrorism" is, as such, mislabeled and should be rethought. I maintain that terrorism is a technological concept but that the problems we face are not primarily technological. Second, I suggest that we tend to rely so heavily upon high-tech solutions to the problem because of the particular ways in

---

[1] Though the proximal weapons were highly advanced jet aircraft, the attackers were able to take control of them with exceptionally low-tech means that easily avoided the relatively high-tech means employed at the time to keep aircraft safe. On the relationship between September 11 and missile defense, see, for example, Philip H. Gordon and Michael E. O'Hanlon, "September 11 Verdict—Yes to Missile Defense, But Don't Alienate Russia or China," *Los Angeles Times*, October 17, 2001, http://www.brook.edu/views/op-ed/Gordon/20011017.htm.

which terrorism and technology are situated within an ideology of progress.

First we must say a word or two about "technology." "Technology" is, in English, a notoriously ambiguous word. Viewed etymologically it should mean "the theory of crafts," that is, the *logos* of *techne*, and some authors have defined "technology" as the theory or systematization of innovation. This usage, however, is neither typical nor clear. In common usage the term has come to mean "gadgetry," and, in particular, novel or complex gadgetry. This definition, while familiar, is imprecise (What counts as a gadget?) and relative, since a thing's perceived novelty and complexity are dependent upon one's experience. Philosophers of technology have advanced a number of definitions of "technology" and the field remains largely concerned with this issue. Rather than attempt a final and comprehensive definition of technology, I will offer two simplifications. First, I will restrict myself primarily to the adjective "technological" and observe that the "technological" is that which is concerned primarily with the means of achieving something, especially as these means involve artifacts. Second, I will adopt the popular usage of the terms "high tech" and "low tech" to mean "complex and novel" and "simple and traditional" technological artifacts respectively. "High-tech" artifacts are by definition artifacts with which we are unfamiliar, which require complex systems to produce and sustain, and which can often (I will argue) be thwarted by relatively "low-tech" means.[2]

The first part of my argument seeks to establish that although it is not ordinarily thought of as one, "terrorism" is a technological concept rather than, say, an ideology. Though having an almost universally negative moral value attached to it,[3] "terrorism" is not an ideology, despite its grammatical similarity to words that signify ideologies, which typically end in "ism." Unlike an ideology, "terrorism" refers not to an end that is sought by a group of people but rather the means of achieving any number of distinct ends.[4] Framing the problem in terms of means employed rather than ends sought allows us to

---

[2] On the definition of "technology" see, for example, Carl Mitcham, "Types of Technology," in *Research in Philosophy and Technology*, vol. 1, ed. Paul Durbin (Greenwich, CT: JAI Press, 1978), 229–94.

[3] Haig Khatchadourian, "Terrorism and Morality," in *Applied Ethics: A Multicultural Approach*, ed. Larry May et al. (Upper Saddle River, NJ: Prentice Hall, 1998), 286.

[4] Unlike "capitalism," "communism," or "Protestantism," "terror*ism*" is not an ideology or a cause but a strategy, a fact that has only lately come to be acknowledged by

collect together under a single term groups whose aims are as disparate as those of North Korea, Iraq, Al Qaeda, Russia's Chechen rebels, militant Palestinians, and the Irish Republican Army, whether these groups have much in common or not.

Terrorism *seems* as if it were an ideology rather than a technology for a number of reasons. (1) Terrorism is typically employed in the service of political rather than more narrowly economic or other goals. (2) Terrorism appears to be more compatible with some political commitments than others (e.g., it is a technology that appears to be fundamentally undemocratic due to its tendency to silence rather than encourage open debate). (3) Terror is not a particular means but a category of grouping other, more specific, means. Thus, from one point within the means-end continuum, terrorizing a population appears as an end that could be pursued by various more specific means, such as blowing up a building or gassing a subway. However, this does not make terrorism an end in itself. For example, when a nerve agent is released in a subway car to terrorize a city or a nation, the nerve agent is the technological means of achieving terror, a proximal end. Nonetheless, terror is not an end in itself but a means to some other, more ultimate (and often political) end. We can clarify this situation by referring to proximal and ultimate means and ends. In this situation, the nerve agent is the proximal means of causing terror, which is the ultimate means of, for example, achieving the end of countering government repression of one's religious group. Finally, (4) we are in the habit of identifying groups of people by their ideological commitments rather than by the technologies that they employ, and the "*-ism*" in "terror*ism*" lends itself to this tendency.

With this in mind, consider that "terrorism" is a term that is defined with reference to means employed rather than ends sought. A

---

our political leaders. Since terrorism is not an ideology, its opposite, antiterrorism, is viewed as ideologically neutral. This is not the case, for example, with other "-isms" such as capitalism and communism. Apart from the general way in which political ideologies can be thought of as disagreements not about the proper end worth seeking, conceived as human happiness, but about the means of achieving it, political ideologies are disagreements about ends rather than the means of achieving them. Even anarchism, which is the closest political analogue to terrorism, is framed in terms of an end rather than the means of achieving that end, despite the fact that anarchists were popularly conceived, much like terrorists, as bomb-throwers and creators of havoc rather than in terms of the ends that they pursued. Anarchism seeks the end of eliminating or radically reducing the scope and influence of government. Terrorism *qua* terrorism is not about ends. It refers to a choice of means.

disagreement about means rather than ends is a technological rather
than a social or political disagreement. A disagreement about the relative merits of solar or nuclear power is a disagreement about the best
means of producing energy rather than about the desirability of
energy as such. (This is true despite the fact that the choice of means
is often influenced by the relative importance assigned to ends that
are differentially achieved by different means.)[5] Thus, terrorism and
antiterrorism characterize technological rather than social or political
positions. The terrorist is someone who proposes or, more typically,
puts into practice the view that "terror" is a good means of achieving
his ends, whereas the antiterrorist is someone who presumably does
not or, more typically, who attempts to prevent the employment of terror as a means. Insofar as it is a question about the means of achieving change, not the desirability of change itself, the question of
terrorism is a technological question.

Another barrier to conceiving of terrorism as a technology is that
doing so violates the common assumption that technologies are
morally and politically neutral whereas terrorism clearly is not. A typical stance toward technology is that what is good or bad about it is
not technologies themselves but the ends to which they are put. The
popularity of this view, apart from its ability to shield technologists

---

[5] I do not mean to imply that technologies cannot be political or that politics cannot
be technological. With regard to technologies as political, Langdon Winner and
many others have argued that because technologies tend to alter the character of
human relationships and because they tend to sediment choices with political implications, technologies are political. See Langdon Winner, *The Whale and the Reactor:
A Search for Limits in an Age of High Technology* (Chicago: University of Chicago
Press, 1986). With regard to politics as technology, Larry Hickman, following John
Dewey, has proposed an expanded definition of technology which would include all
manner of technical, social, and sign systems. See Larry Hickman, *John Dewey's
Pragmatic Technology* (Bloomington, IN: Indiana University Press, 1990).
Moreover, Dewey rightly argued that means and ends necessarily interpenetrate and
that it isn't possible to think completely about means without reference to ends and
vice versa. It is not possible to employ means intelligently while ignoring the ends
sought, and ends conceived wholly apart from the means of achieving them are
utterly indeterminate. See, for example, John Dewey, *Human Nature and Conduct*
(New York: H. Holt and Company, 1922). Neither of these perspectives alters the fact
that it makes sense to draw a conceptual distinction between technology and politics
or at least between the technological and the political. While it is true that means and
ends necessarily interpenetrate, the technological *qua* technological is primarily a
question of means whereas the political *qua* political is about ends. It is only with
reference to some such distinction that it would make sense to talk about the political aspects of technology or about the technologies of the political.

from being implicated in moral or political questions, stems from what Langdon Winner calls the *promiscuous utility* of technologies.[6] Because I can use a hammer either for driving nails or for knocking people over the head, the hammer appears to be morally neutral. Any value that pertains to the technology seems to be attached to the user of that technology rather than to the technology itself.[7] Thus, on the standard view a tool cannot be good or bad in itself. Rather, one must evaluate the uses to which it is put.

According to this reasoning, because terrorism is, on most accounts, not morally neutral, terrorism cannot be a technology. Not all technologies are regarded as morally neutral, however. Supposing that we assume the value-neutrality of technologies in general, this leaves open the possibility that terrorism is a technology of this sort.[8] For example, most people regard landmines and most Weapons of Mass Destruction (WMDs) as morally problematic technologies. With the exception of the United States, the international community is virtually unanimous in its opposition to the possession and deployment of landmines. There is also virtual unanimity with respect to the creation, stockpiling, and deployment of biological and chemical weapons, with most nations decrying these technologies as morally bad.[9] The negative moral value is ascribed not to their use but to the technologies themselves because it is inconceivable that such

---

[6] Winner, *The Whale and the Reactor*, 6.

[7] On the other hand, as Abraham Maslow observed, "If the only tool you have is a hammer, you tend to see every problem as a nail."

[8] The belief in the alleged value-neutrality of technology is more common among the lay public and technologists than philosophers of technology. Often this belief is accompanied by a nondescript positive value that many people attach to various technologies, concomitant with a belief in "progress" even as they harbor vague foreboding about other technologies despite the fact that these various views are mutually contradictory. Even so, most popular discussions of technology implicitly affirm the value-neutrality of technology since they tend to focus on the uses to which the technologies might be put or the appropriateness of the ends sought, not the value relations created and sustained by the technologies themselves.

[9] Nuclear weapons, also WMDs, are not always viewed in the same way as biological or chemical weapons. While virtually every nation regards the manufacture and possession of chemical and biological weapons as immoral, the possession of substantial nuclear arsenals—stockpiles large enough to wipe out the population of the planet many times over—is not so regarded, at least by some nations. Is there something about the high-tech nature of nuclear weapons and the character of a nation advanced enough to develop them that accounts for this moral difference, something beyond the realpolitik involved in maintaining the status quo of the nuclear club? The second half of this essay answers this question in the affirmative.

weapons could be used for worthy ends or that any end could be good enough to redeem the evil that necessarily accompanies their use. So there exists a class of technologies, probably not limited to the examples above, that are viewed not as morally neutral but as positively evil. It is possible that terrorism is a member of this class.[10] This raises the question of why, unlike most technologies, terrorism and these other technologies are regarded in this way, a question that pertains to the definition of "terrorism."

"Terrorism" can be defined in a number of ways. According to a relativist view, the difference between "terrorists" and "freedom fighters" depends wholly or largely upon one's sympathies with the people involved. Such a definition is inconsistent, however, because the term "terrorist" focuses upon the means employed, whereas "freedom fighter" is a rather vague way of focusing on the end sought (and signaling approval of that end). Such a definition assumes that there is no feature by which we may identify terrorists apart from our (dis)approval of the ends they seek. On the other hand, we can readily group terrorists according to the means they employ, without having to decide first whether or not we approve of the ends they seek. This further suggests the appropriateness of a technological definition of terrorism.

We might define terrorism as "a technology that employs the indiscriminate use of violence used to terrorize a population." In order to see what kind of technology terrorism is, and what distinguishes it from other varieties of technology, we should examine this proposed definition in detail. That terrorism involves the use or threat of violence seems self-evident. While other kinds of harm (as, for example, to property) might be sufficient to intimidate or extort some desired outcome from a person or population, most other kinds of harm would appear to be insufficient to incite terror.[11]

---

[10] Torture and genocide may also fall into this category. There are probably others.

[11] Thus, when Secretary of Education Rod Paige called the National Education Association a terrorist organization, he was clearly engaging in hyperbole. The NEA may, as Paige argues, use its political power to intimidate individual teachers, but because it does not use or threaten violence, it cannot properly be labeled terroristic. See "Paige Calls NEA Terrorist Organization," CNN.com, February 23, 2004, http://www.cnn.com/2004/EDUCATION/02/23/paige.terrorist.nea/. The FBI includes "violence against property" in its definition of terrorism when such violence is used to achieve social or political objectives. However, in my view, this definition is overly broad and fails to distinguish terrorism from run of the mill extortion and vandalism. Granted, certain acts involving damage to property might be properly called

The indiscriminate nature of terroristic violence appears to be an important part of the definition and might explain why, unlike most other technologies, both terrorism and, for instance, landmines and some WMDs are not considered to be morally neutral. The problem with acts of terrorism, landmines, and WMDs is that they do not generally discriminate innocents from combatants. When a landmine is buried, one never knows whether its victim will be a soldier or a civilian.[12] We might distinguish WMDs from Weapons of More Particular Destruction (WMPDs) which include artillery rounds, so-called smart bombs, and bullets, due to their ability to discriminate their targets. When one targets someone with WMPDs, one generally knows who one is targeting and the likelihood of "collateral damage" (though the very existence of this term as a regular military concept suggests that the discrimination criterion is problematic). One of the moral problems with terrorism is that terrorists flout the rules of war by failing to distinguish between civilians and enemy combatants. Even worse, terrorist acts typically expressly target civilians.[13]

However, when we examine cases, we see that neither indiscriminate violence nor violence expressly targeted toward civilians is a necessary or sufficient condition for a terrorist act. If we attend to usage and assume that the term is employed consistently, we find that failure to discriminate is not necessary because acts of violence toward military targets are often referred to as terrorist acts. Apart from the question of whether the Pentagon represented a military or a nondiscriminated target for the September 11 hijackers—plenty of civilians work at the Pentagon—many recent attacks on soldiers in Saudi Arabia, Afghanistan, Kuwait, and Iraq have been called terrorist

---

terroristic, such as burning down a person's house or burning a cross on his lawn, but these acts are terroristic not because they destroy property but because they function as threats of violence to persons. See the Federal Bureau of Investigation's publication #0308, "Terrorism 2000/2001," FBI website, http://www. fbi. gov/publications/terror/terror2000_2001.htm.

[12] In fact, most victims of landmines these days tend to be civilian and, quite often, children. This is the main impetus behind the international convention against the use of landmines. See Philip Winslow, *Sowing the Dragon's Teeth: Land Mines and the Global Legacy of War* (Beacon Press, 1998).

[13] It is arguable that these two points are really one: Terrorists justify the targeting of civilians because civilians, by supporting or failing to act against a regime or system that is regarded as one's enemy, possess collective guilt and are rightly regarded as enemy combatants. Thus, according to this argument, there is no real distinction. See, for example, Burleigh Wilkins, "Can Terrorism Be Justified?" in May, *Applied Ethics*, 295–302.

attacks, as was the attack on the Marine barracks in Beirut in the 1980s.[14]

A counterargument might be made that the term "terrorist" is being employed in the following way: (1) A "terrorist act" is any violent act committed by a terrorist[15] and (2) a "terrorist" is someone who does not discriminate between civilian and military targets. The problem with this definition is that it focuses upon the person committing the act rather than the act itself and ignores the possibility that someone might be both a terrorist and a legal combatant. Such a definition would seem to imply that the legal violent acts of, say, an executioner or a soldier are acts of terrorism if such a person happens to be a terrorist in his spare time. Thus, again, for the sake of consistency it appears that in defining terrorism we must focus upon the means employed (i.e., the technology) rather than the person who employs those means and then define the latter in terms of the former rather than vice-versa.

The express terrorizing of civilians is not a sufficient condition, because there have been times when acts of violence that tend not to be defined as terrorist acts seemed to be intended to terrorize civilians. The bombings of Dresden, Hiroshima, and Nagasaki during World War II might fall into this category. None of these cities represented serious military targets, and the goal of the bombing appeared to be the weakening of civilian morale through the incitement of terror. Such actions, undertaken by nation-states in times of total war, while not necessarily justified, do not fit the standard ways that "terrorism" is typically employed. Such acts can be called terrorist acts only if we are willing either to label the leaders of the Applied Powers during World War II as war criminals or to say that acts of terrorism

---

[14] One might limit "terrorist" attacks on military targets to those that also target civilians or that occur in peacetime. However, considering the second possibility, in an age of frequent and numerous undeclared wars, such a distinction would appear to be of very little value. Moreover, the military quite often employs civilian contractors in any number of roles, ranging from logistical to security support to acts that have more traditionally been those of soldiers. Are the CIA agents who pilot drone aircraft civilians or soldiers? Are contractors who launch assaults on insurgent groups in order to provide "security" for oil platforms civilians? For a recent example of the term "terrorist" applied to people targeting soldiers in a time of war, see Thom Shanker and David Johnston, "CIA Warning of Terror Risk to GIs in Iraq," *New York Times*, March 9, 2003.

[15] I limit this to "violent acts" because a terrorist brushing his teeth, though an act of a terrorist, is clearly not an act of terrorism.

are sometimes morally justified, both of which go against standard accounts.[16]

One way of excluding these acts would be to specify that the perpetrators must be nonstate actors. However, in addition to rendering the term "state-sponsored terrorism" oxymoronic, such an approach again focuses on the status of the actors rather than the means employed in the act. To define terrorism in terms of a person's political commitments or sponsorship would return us to the relativistic distinction between "terrorist" and "freedom fighter" rejected above. Although the indiscriminate nature of the means employed, the targeting of civilians, and the employment of terror appear to be important aspects of the general concept of terrorism, such distinctions do not appear to function entirely consistently in determining the class membership of terrorist acts. Although it is probable that these difficulties stem from the fact that the term is not employed consistently, and that political judgments cannot be excluded entirely from determination of class membership, we should still be able to find a basis for making such distinctions that are relatively coherent at a conceptual level.[17] In what follows I will argue that this basis is to be found in the exploration of "terrorism" as a technological concept, specifically in the nature of the technologies employed and the ways in which they are embedded within a morally-charged ideology of progress.

*   *   *

Considered as a technology rather than an ideology or a characteristic of persons, a pattern emerges in the character of terrorist technology. In general, terrorist acts tend to employ relatively low-tech

---

[16] Such examples are not confined to WWII. Madeleine Albright's comment to Leslie Stahl of CBS news that the loss of 500,000 civilian lives as a result of sanctions against Iraq is a price worth paying for the removal of Saddam Hussein seems to indicate a similar strategy. One purpose of sanctions, which disproportionately affect civilians rather than the Iraqi leadership, appears to be to attempt to cause the citizens of Iraq to turn against their leaders. Although they utilize butter rather than guns, it might be argued that economic sanctions result in violence to the extent that they deprive people of the conditions that are necessary to sustain life. See Rahul Mahajan, "We Think the Price Is Worth It," *Extra!* November/December 2001, http://www.fair.org/extra/0111/iraq.html.

[17] Like others who have addressed this issue, I am claiming that while being an essentially contested concept, terrorism nevertheless has a common core of meaning. My contribution is the identification of this common core as involving technology.

means of achieving their ends. Tools as simple as box-cutters, Molotov cocktails, conventional (and often homemade) explosives strapped to suicide bombers, and relatively simple antipersonnel weapons such as hand grenades, small arms, and shoulder-mounted rockets tend to be the favored tools of terrorists. This tendency toward the low tech is more striking when one considers the high-tech means employed in the "war against terror": fighter jets; satellite- and laser-guided bombs; extensive computerized systems for information collection, storage, and retrieval; cruise missiles; and all of the other advanced weaponry and support gear of modern armies. In general, terrorist acts tend to be violent acts that employ relatively low-tech means in order to terrorize people, either military or civilian, whereas violent acts that are not considered to be terrorist tend to use high-tech means even as they not only strike physically at their targets but strike terror into them and people in their vicinity. While I do not wish to argue that low-tech means are a necessary feature of terrorism, I do want to suggest that the relatively primitive nature of means employed contributes both to the categorization of certain acts as terrorist acts and to the negative moral judgment ascribed to them. Moreover, and this is a more important point, the low-tech nature of terrorism and the negative value judgment that I will argue attaches both to low technology and to terrorism are factors dictating a response to terrorism that is almost exclusively technological and that tends to be high tech.

The low-tech nature of terrorist technology is hard to miss. The principal weapons of the September 11 hijackers were box-cutters and duct tape. Palestinian bombers employ sticks of dynamite and grenades made in home-made labs. Timothy McVeigh used a truck full of fertilizer and diesel fuel to blow up the Federal Building in Oklahoma City. The "shoe bomber" attempted to use conventional explosives hidden in his shoes to bring down an airliner. The IRA has employed, among other things, pipe bombs and Molotov cocktails. Radical antiabortion groups use small arms to terrorize abortion providers, clinic workers, and patients. The KKK uses gasoline, wood, and rope. Even the so-called dirty bomb that many fear might explode in an American port or city is a relatively low-tech affair: conventional explosives packaged with a radiological agent.

My claim is that the association of low technology and terrorism is more than accidental. I mean to suggest that the category of terrorist acts as terrorist is built upon the employment of low technology, and that whether low- or high-tech means are employed plays a role in determining whether a given case gets assigned to the class of terrorist acts.

An obvious response to this claim is that while not accidental, the reason terrorists have tended to favor low-tech means is that they have not been able to get their hands on high-tech means, and that if they could, they would. Moreover, terrorists' lack of respect for human life and fundamental morality makes such means entirely appropriate to their ends. Unlike nonterrorists, who must discriminate between civilians and military personnel, who are committed to limiting violence to the absolute minimum necessary to achieve their aims, and who therefore must expend considerable effort and resources to develop precision weapons and armaments, terrorists, who are not so constrained, may use nondiscriminating, low-tech means. Moreover, one might argue, those fighting terrorists, being governments rather than independent groups, typically have a technological advantage, which it is perfectly sensible to want to leverage. Thus, the relative use of low- as opposed to high-tech means by terrorists and nonterrorists, respectively, is a function of what sorts of means are available and what sort of people fall into these groups, rather than a factor in the way that the groups get divided up in the first place.

I should first say that I have no doubt that many terrorists would be quite pleased to have high-tech as well as low-tech means at their disposal. It does not follow from this that their categorization as terrorists has nothing to do with the means they have heretofore employed. Once a group gets classified as terrorist (in part, as I shall argue, on the basis of the employment of low technology), they are not likely to cease to be called terrorists once they switch to high-tech means.

Another objection stems from the observation that an act of violence is not deemed terrorist simply because it involves low technology. A soldier employing a knife or a bayonet in pursuit of his duty is not a terrorist despite the low-tech means employed. Such is not my claim. What I do want to suggest is that the relative height of technology (low or high—and it does make sense to talk in this way because we are talking about a conceptual ladder or golden chain[18]), along with cultural and moral associations that accompany low and high technology as embedded in an ideology of progress, play some role in determining whether an act will be classed as terrorist or not

---

[18] See J. B. Bury, *The Idea of Progress: An Inquiry into its Growth and Origin* (New York: Dover Publications, 1932).

and in dictating the response to such acts. I want to suggest that there is something else going on here, that we make a covert value assessment of high and low technology as technologies, and that this value assessment could help determine who gets classed as a terrorist and who does not, based on what the technologies they are willing and able to deploy reveals about them. In other words, we tend to identify terrorists as terrorists on the basis of the "primitive" technologies they employ and, as I shall argue later, this factor shapes the nature of our response to terrorism.

Assuming that I have established or at least rendered plausible the view that "terrorism" is an essentially technological concept, we must turn to the idea of "progress" in order to see how it is implicated in our response to the problem of terror, defined technologically. Although the relationships between technology and values are complex and have been explored extensively, and despite the fact that specific technologies are often accompanied by multivalent moral modalities, it is possible to identify some basic associations that attend high and low technology.

High technology is generally associated with relatively advanced civilization, whereas low technologies are a mark of the primitive. As historian Michael Adas points out, perceived technological superiority has long been taken as a sign of moral superiority. Interestingly, technical achievements not only in the pacific arts of science and medicine but also, in particular the martial arts, in the form of high-tech weapons systems, have been taken as a sign of superior civility and, indeed, of the blessings of the Creator and of being in harmony with the universe.[19] Moreover, Adas writes, during the age of industrialization,

---

[19] Weapons systems: For example, Thomas Babington Macaulay averred that ". . . the English were 'the greatest and most highly civilized people that ever the world saw.' [He] . . . drew attention to Britain's vast empire and its powerful maritime fleet, which, he argued, could 'annihilate in a quarter of an hour the [preindustrial] navies of Tyre, Athens, Carthage, Venice and Genoa together.' He also stressed as proof of Britain's greatness the great advances that had been achieved in medicine, transportation, and 'every mechanical art, every manufacture . . . to a perfection that our ancestors would have thought magical.'" Michael Adas, *Machines as the Measure of Men: Science, Technology, and Ideologies of Western Dominance* (Ithaca, NY: Cornell University Press, 1989), 134. Harmony with the universe: Lancelot Smith, the protagonist of Charles Kingsley's best-selling Victorian novel, *Yeast*, avers that technological advances are "signs that we are on some points at least, in harmony with the universe; that there is a mighty spirit working among us, who cannot be your anarchic and destroying Devil and therefore must be the ordering and Creating God" (quoted in Adas, *Machines as the Measure of Men*, 139).

Europeans and (increasingly) Americans grew more and more conscious of the uniqueness and, they believed, the superiority of Western civilization. . . . [They] came to view scientific and technological achievements not only as the key attributes that set Europe off from all other civilizations, past and present, but as the most meaningful gauges by which non-Western societies might be evaluated, classified, and ranked.[20]

Thus high technology came to be the principal sign of civilization, which carried, in turn, the expectation of "civility" and moral superiority, whereas low technology was a marker of the primitive, the brute, and the moral inferiority of other cultures. This hierarchical ordering of civilizations based on technological achievements linked with moral stature continues to this day. High technology, culture, and civility form a cluster of concepts that finds its antipode in low technology, nature, and brutality. Thus, despite negative practical "side effects" that often accompany high technology, because of the embeddedness of technology in an ideology of progress that is already a moral scale, high and low technology generally carry positive and negative moral modalities, respectively. High technology as the product of systematized intelligence that aims at human good implicitly carries connotations of humanity, at least when the principal distinctive attribute of the human is conceived as the rational, while low technology is conceived as closer to nature. The violence of nature—even human nature, as opposed to human culture—is viewed as, at best, morally neutral and, at worst, an instance of positive evil.

Of course, high technology does not carry uniformly positive associations. Observers have routinely noticed the ability of high technology to carry out violence on an unprecedented scale, most notably, for example, the Gatling gun, mustard gas, V2 rockets, and nuclear weapons. Moreover, it was the (then) high technology of the industrial revolution that cased the Romantics to find respite in the supposedly unspoilt nature of primitivism. However, these observations are not counterexamples to the associations of high technology with moral goodness and opposition to brutality and moral evil. Rather, the idea that advanced culture can be at least as—if not more—violent than primitive life gains its ironic force from the strength of this association. Although the Romantics were often concerned with the inhumanity of technology, they simultaneously

---

[20] Adas, *Machines as the Measure of Men*, 144.

mourned the loss of a primitive violence. In other words, the Romantics did not cease to regard high tech as rational, civilized, and pacific, and low tech (or raw nature) as irrational and brutal. Rather, in the context of concerns about losing the "dark side" of our humanity, they revalued violence, thus preserving and possibly even reinforcing these associations.

This contrast of primitiveness and brutality with advanced civilization and civility and the concomitant associations with low and high technology, respectively, is relevant because the first set of concepts is associated with terrorism, or at least with terrorists. Both sets of concepts are situated in the context of a general tale of progress that depicts (most) human beings as having emerged from an early, primitive, and violent state of nature into a state of advanced civilization that is based upon reason and peaceful coexistence.[21] Terrorism is conceived as a relapse into a more primitive state of violence and, more importantly for my argument, this atavism is identified by the employment of low as opposed to high technology.

To reiterate, I do not claim that low technology is a necessary condition for terrorism. The possibility that terrorists will gain access to relatively high-tech means of violence, such as nuclear weapons, is certainly a legitimate concern. However, I am claiming that in addition to being framed as a technological problem, acts of terrorism tend, on the whole, to be identified through their use of low technology and that this tendency plays a role in framing the response to terrorism. While low technology is not a necessary feature of terrorism, it is not accidental that acts of terrorism tend to employ low rather than high technology. Nor is it accidental that terrorism appears to call for a high-tech response. The nonaccidental nature of this association is made clear by the fact that the negative associations with terrorism are borne by the technology of terrorism itself and thus can be taken as signs of an ideology, in opposition to positive features that are borne by high technology itself that also can be taken as indicative of the ideology held by those who employ it. Specifically, the low technology of terrorism bears the marks of a lack of respect for human life in general, for individualism, and for freedom whereas high technology as located within an ideology of progress is under-

---

[21] Edward Said's discussion of "Orientalism" is relevant here, more so with respect to the dehumanization of racial or ethnic groups who have commonly been associated with terrorism, such as Arabs and the Irish. See Edward Said, *Orientalism* (New York: Vintage Books, 1979).

stood as leading directly to a greater respect for human life, individuality, and freedom.

Consider the contrast between the media portrayal of the technologies of terror and the alleged pinpoint accuracy of the high-tech weaponry of the United States military. Although box-cutters and gasoline cans kill far fewer people than cruise missiles and smart bombs, and despite the fact that more civilians have been harmed by the latter than the former, the more primitive forms of violence are portrayed as more brutal. Although in terms of sheer numbers more people and more civilians die as a result of the employment of advanced military weaponry than from the primitive tools of terrorism, we experience a more visceral reaction to those who would employ knives and bombs at close range than to fliers and military planners who "precisely" drop weapons from a distance. Setting aside questions of who is acting in self-defense and who is not, and the extent to which "collateral damage" is tolerated or advocated, the notion of high-tech violence as opposed to the more direct, low-tech variety carries a sense of moral superiority, largely because mediation via high technology makes these acts seem less violent. Since violence bears an implicit-unless-mitigated negative moral modality, the more direct connection to it that accompanies low-tech violence tends to reflect poorly on the human and moral status of the person who carries it out. (Thus, the capacity of a person, even a nonterrorist, to commit violence using low-tech means prejudices judgments about his character.) Despite the fact that cruise missiles and car bombs are equally effective instruments of terror and tend to have relatively indiscriminate effects on civilians, car bombs seem more violent because the car bomber is closer to the violence, and is therefore viewed as less moral and less humane. Thus, acts that are mediated by low technology and that place the perpetrator closer to the action are more likely to be regarded as terrorist acts. Additionally, because acts of violence that utilize low technology typically require the perpetrator to be closer to the action, they seem more violent because the actor is himself directly involved in the violence, occasionally so directly that he commits suicide in carrying out the act. By contrast, the mediation and distance of high tech means helps to insulate the precision bomber from the brutality associated with the suicide bomber even though the former kills many more people.

Another related feature is the tendency of low technology to be perceived as robbing people of their individuality, while high technology is seen as enhancing it. The indiscriminate violence of car bombs and WMDs provides stark contrast to the highly discriminating nature of satellite and laser guided smart bombs and so-called surgical strikes. Moreover, because the low-tech weapons of the terrorists tend to involve the perpetrator more closely in the violence itself, quite often subjecting him to its terrible results, this form of technology is seen as inherently anti-individual, not even discriminating the victim from the aggressor. Contrast this with high-tech weapons whose high cost is justified by their advertised ability to discriminate targets with absolute precision and to keep the aggressor as far as possible from the effects of the violence.

This shift in the perceived effects of technology on individuality is relatively recent. Whereas older, lower, industrial-age technologies were regarded as fundamentally disindividuating and dehumanizing, with their one-size-fits-all approach to problem-solving, the advent of information technology with its ability to use feedback loops to generate highly tailored products has made high technology appear as the savior of individuality. In the area of consumer products, the introduction of information technology to the industrial process purports to reinforce one's individuality by, for example, allowing one to order a custom-designed sofa rather than having to accept a product that is designed for everyone and therefore no one. Customized tools and technologies, which since the decline of craft industries have become possible only through the introduction of high technology, may be viewed therefore as enhancing individuality rather than limiting it. Consider the Army's recent "Army of One" advertising campaign, which portrays high-tech weaponry as enhancing both the effectiveness and the individuality of the individual soldier. The soldier as an Army of One stands in stark contrast to the GI, the abbreviation for "General Issue," which refers to mass-produced and often ill-fitting boots, fatigues, and food. The Army of One stands in even starker contrast to the image of thousands of poorly equipped terrorists subordinating their individuality to their cause in the extreme case of sacrificing their lives to it.

Similarly, high technology connotes the enhancement of freedom, whereas low technology is tied to notions of drudgery and bondage. For instance, we associate freedom with innovations as diverse as automatic washing machines and cellular telephones. By increasing flexibility and freeing the individual from specific ties to embodied labor, high technology seems to enhance our freedom while low tech appears to rest fundamentally on embodied labor. Thus the technology employed by the high-tech warrior functions symbolically, emphasizing the liberating potential of technology and directly opposes the freedom-limiting low technologies of terrorists, whose actions are (not surprisingly) attributed to their hatred of freedom.[22] Thus, the trend toward identifying people as enemies of civilization less by their ideological commitments and more by the technologies and techniques they employ (which function as proxies for the former) is consistent. The missing premise is "by their tools ye shall know them."

I have argued thus far that "terrorism," though guised as an ideology, is rather a technological concept that functions as a proxy for ideology in virtue of its embeddedness in a morally charged narrative about progress. When we identify groups of people as "terrorists," we do so, in part, on the basis of the level of technology they employ and thereby, without realizing it, import another layer of cultural meanings related to progress and civilization as a result of the way in which we have framed the problem. In the rest of this essay I will explain what's wrong with this approach, specifically how it has limited and oversimplified our response to a complex and essentially nontechnological problem.

*   *   *

The problem with defining the set of problems we face as "terrorism," which, as I have argued, is a technological concept, is that it limits our response in two ways. First, because technological problems necessitate technological solutions, we unnecessarily limit our range of responses to the arena of the technical and thereby occlude social, political, and other responses we might otherwise undertake. Second, because of the positive cultural associations with high technology and the negative associations with low technology, we tend to further restrict our responses to high-tech interventions as a way of distinguishing ourselves morally and culturally from those with whom we struggle. Both responses are short sighted and dangerous.

It is the nature of technological problems that they call for technological solutions. This is because when we define problems technologically—that is, we define them strictly in terms of means rather

---

[22] Viz., President Bush's remarks on September 17, 2001: "The focus right now is on Osama bin Laden, no question about it. He's the prime suspect and his organization. But there are other terrorists in the world. There are people who hate freedom. This is a fight for freedom." From "Bush: 'There's No Rules,'" CNN.com, http://archives .cnn.com/2001/US/09/17/gen.bush.transcript/.

than ends or the contexts from which they emerge—we limit our frame of reference to the realm of technological intervention and exclude the wider economic, political, and ethical context. Take the problem of accidental deaths due to the mishandling of firearms, particularly when they fall into the hands of children, for example. Viewed technologically the problem is defined in terms of the technological limitations of handguns. Handguns, by and large, lack the ability to discriminate between their rightful owners and others into whose hands they might fall. So, a technological solution might involve installing biometric trigger locks so that a handgun will discharge only when held by (and pointed away from) its owner. Another aspect of the problem of accidental discharge, viewed technologically, is the difficulty of determining whether a firearm is loaded. Viewed in this way, another technological solution presents itself: install a light emitting diode or some other easily viewed sign indicating whether the firearm is loaded. These solutions are fine as far as they go. But note how the technological frame artificially limits our understanding of the problem. By defining the accidental discharge problem technologically, we accept the current technological frame and are left with limited alternatives that involve tweaking current technologies rather than further interrogating the problem. Our inquiries are thus directed away from other possible responses, such as asking why Americans feel the need to keep so many firearms around in the first place, whether other approaches might eliminate or mitigate the perceived need for handguns, thus avoiding or substantially limiting the accidental discharge problem to begin with.

The point is that by accepting the technological frame, we tend to artificially restrict our range of responses to technological interventions that operate within that frame. So, with respect to the question at hand, when we define the problems we face in the "war on terror" as a problem of terrorism, thereby defining the problem, technologically, in terms of the means employed, we limit our range of response to interdiction of those means rather than attending to the social, political, and economic contexts from which the problem arises. By defining the problem in this way we artificially restrict our angle of vision at the precise moment when creativity and a wider set of options are needed.

Worse, given the moral modalities of high and low technologies, we have a tendency to limit our responses not only to the domain of technology but to high technology, a limitation that is costly, prone to failure, and likely to lose in a war of attrition. Once we have settled on a technological response to a technological problem (because defined in terms of the tool: terror-inspiring violence), we tend to choose high-tech means to distance ourselves from the low-tech approaches of the terrorists. This is more than merely the attempt to leverage a technological advantage. If what defines terrorists is the low-tech means that they employ, we can and must distinguish ourselves from them by employing high-tech means. To employ high-tech means reinforces our civility and pacifism in contradistinction with the terrorists' brutality. The notion of precision implicit in high technology in general and explicit in the terminology of "surgical strikes" and "smart bombs" in particular attaches positive moral value to high-tech violent means in two ways. First, the idea of precision carries with it the positive connotation of advancement, civilization, and progress as distinct from the idea of imprecise and "brute" force that connotes primitiveness and brutality. Second, the idea of "precision" implies the satisfaction of the principle of discrimination, one of the conditions of *jus in bello*, the prosecution of a just war, which prohibits deliberately harming innocents.[23] By stressing this attribute, the high technology employed by antiterrorism amplifies the moral distance from the characteristically low-tech means of terrorists.

Two principal responses of the United States government to the attacks of September 11 provide examples of this. First, there is the otherwise inexplicable claim that the attacks, which were carried out with extremely low-tech means, provide evidence that we need to spend vast sums of money on a national missile defense system, despite the rather obvious fact that such a system would not have prevented the attacks. Second, the ideological need to employ high-tech fixes helps explain the government's insistence that we must respond to the attacks with a strike on Iraq despite the fact that no one has plausibly claimed that the government of Iraq had anything to do with the September 11 attacks. Recall that it was in the first Gulf War that the intelligent, high-tech weaponry of smart bombs and advanced weapon systems was displayed so prominently in the theater of television news. Thus, another "video game war" provides us with ample means to demonstrate the moral distance that separates us from terrorists.

---

[23] Khatchadourian, "Terrorism and Morality," 289. As previously noted, the use of the principle of discrimination to define terror is problematic in the context of undeclared war and the extensive use of civilian personnel in military operations, two prominent features of the current "war on terror."

This analysis has several concrete implications. The first and most important stems from the observation that the identification of the problem as "terrorism" limits us to attempting technological fixes since, as I have argued, terrorism is an essentially technological concept, despite the fact that it is not recognized as such. Because technological problems call for technological solutions, combating one technology with another, the identification of the problem as "terrorism" necessitates a technological fix and tends to obscure other approaches—political, economic, and social—from the outset. This is problematic because there can be no technological fix to the problems that manifest themselves in terrorist acts. The fact that it is the means that are most striking and that make the most vivid impact on the imagination further occludes the complex context that must be considered in order to adequately formulate, not to mention respond to, the problem.

The second implication relates to our apparent need to differentiate ourselves from terrorists through a commitment to high-tech as opposed to low-tech approaches. Given that the war on terror is ongoing with no discrete end, a reliance on high-tech solutions does not present a viable long-term strategy against low-tech aggressors. Despite the apparent advantages that high- as opposed to low-tech approaches provide over the short term, the fact is that the higher the technology, the more vulnerable, costly, and nonsustainable it tends to be in the long run. Because they can be sustained only by highly complex and far-flung networks and because of their inherent complexity, high-tech systems are more vulnerable than low-tech approaches. In addition, the difference in relative cost between high-tech and low-tech solutions makes the former unlikely to succeed in long-haul efforts. The space program provides good examples of both points. Although the United States "won" the race to the moon, by responding to the relatively low-tech approach of the Soviets with an approach that emphasized cutting-edge technologies, Russia, despite ongoing and severe budget crises, maintains a far firmer foothold on space through a reliance on less complex and less costly technologies. Ongoing problems with the Space Shuttle indicate the relative merits of simple and cheap systems in contrast to complex and expensive ones over the long term. The situation with terrorism is no different in this respect. Even if the United States were willing to commit massive resources to the development of high-tech responses to terrorist threats both with respect to homeland security and military engagements abroad, how sustainable is such a commitment over the long run?

Also, in the context of security, high-tech responses pose more of a threat to democracy and civil liberties. Apart from interdiction and retaliation, the primary response to terrorism viewed as a technological problem involves risk assessment and a concomitant "hardening" of likely targets. These approaches require very specialized expertise. Although the employment of experts presents a problem for democratic societies in general because the general public tends to be excluded from debate of issues deemed too complex to be comprehensible to the average citizen, the problem of terrorism poses a special problem. This is because the dangers of overreliance on experts are best mitigated by extensive public education and free and open criticism. However, once terrorist risks are evaluated, the risk assessments and the responses that they entail must, in order too be effective, be kept secret. Out of a concern for its safety, the public must be kept in the dark and thus deprived of the ability to exercise oversight over measures taken. Moreover, secrecy endangers the ongoing viability of technology in general because technological development can proceed effectively only in the context of free and open critical discourse. The proliferation of secret threat analyses, weapons and surveillance systems, and security initiatives is, in the end, more likely to harm democracy than to save it.

These problems are not simple, and neither are the solutions. The first step in finding solutions to the vexing problems that we face is recognizing the problems for what they are. The identification of our problem as one of "terrorism" incorrectly identifies the problem as technological rather than political, economic, and social and dangerously suggests that there is a technological fix. The problem with the identification of the problem as "terrorism" is that it identifies a complex situation in terms of a single class of symptoms in place of efforts to identify and respond to a complex and diverse etiology. One might compare the war on terror to a campaign to wipe out nosebleeds. While one may succeed in applying a fix to a symptom whenever it crops up, such an approach diverts attention away from an extremely diverse set of underlying causes. There is no technological fix to the problems that we face. Rethinking the problem and understanding the sources of our propensity to prefer high-tech solutions can help us to avoid costly, dangerous, and ineffectual responses and pave the way toward a more mature understanding of and response to the world in which we live.

Violence, Terrorism, and War

| 5 |

Defusing Fear: A Critical Response to the War on Terrorism

ANDREW FIALA

At protests and rallies aimed at dissuading the Bush administration from going to war in Iraq, a common sign read War Is Terrorism. At first glance, this seems to be another example of the way in which political rhetoric oversimplifies complex ideas. Protest rallies demand pithy sayings designed to provoke action but they are not known for their philosophical complexity. However, upon reflection one wonders where the difference between war and terrorism exactly lies. It is clear that wars fought during the twentieth century have employed terror tactics to attain military and political objectives. One need only mention Dresden, Hiroshima, and Nagasaki to make this point. Consequentialist forms of military realism can be used to argue that terrorism might be justifiable in fighting a war.[1] Indeed, on some interpretations of just war theory—such as those of Michael Walzer and John Rawls—terrorism might be justifiable under the rubric of the "supreme emergency principle."[2] This possibility should make us think critically about the very idea of a "war on terrorism." If we are concerned to eliminate terrorism, then we should also be concerned to eliminate war or at least to restrain the tendency of military strategists to see terror tactics as an option. If terrorism is wrong, then it is wrong regardless of who practices it. In light of this, I argue that we

---

[1] For arguments that do just this see Kai Nielsen, "Against Moral Conservatism," *Ethics* 82 (1972): 219–31, and Virginia Held, "Violence, Terrorism, and Moral Inquiry," *The Monist* 67:4 (Oct. 1984): 605–26.

[2] Michael Walzer, *Just and Unjust Wars* (New York: Basic Books, 1977) and John Rawls, *The Law of Peoples* (Cambridge, MA.: Harvard University Press, 1999).

must carefully guard the rhetoric of war, that we should avoid the militaristic tendency to slip beyond the limits imposed by the just war theory, and that we should insist that terrorists be prosecuted in a legal context that is as open as possible. In order to support these points, I argue that we should critique the rhetorical maelstrom that has created a state of anxiety and panic in the aftermath of the 9/11 attacks. Indeed, statistical analysis shows us that things are not as dire as most of us fear. Although I do not intend to downplay the evil of terrorism, I do intend to defuse our fear of it. Fear is a useful emotion. But terrorists abuse our fears and use them against us. Thus by defusing our fear of terrorism we can begin to think about it more rationally and more justly.

Defining Terrorism

Rhetorical problems intrude as we try to define both terrorism and war. Those who want to advocate and support certain activities use euphemisms to describe them; those who want to condemn certain activities use dysphemisms to describe them. We condemn "terrorists" and are fighting a "war on terrorism." However, for the supporters of Al Qaeda or for supporters of the Palestinians, "terrorists" may be considered as "freedom fighters" or "martyrs." Indeed, the U.S. has supported "freedom fighters" in Central America and in Afghanistan, whose destructive power was justified by the higher cause they served—although one supposes that from the opposite side, these looked like terrorists. The word "martyr" as used by supporters of recent suicide bombers is telling: it assumes that the suicide bomber is dying for a higher cause and that his use of violence is justified. Terrorism, on the other hand, is a dysphemism used as a rebuke that indicates that the terrorist's acts are unjust.

We must think critically about our use of rhetoric. In times of distress, we have a tendency to manipulate language and to be manipulated by it.[3] War and terrorism are both horrible and violent, involving

---

[3] One problem is the way in which rhetorical forces can blind us to the horrors of war. Orwell noted that "political language has to consist largely of euphemism, question-begging and sheer cloudy vagueness. Defenceless villages are bombarded from the air, the inhabitants driven out into the countryside, the cattle machine-gunned, the huts set on fire with incendiary bullets: this is called pacification." George Orwell, "Politics and the English Language," in *George Orwell: Essays* (New York: Knopf, 2002), 963. Likewise, Aldous Huxley wrote, "All war propaganda consists in the last resort, in substituting diabolical abstractions for human beings. Similarly, those who

harms to innocent people, including children. We must be careful as we discuss the justification of violence, terrorism, and war not to be misled by the rhetoric and ideology that can make these seem to be good things. At best violence is a regrettable means of last resort. When we must use violence, this is a tragedy, not a triumph. Osama bin Ladin's fatwas are filled with religious rhetoric and pretentious claims designed to inspire his followers. And the language of supporters of military solutions to terrorism also utilizes religious and other rhetorical flourishes. But critical thinkers must attempt to see through euphemisms, which attempt to disguise the ugliness of war and the despicable wickedness of terrorism. We all have a tendency to blindly adhere to myths that portray "our" side as the side of truth and justice. And we easily succumb to negative, sometimes overtly racist, views of the "other" side. Such tendencies create a potential disaster for serious moral reasoning. As Chris Hedges has recently concluded: "Destruction of honest inquiry, the notion that one fact is as good as the next, is one of the most disturbing consequences of war."[4] This potential for bad judgment and self-deception is found on all sides in war.

But let us turn more explicitly to the question of terrorism. Terrorism, like violence, is a normative concept. It is, by definition, thought to be wrong. Terrorists are those who commit criminal acts including kidnapping, hijacking, and murder. Thus, as a report issued in 1999 by the RAND corporation states: "an act of terrorism is first of all a crime in the classic sense."[5] Thus, even within war, terror tactics are usually ruled out by the principles of justice in war. Terrorism is destructive force deliberately directed at innocent targets, usually with the intention of instilling fear into the general population. The just war doctrine says that it might be permissible to harm innocent civilians if this harm is an unintentional side effect of a legitimate military goal. Such unintended killing might be justifiable by way of the "principle of double effect." Terrorism, however, is not justified

---

defend war have invented a pleasant-sounding vocabulary of abstractions in which to describe the process of mass murder." Aldous Huxley, "Pacifism and Philosophy," in *The New Pacifism*, ed. Gerald K. Hibert (New York: Garland Publishing, 1972), 35.

[4] Chris Hedges, *War Is a Force That Gives Us Meaning* (New York: Public Affairs, 2002), 149–50. For further discussion of the way in which propaganda is used in war (with a focus on the Gulf War), see Jonathon Glover, *Humanity: A Moral History of the Twentieth Century* (New Haven, CT: Yale University Press, 2001), chap. 20.

[5] Ian O. Lesser et al., *Countering the New Terrorism* (Santa Monica, CA: RAND Corporation, 1999), v.

by the doctrine of double effect because it aims directly at killing innocents.[6]

It should be noted that the discussion of the idea of justice in war assumes that some forms of violence can be justified and that others are not. A "war on terrorism" that was guided by the principles of just war thinking would thus be guided by ideas about appropriately limited uses of force. There are other approaches to violence. Some argue that in war any means are suitable for intended ends. This perspective, usually known as "realism," might be appealing in the context of the war on terror, if it seems that terrorists whom we are fighting have no respect for ideas about justice in war. Terrorist's acts are, according to standard definitions of justice in war, war crimes. "Terrorist tactics, in most cases, violated the rules that governed armed conflict—for example, the deliberate targeting of noncombatants or actions against hostages."[7] The assumption here is that it is possible for just warriors fighting a war against terrorism to adhere to the principles of justice in war so that the war on terrorism does not itself become another form of terrorism.

One of the questions raised by the war on terrorism is whether we want to classify terrorists as ordinary (if horrible) criminals, as war criminals, or according to some other classification scheme. The issue of classification is important for a number of reasons.[8] One issue has to do with the rhetoric of war. Those we call "terrorists" may see themselves as engaged in a war. These terrorists may thus want to be afforded a certain status as warriors whose actions could be dignified by the idea of a just or holy war, despite the fact that they do not have the power or authority of a state agency. More importantly, the question of criminality brings up issues about proof, jurisdiction, and due process. The Bush administration's policy is to use military tribunals to prosecute terrorists, thereby treating terrorists as war criminals. Moreover, as we've seen in the Abu Ghraib prison scandal in

---

[6] Alison McIntyre has recently clarified that the doctrine of double effect only applies to those rare occasions when the harm caused is indeed unintended, is only a side effect (and is not a direct means), is unavoidable given the intention, and is proportional to the good intended. She uses terrorism as an example and contrasts terrorism with strategic bombing campaigns—a distinction that I am calling into question in the present essay. See Alison McIntyre, "Doing Away with Double Effect," *Ethics* 111 (January 2001): 219–55.

[7] Lesser et al., *Countering the New Terrorism*, v.

[8] This paragraph builds on some ideas defended by Mark A. Drumbl in his "Judging the 11 September Terrorist Attack," *Human Rights Quarterly* 24 (2002): 323–60.

Iraq, the Bush administration has utilized methods of coercion that go beyond the limits imposed by just war convention. From a realist perspective, there may be no intrinsic reason not to abuse prisoners in this way: any means are necessary in order to attain the end of eradicating terrorism. But for those who accept the principles of just war theory, such methods themselves begin to look suspiciously like terrorism.

Military tribunals are the preferred method for dealing with those captured in the war on terrorism because they allow for easier trials and convictions, while also ensuring the possibility of the death penalty. Those who object to this approach might insist that we ought to try suspected terrorists in nonmilitary courts, whether domestic or international. I am sympathetic to this latter approach for two reasons. Just as we should not become terroristic in our pursuit of terrorism, we should also not let the terrorists make us lose faith in the fairness and efficiency of either the domestic or international legal system. Nor should we support the use of military tribunals because we should not set a precedent that encourages their use in other, more mundane, domestic cases. While I am in no way condoning acts of terror, I am interested in protecting liberty from the expansion of the military and the security state. Moreover, open criminal proceedings are important political strategies aimed at legitimizing the condemnation of terrorism by disclosing the truth. Terrorists should be tried as openly as possible in order to show the world the atrocity of terrorism. Unbiased prosecution is essential to eliminate the misconception that "might makes right," a thesis that undergirds terrorist strategy. At the very least we need to work to ensure the appearance of impartial justice—perhaps only available in an international court that included at least some Islamic jurists—in order to get the message out that the vast majority of the world condemns such actions. Finally, an appeal to universal principles of justice that go beyond the law of the sword is crucial if we want to show potential terrorists that what they propose to do is wrong based on principles that they themselves would accept.

War and Justice

My worry about rhetoric extends to the idea of a "war on terrorism." In declaring war on terrorism the condemnation and pursuit of terrorists becomes confused with a military strategy aimed at supremacy, rather than an approach that is aimed at justice. At the very least one hopes that in declaring war on terrorism, our leaders—

civilian and military—would explicitly and forcefully disavow the use of terror tactics in the prosecution of the war. Just means must be employed to bring terrorists to justice. We must be careful about the propagandistic tendency of political language here. The distinction between terrorism and justifiable force is a slippery one that depends upon the question of whether civilian casualties are directly intended. During World War II, terror tactics were employed by both sides: deliberate bombing of civilian population centers is a form of terrorism. The fire bombings of Tokyo and Dresden were terror attacks. And the two atomic bomb blasts that destroyed Hiroshima and Nagasaki represent perhaps the most destructive terrorist attacks in history.[9] It might be the case that in the era of total war—in which whole populations are mobilized in the war effort—the distinction between combatants and noncombatants has been effaced. In which case, either there is no such thing as terrorism per se or all war is terrorism. Realists might adopt the first part of this disjunction, when they claim that any means are suitable to the end of victory. Pacifists, of course, worry about the other side of the disjunction. This can be seen in those signs that read, War Is Terrorism. The just war theory attempts to find a third option that distinguishes between justifiable and unjustifiable uses of violence. Justifiable use of violence would not be terroristic, while unjustifiable uses would be.

It is important to note that the realist approach that would allow terrorism is not irrational. Most politically motivated terrorists are not merely pathological. Political terrorists should be distinguished from what we might call "nihilistic terrorists," that is, those who, like the shooters at Columbine High School in Colorado, aim only at disrupting and destroying.[10] Political terrorists are rational agents who utilize what might be called a calculus of terror. The terrorist uses destructive force in order to antagonize a people and destabilize a social structure in order to make a political point aiming at some future political end. This is why political agents who use terrorism are rational: they know how to do cost-benefit analysis in order to maximize the results of their activity. Like those who planned the bombing of

---

[9] For a discussion of the morality of the atomic bomb blasts and the erosion of moral resources that paved the way see Glover, *Humanity*, chap. 12.

[10] For a discussion of the distorted view of reality of Harris and Klebold, the Columbine, Colorado terrorists, as well as other terrorists such as McVeigh and Kaczynkski, see Suzanne Laba Cataldi, "Making a Game of Killing," *Philosophy in the Contemporary World* 9, no. 1 (2002): 19–26.

Hiroshima and Nagasaki, the September 11 terrorists were quite efficient. This one act, which involved only a handful of Al Qaeda operatives, resulted in a radical change in U.S. policy and a sense of anxiety and destabilization that continues today.[11] Since consequentialist reasoning can support terror as a tactic, if we are to condemn it, we must appeal to some deontological principles such as the *in bello* limitation on means found in the just war theory.

Some philosophers have argued that terrorists might justify their actions as necessary for the good they intend or they might redescribe their activities in an effort to appeal to something like the doctrine of double effect.[12] I think that, ultimately, these efforts to justify terrorism must fail because terrorists aim directly at creating civilian casualties as a means. Thus the doctrine of double effect does not apply. I doubt that the World Trade Center bombers only meant to destroy the buildings and create panic without directly intending to kill innocent human beings, as would have been required if this act could have been justified by the principle of double effect.

It is not only the physical pain and death caused by terrorism that is bad, but terrorism is also an assault on the integrity, autonomy, and dignity of its victims.[13] The spiritual harm that results from terrorism is ultimately more important than whatever physical harm is caused by violence. The result of terrorism is both death and terror. The aim of the terrorist is to intimidate and overwhelm by strategically creating fear and panic. Thus terror tactics are not primarily aimed at military targets—although, of course, the destruction of important strategic targets can produce terror effects. Rather, terror targets are those that have some symbolic significance. On 9/11 the targets were large substantial buildings, symbolizing the invulnerability of America. In Israel, Palestinians target civilians in buses and in other public places, because these produce the feeling of fear that is the main goal of terrorism.

---

[11] Of course, it is possible that the changes in U.S. policy brought about by the terrorists were counterproductive to their ends. The declaration of a war on terrorism and the destruction of the Taliban regime were undoubtedly unanticipated negative outcomes for the terrorists.

[12] Viginia Held ("Violence, Terrorism, and Moral Inquiry," 619–20) has suggested that terrorism may be justifiable in light of the just war tradition.

[13] This idea derives in part from Jonathan Glover, *Causing Death and Saving Lives* (London: Penguin, 1990), chap. 5, and Peter Singer, *Practical Ethics*, 2nd ed. (Cambridge: Cambridge University Press, 1993), chap. 4.

Because terrorism aims to create massive spiritual disruption with minimal exertion, it might be justifiable on consequentialist grounds. Kai Nielsen, for example, has argued, "There are circumstances when such violence must be reluctantly assented to or even taken to be something that one, morally speaking, must do."[14] The example he has in mind here are those "terrorists" or "freedom fighters" who fought for Algerian independence in the 1960s using terror tactics. One assumes that Palestinian suicide bombing and perhaps the World Trade Center bombings could be justified on consequentialist grounds as promoting the general welfare of the Palestinian people or as working toward the freedom of Islam from foreign intervention. A consequentialist might argue that if these actions serve some further legitimate purpose for a person or group, then they are justifiable. However, if violence is always a violation of autonomy, and if autonomy is something to which we all have a right by virtue of being human, then violence against innocents can only be indirectly justified by something like the principle of double effect.

I must admit here that I am suspicious of the just war tradition's doctrine of double effect, just as I am suspicious of those who would argue that anyone should be willing to sacrifice oneself for a larger political end. I have a hard time imagining how it might be possible to justify actions that cause harm to innocents without their consent, even if these actions are not intended, or if these harms can serve some higher purpose.[15] I think we are safer adopting something like a presumption of nonviolence and setting a very high burden of proof to justify all forms of violence. I thus argue for what I call "practical pacifism." This idea is derived from the idea that modern warfare— with its mechanized means of killing, its use of terror bombing, and

---

[14] Kai Nielsen, "Against Moral Conservativsm" *Ethics* 82 (1972): 222.

[15] The doctrine of double effect is complex and includes issues such as the problem of defining negative vs. positive actions; the distinction between killing and letting die; the problem of intentionality of harm vs. foreseeing harm; and the question of whether or not the numbers matter (see McIntyre, "Doing Away"). There are no easy answers to these questions, but I assume that there is a prima facie obligation not to harm innocents without their consent. In this regard I am also sympathetic to Wolff who holds that no violation of autonomy can be justified and who thus roundly condemns violence: "If 'violence' is taken to mean an unjustified use of force, then the answer to the question [of when it is permissible to resort to violence] is obviously never. If the use of force were permissible, it would not, by definition, be violence, and if it were violent, it would not, by definition, be permissible." Robert Paul Wolff, "On Violence," *Journal of Philosophy* 66 (October 1969): 601–16; 608.

its general tendency to exceed the limits of *in bello* proportionality and discrimination—is prima facie wrong based upon commonly accepted just war criteria. It is up to those who propose wars to ensure us that these wars will be fought justly; and it is up to ordinary citizens to question and resist until we are sure that a war fought in our names will be fought justly.[16]

The further problem is that recourse to war or terrorism represents a breakdown of consensus about ideas and ends. We fight because we disagree. Thus again, we return to the problem that one man's terrorist is another man's heroic martyr. And terror tactics that are thought to be necessary according to the objectives of those on one side of the war might be viewed as evil from the perspective of those on the other side. Military strategists deliberately plan the killing of innocents in designing bombing campaigns. A rhetorical disconnect makes us find "terrorism" unimaginable, while allowing us proudly to celebrate the accomplishments of our military forces by hiding their destructive force behind the doctrine of double effect. I think we would be better off admitting that both terrorism and war are violent and can intentionally cause the destruction of innocent lives. Likewise, even the use of economic sanctions can be a form of violence that deliberately causes the destruction of innocents, by depriving them of the means of life.[17] It might be that by appealing to the just war theory we might accept certain of these activities as justifiable. But if violence is bad and if unjustified uses of violence are wicked, we must be very careful to be certain that any proposed

---

[16] I defend this thesis in *Practical Pacifism* (New York: Algora Publishing, 2004) and in articles such as "Practical Pacifism and the War on Terror," *The Humanist* 62, no. 6 (November/December 2002): 14–16, and "Citizenship, Epistemology, and the Just War Theory," *Logos: A Journal of Catholic Thought and Culture* 7, no. 2 (April 2004). For a related view see Paul J. Griffiths, "Just War: An Exchange" (with a reply by George Weigel) in *First Things*, no. 122 (April 2002): 31–36. Also see Stanley Hauerwas, *Should War be Eliminated?* (Milwaukee, WI: Marquette University Press, 1984). In the background of this discussion is The U.S. Catholic Bishops' pastoral letter of 1983, "The Challenge of Peace: God's Promise and Our Response." Also see Richard Wasserstrom, "On the Morality of War," *Stanford Law Review* 21: 1627–56, reprinted in *Moral Problems*, ed. James Rachels (New York: Harper and Row, 1971), and Martin Benjamin, "Pacifism for Pragmatists," *Ethics* 83:3 (1973): 196–213. Perhaps the most forceful argument made in this regard is by Robert L. Holmes, *On War and Morality* (Princeton: Princeton University Press, 1989).

[17] This argument has been forcefully made by Joy Gordon in "Economic Sanctions, Just War Doctrine, and the 'Fearful Spectacle of the Civilian Dead,'" *Cross Currents* 49 (Fall 1999), no. 3.

use of violence is in fact justifiable. Moreover—and here we return to the tragic element in the use of violence—we must recognize that the terrorist has a theory of justification of his own.

To be clear, I am not claiming that terrorism, such as occurred in Oklahoma City or on September 11, is justifiable. And I am not claiming that all uses of military force are unjustifiable. The just war theory should be interpreted as aiming to prevent justifiable military force from becoming terroristic. Thus my thesis is that we must be very careful when we propose using military force, so that on those tragic occasions when we must resort to violence, we do not become terroristic in our pursuit of a war against terrorism. One way of ensuring that we do not become terroristic is to be very clear about our language and our methods. We should avoid euphemism and frankly describe the facts of violence. We should also demand transparency and honesty from our political and military leaders, so that we can assess military actions done in our names and on our behalf. Finally, when we are unsure that certain military actions are not terroristic, we should protest and resist.

The Problem of Fear

A further problem arises if we feel that the just war theory is simply not sufficient to respond to the magnitude of the threat posed by terrorists. Indeed, Huntington's notion of the clash of civilizations might make it seem as if 9/11 was the beginning of a final war in which our very existence was at stake.[18] In such a case one might follow Walzer and Rawls by invoking the idea of a "supreme emergency," which would exempt us from the limits imposed by the just war theory. A supreme emergency is one that confronts a people with the impending fact of their own annihilation. The example, which Rawls borrows from Walzer, is Great Britain in the early 1940s. The phrase "supreme emergency" draws upon Winston Churchill's rhetorical flourish in which he called Britain's predicament in 1939 a "supreme emergency." The point of this is that in case of a supreme emergency, violations of the standard principles of *jus in bello* could be justified. As Walzer describes this, it is the "back-to-the-wall" argument: "when conventional means of resistance are hopeless or worn out, anything goes (anything that is 'necessary' to win)."[19] When a supreme emer-

---

[18] Samuel P. Huntington, *The Clash of Civilizations* (New York: Simon and Schuster, 1996).
[19] Walzer, *Just and Unjust Wars*, 252.

gency is recognized, we are thrown back upon the laws of necessity and, as Walzer indicates, "necessity knows no rule."[20] Walzer's discussion of the supreme emergency indicates a point at which consequentialist reasoning mixed with a dose of political realism overrides other principles of justice. This form of reasoning seems to be found in much of the Bush administration's recent reasoning about the necessity of expanding the war on terror to include Iraq, where Iraq's supposed possession of weapons of mass destruction was the primary rationale behind a war.

There are epistemological problems that should make us reluctant to invoke the idea of a supreme emergency. It is very difficulty to know that the present moment is really a supreme emergency of world-historical significance. Moreover, our judgments about such matters are often biased by emotions, especially fear. Fear can be a useful emotion: it can serve as a "wake up call" (to use the language that many Americans used to describe the events of September 11). But fear that is unanalyzed from a less emotional and more rational perspective should not guide our actions. This is a truism about how to make good judgments. But it is important to remember when thinking about terrorism because terrorists deliberately aim to provoke fear, hoping to use fear against us. We can avoid being misled by fear by employing reason. We must stick to principles that the cool light of reason tells us are right. And we must dispassionately examine the facts.

Thus we must remain committed to the principles of just war theory as we combat terrorism. To employ terror tactics against terrorists is to become terroristic. We should not let fear and the heat of battle distract us from principles we know are right. And we should consider the true risks of terrorism and admit that the facts do not support the idea of a supreme emergency in the case of terrorism. One analysis of the statistical risk of death by terrorism in the United States after September 11 concluded: "Even the terrible death toll of September 2001 implies a risk of death from terrorist attack that is well below that of death from ordinary murder or traffic accident in the United States. Indeed, even in that year, the probability of being killed by terrorism in the United States was less than that of being run over by a car while walking."[21]

---

[20] Walzer, *Just and Unjust Wars*, 254.

[21] Roger D. Congleton, "Terrorism, Interest-Group Politics, and Public Policy," *The Independent Review* 8:1 (Summer 2002): 59. Along these lines, Richard Rorty has recently argued that terrorism is perhaps more similar to a natural disaster such as an

This conclusion should be reassuring and should make us question whether in fact the vigorous response of the war on terror is justified. I am not saying that we should ignore the risk of terrorism. Rather, we should keep a sane perspective on the problem. Terrorism is a horrible thing; indeed, the idea that terrorists could obtain weapons of mass destruction is even more horrifying. Thus we should act vigorously to combat terrorism. But we should not let the fear generated by terrorism cause us to give up on our principles; nor should we let our fear of terrorism drive us into an unnecessary series of foreign adventures.

Conclusion

Understanding terrorism can help us to defuse our fears and ensure that in waging a war on terrorism we do not resort to terror tactics ourselves. The key to understanding terrorism is to recognize that terrorists utilize small amounts of force to produce large amounts of fear and that the impact of terrorism is linked to the perception of fear on the part of the masses. We should also note that the government and the media can magnify our fears, either inadvertently or deliberately. When we understand this, we may begin to react more rationally and more easily uphold the idea that the war on terrorism should proceed in a principled manner that aims to prevent terrorism and bring justice to terrorists without violating the principles of justice.

After September 11, cynics have argued that the Bush Administration has cultivated fear in an Orwellian bid to gain support for its foreign and domestic agenda. Such a conspiracy theory approach is ultimately a matter of unfounded speculation that itself requires careful critical analysis. It has not, then, been my intention to engage in such speculation. Rather, my point is that what is needed in general is critical analysis and education about the risks of terrorism and about the principles of justice that would restrain our use of force. Education can decrease our anxieties, reinforce the basic principles of justice, and help us begin to imagine creative responses to the terrorist threat.

The "war on terrorism" is not a war between peoples or states. Because of its very unconventional nature it risks becoming unprin-

---

earthquake or hurricane than it is to any other form of political violence: it is unpredictable and ultimately unpreventable—given the fact that a few individuals with a little bit of money and organization can threaten massive destruction (Richard Rorty, "Fighting Terrorism with Democracy," *The Nation*, October 21, 2002).

cipled. Ideally the war on terrorism would be understood as a law-enforcement concern aimed at infiltrating, arresting, and prosecuting terrorists while also establishing security systems to prevent further attacks. This means that it should be conducted within the limits established for law enforcement, including restraint of force, due process, certain conventions about the burden of proof, and a great deal of respect for individual liberty. The U.S. has previously supported established legal channels—both domestic and international courts—to prosecute terrorists (as we did, for example, in the response to the 1988 terrorist attack on the Pan Am flight over Lockerbie, Scotland). The current situation may require a more creative, active, and perhaps militaristic approach. However, in dealing with Islamic terrorists, we should appeal to Islamic jurists to pass judgment on terrorism, so that the war on terrorism will be perceived as legitimate by Muslims, who may feel threatened by a more unilateral approach. Only in this way—by condemning terrorism on principles that terrorists themselves and citizens of the world might agree to—will potential terrorists be deterred (if those who are willing to commit both suicide and homicide can ever be deterred).

The rhetoric of war must be carefully guarded in order to avoid what Jonathan Glover has called "military drift."[22] Once a war is declared we tend to slip toward the perspective that aims at victory at any cost. However, if we are committed to ideas about restraint of force, we should always be careful about using the indiscriminate destructive force of modern warfare. And we must be judicious about using the rhetoric of war, lest we become too willing to sacrifice principles of justice for success in killing. The rhetoric of war tends to incline us toward a realist point of view where supreme emergencies loom. War utilizes violent methods and these methods can easily become terroristic, as we've seen, for example, in the excesses of the Abu Ghraib prison. We should thus be skeptical of the rhetoric of war and conclude that war is prima facie to be avoided. And we must demand that our military and civilian leadership does their best to uphold the same principles of justice, which we use to condemn terrorists. If we are not to become terrorists ourselves, we must demand that the war on terrorism be conducted in a just manner, that terrorists be tried in open courts so that the truth might come out, and that our leaders honestly apprise us of the real risks of terrorism so that we are not seduced by fear to demand more than justice requires.

---

[22] Glover, *Humanity*, 75.

| 6 |

Physical Violence in Political Contexts: Grounds for a Strong Presumption against Violence

TRUDY GOVIER

Introduction

In this essay, I want to explore the common presumption that those who resort to physical violence as a response to conflict bear a burden of justification and are acting wrongly unless they can show otherwise.[1] Although the presumption against physical violence is not universal, it can be argued to be fundamental, due to its role in protecting physical security and structuring a decent civil society with respect for human rights and the rule of law.

Despite talk of institutional violence, psychological violence, structural violence, verbal violence and so on, the term "violence" ordinarily refers to physical violence. There are good reasons to resist extensions of the notion of "violence" away from the physical paradigm: the stipulated usages are contrary to ordinary convention, potentially vague and confusing, and unnecessary as a means to defend the norms people have sought to buttress by persuasive definitions. To object to a policy or action, we need not brand it a form of violence. Such actions as lying or stealing are often nonviolent but there are nonetheless good reasons for regarding them as generally wrong. In any event, it is physical violence that will be the focus of attention here.

In acts of physical violence, agents apply external force so as to suddenly and intensely damage or destroy persons or other entities.

---

[1] The term "resort to" actually suggests that there is this burden of proof. People are said to *resort to* violence as a means, and not simply to use or adopt physically violent methods.

Physical violence against persons characteristically injures or harms them and may kill them. Animals can be killed or injured by physical violence, and damage or destruction can also be wrought against natural environments, economic resources, and cultural artifacts. Clearly, the violent use of physical force is not the only way to damage these entities, but it is a prevalent and striking one. The concept of physical violence is evaluative because of the centrality of the notion of harm, and it is plausible to say that all acts of physical violence are prima facie wrong because of their harmful character.[2]

My own interest is in the use of physical violence as a response to conflict between human beings and, more specifically, in its use as response to political conflict.[3] People are involved in a conflict when they have, or believe themselves to have, opposed and incompatible goals. It would appear that not all can win. Each party presumes that it needs victory to be gained by the defeat of the other, and a struggle for power results. Conflicts are political when they concern relations between individuals and groups involving arrangements about governance, power over entitlements and resources, and the distribution of goods.[4] Physical violence is not an inevitable response to conflict, not even (as is often assumed) to serious political conflict. Nor is the assumption that in any serious conflict only one party can win strictly correct: goals that appear to be incompatible may turn out to be reconcilable in the end, when the circumstances and interests of the parties are more thoroughly understood. Thus some conflicts can be altered or transformed as a result of negotiation, dialogue, mediation, and other nonviolent responses. Sometimes cooperation and compromise achieve results acceptable to contending parties and no physical

---

[2] Robert L. Holmes, "The Concept of Physical Violence in Moral and Political Affairs," *Social Theory and Practice* 2, no. 4 (Fall 1973): 387–408. Quoted passage is on p. 403.

[3] This is not to say that there is no presumption against violence between persons or groups when the conflict is *not* political. In fact, I think that such a presumption is more solid than that against political violence, and I grant it. Some of my arguments here would apply to this case, but some would not. It is political contexts such as wars between and within states, terrorism as a political tool, and violent resistance to oppression that are my main concern.

[4] Gerald C. MacCallum, Jr., "What's Wrong with Violence?" in *Legislative Intent and Other Essays on Law, Politics, and Morality*, ed. Marcus G. Singer and Rex Martin (Madison: University of Wisconsin Press, 1993), emphasizes the sudden nature of the physical force and the radical nature of change; he also points out that our sense that doing violence to an entity, E, is prima facie wrong will depend on how we value that entity.

violence is used by either side; in such a case, there has been a con-flict but it has not been characterized by physical violence. Even in adversarially constructed situations that seem to require something like victory by one side or the other, the struggle may be conducted by other means such as legal proceedings or exercises of nonviolent social power in the form of demonstrations, strikes, boycotts, and other people power campaigns. Thus it is by no means inevitable that physical violence be the means of waging political struggle.

In most circles in a tolerably well-run civil society, people share the presumption that resorting to the use of physical violence is gen-erally wrong—which is to say, that it is wrong, other things being equal. In fact, such a presumption is presumed by the common expression "*resorting* to violence." The demand for a justification is typically met by an argument claiming that violence is a necessary means to a good end and that realistically, there is *no alternative* to it: the implication of this sort of response is that if there were an alter-native, that alternative would be preferable. This again is just to say that a presumption against violence is common.

But *Is* There a Presumption against Physical Violence?

Before exploring the values and assumptions that underlie the pre-sumption against physical violence, we must acknowledge that doubts can be raised on this topic. Indeed, the claim that there exists a solid general presumption against violence is in significant respects an oversimplification.

Some theorists regard violence as good by merit of having posi-tive biological or historical functions. To some, the violence of wars has seemed a force that serves as an agent of the inevitable in human history, operating in the direction of historical progress. For example, they see war as "the engine by which the best that is in humankind" can be made to "flourish."[5]

Many who do not regard violence as generally good—or in some positive sense "normal"—may see it as good in some competitive

---

[5] The idea that the Western presumption against violence is not as strong as one might assume is explored by Robert L. Holmes in "A Western Perspective on the Problem of Violence," in *Social and Political Philosophy*, ed. David M. Rasmussen, Proceedings of the Twentieth World Congress of Philosophy, vol. 11, 193–205 (Bowling Green, OH: Philosophy Documentation Center, 2001).

contexts, with group struggles for power and resources being cases in point. While there may, within a culture, be a general presumption that violence is wrong and should be used only when absolutely necessary, that presumption may not operate in all contexts within that culture. In dramatic contexts, for instance, we often assume that violence is desirable because it makes for adventure and excitement and provides a decisive narrative resolution to a conflict. Some people engage in violence as a beautiful form of destruction, an attitude exemplified by the novel *A Clockwork Orange* where the central character Alex exalted in violence as a beautiful reaction against an ugly society.[6]

In his book *The Wretched of the Earth*, Frantz Fanon seems to exalt physical violence. Far from deeming such violence as regrettable, Fanon maintains that colonized peoples need to use it against white settlers and settler societies. Fanon understands physical violence as something that would be valuable in a context where oppressed and humiliated people are struggling to restore their dignity and humanity. Fanon assumes that violence has a positive value because of its role in asserting an uncompromising rejection of colonial values.

> The shantytown sanctions the native's biological decision to invade, at whatever cost and if necessary by the most cryptic methods, the enemy fortress. The *lumpenproletariat*, once it is constituted, brings all its forces to endanger the "security" of the town, and is the sign of the irrevocable decay, the gangrene ever present at the heart of colonial domination. So the pimps, the hooligans, the unemployed, and the petty criminals, urged on from behind, throw themselves into the struggle for liberation like stout working men. These classless idlers will by militant and decisive action discover the path that leads to nationhood. They won't become reformed characters to please colonial society, fitting in with the morality of its rulers; quite on the contrary, they take for granted the impossibility of their entering the city save by hand grenades and revolvers. These workless less-than-men are rehabilitated in their own eyes and in the eyes of history. The prostitutes too, and the maids who are paid two pounds a month, all the hopeless dregs of humanity, all who

---

[6] This case is discussed in Joseph Kupfer, "Ultra-Violence," *Journal of Social Philosophy* 11 (1980): 15–22. He describes the violence of Alex as ultra-violence in the sense that there is nothing that would limit it because it "requires and reflects a loss of the social connectedness in which human living and even violence consists" (17). Alex's devotion to an aesthetic of violent destruction is monstrous and yet it expresses his response to the ugliness and injustice of his society.

turn in circles between suicide and madness, will recover their balance, once more go forward, and march proudly in the great procession of the awakened nation.[7]

For these people, there is only one duty, to throw out colonialism by every means in their power. According to Fanon, the use of physical violence in such a context would be positively redemptive, marking a constructive distinction between the downtrodden *us* and the oppressive *them*, and that distinction has to be marked because colonialists are purely and simply *evil*. No display of humanity would possible or desirable in the pursuit of the anti-settler cause.[8]

Fanon's account was (notoriously) endorsed with enormous enthusiasm by Jean-Paul Sartre. In a preface to *Wretched of the Earth*, Sartre referred to Fanon as the authentic voice of the Third World, a doctor diagnosing Europe's illness and imminent death. Pointing out that European people had permitted the massacre, in their name, of brown and black skinned people in the colonies, Sartre proclaimed enthusiastically that the only true culture was the culture of the revolution. Fanon, he said, was showing the responsive processes of history in the clear day. "Hatred is their only wealth," Sartre said of Third World peoples, and "by this mad fury, by this bitterness and spleen, by their ever-present desire to kill and by the permanent tensing of powerful muscles which are afraid to relax, they have become men."[9]

Quite apart from the conduct of competition, a society might selectively favor violent acts for their expressive value, as dramatic acts enacting its own sense of desperation, revenge, and willingness to sacrifice. The Palestinians claim, in the period 2001–2004, to be engaged in a war against an occupying power and to be justified in using any means to resist and retaliate against Israeli soldiers and citizens. Young people who commit suicide bombings are deemed to be martyrs or *shuhada* fighting for Islam and the Palestinian nation and are glorified by many in Palestinian society. Violence against Jews, in this context, is not something against which there is a standing presumption in this society. For better or for worse, such violence is

---

[7] Frantz Fanon, *The Wretched of the Earth*, trans. Constance Farrington (New York: Grove Weidenfelt, 1963), 130.

[8] For a philosophically sophisticated explanation of Fanon's ideas, see Olapido Fashina, "Frantz Fanon and the Ethical Justification of Anti-Colonial Violence," *Social Theory and Practice* 15 (1989): 179–212.

[9] Jean-Paul Sartre, preface to *The Wretched of the Earth*, by Frantz Fanon, 17.

exalted. Violence is revenge and an expression of defiance, and resistance to an oppressive occupying power. To many Palestinians, it seems that this violence works: the suicide bombers have killed many Israelis and struck fear into the hearts of all, with everyday activities like shopping, taking buses, and going to beaches and parks fraught with insecurity and uncertainty. One has the sense that the exercise of physical power feels cathartic in a context of extreme frustration and oppression. Through the sacrifices of young men and women, the Palestinian people have gained destructive power and a corollary political power (or so it is assumed): they can kill and maim and inspire fear, and they are not to be dismissed.[10] Many outsiders and some critics from within see highly negative consequences: the number of Palestinians killed in reprisals exceeds the number of Israelis killed by a factor of more than two; the effects on the Palestinian economy and resources are highly negative; and there is concern about children being taught that martyrdom should be their highest goal in life. Nevertheless, the strategy of suicide bombing enjoys wide approval in Palestinian society; one could hardly say that there is a presumption against the use of physical violence in this context.[11]

Not only does the presumption against physical violence fail to exist within some societies and for some theorists, but even where it does exist, the presumption may be selective in scope. Most well-brought-up people in Western societies do not condone the use of physical violence as a response to conflicts in personal relationships or daily social life. Nevertheless, most of these same people regard war between states and perpetual preparation for it as permanent realities of international relations and serious political conflicts over governance—and as so natural and inevitable in these contexts as to require no special justification. Within this framework of assumptions, repugnance toward terrorist acts as *violent* is outrage against *nonstate agents* presuming the right to use physical violence—the assumption being, apparently, that the use of physical violence by *state* agents would not be objectionable. This attitude was satirized in a small poem, "Ethics for Everyman," by Roger Woodis.

---

[10] Much of this analysis is drawn from Avishai Margalit, "The Suicide Bombers," *The New York Review of Books*, January 16, 2003, 36–39.
[11] See, for example, Gal Luft, "The Palestinian H-Bomb," *Foreign Affairs*, July/August 2002.

Throwing a bomb is bad
Dropping a bomb is good
Terror no need to add
Depends on who's wearing the hood[12]

Some people think, and feel, that physical violence in their own neighborhood or society is shockingly wrong, while, as an aspect of international relations, it is entirely normal and respectable. This attitude is depicted in the film *Bowling for Columbine*, when Michael Moore interviews a weapons engineer about high school violence. While finding the Columbine high school massacre horrifying, this man shows pride in his own role supporting weapons systems used to support American military power. He sees shooting as deplorable, when the agents are troubled teenagers in Colorado, but bombing as commendable when it serves the interests of his state. In all probability, this man would be selective in another respect, believing that his *own* government—the "one remaining superpower"—can legitimately use physical power in pursuit of its own interests while *other states* cannot legitimately do so.

In the fall of 2002 and the winter of 2003, there was considerable discussion as to whether Iraq and North Korea possessed weapons of mass destruction. With very few exceptions, it was conducted on the assumption that possession of such weapons by the *United States and other major powers is normal and legitimate*, while their possession by *smaller powers* or others outside the club (Pakistan and India) is not legitimate at all, and calls for immediate verified disarmament, enforced by outside intervention if necessary. We find here an official repugnance toward extreme physical violence by states—but the attitude is selective.

Further aspects of selectivity arise in connection with the range of entities affected by violence. We may restrict our concern to violence against persons, broaden them so as to include animals and the natural environment, or extend them still further to include economic and cultural properties. The most general presumption against violence would make no systematic exceptions, presuming that physical violence is generally objectionable, or prima facie objectionable, for every agent and in every context, because of its damaging character

---

[12] *New Oxford Book of Light Verse*, 1978, as quoted by C. A. J. Coady in "The Morality of Terrorism," *Philosophy* 60 (1985): 47–69.

and devastating effects on human beings, the natural world, and the many things human beings hold valuable.

In the light of all these qualifications, any claim that *we generally* regard physical violence as prima facie wrong is an overstatement. Such a statement stands in need of qualification with regard to who *we* are and what scope and strength *our* presumption has.

Why a Presumption?

Notwithstanding all these qualifications, it still makes sense to explore grounds for a presumption that physically violent means require some special justification.[13] Fundamentally the basis of this presumption is that the entities damaged or destroyed in acts of physical violence have value in themselves or in virtue of their function and use. Persons are believed to have a right to life that should be overridden only when absolutely necessary. Animals have value as sentient creatures and as serving biological or other needs of persons. Clearly persons and animals have a need for the natural environment in which they live; that and other factors show a value to the natural environment as well. Any ethic in which persons, environment, and properties are deemed to possess positive value yields by implication the presumption that it is wrong to harm or destroy them. Thus a presumptive case against physical violence emerges logically from any ethic in which one grants rights to persons, presumptions against harm to sentient creatures, and value to the interests of human beings and other sentient creatures and their need for resources.

Whether something that is presumptively wrong is wrong, full stop, depends on what other factors may be acknowledged as potentially outweighing that presumption.[14] In the context of political vio-

---

[13] I believe that this presumption is common and hope that my description will corroborate that interpretation of common norms. To one who would say that we do not hold it, I would argue—for reasons stated here—that we should.

[14] For a general outline of how one might believe violence to be necessary in pursuit of a good cause, see Kai Nielsen, "On Justifying Violence," *Inquiry* 24 (1981): 21–57 and "Political Violence and Ideological Mystification," *Journal of Social Philosophy* 13 (1982): 25–33. For a reply questioning the effectiveness of violence and arguing for the nonviolent social action, see H. J. N. Horsburgh, "Reply to Nielsen," *Inquiry* 24 (1981): 59–73. Virginia Held also argued that political violence could be justified, in "Violence, Terrorism, and Moral Inquiry," *Monist* 67 (1984): 605–26. Held shows a greater awareness than Nielsen of the negative effects of violence, the difficulty of controlling it, and the possibility of its worsening a situation.

lence in the form of *war* between states, just war theory itself testifies to a strong presumption against physical violence, because it specifies that no state is justified in resorting to war unless a number of strict conditions are met. A state may not rightly engage in war unless it can meet the conditions of being justified in going to war (*jus ad bellum*) and of conducting that war in a just way (*jus in bello*). Clearly, war is not the only context in which there are questions about the justifiability of violence in political conflicts. What about *torture*, used against people of whom there were reasons to believe they were a threat to others, or to the state itself? Or *revolutionary insurrection* involving violence targeted against state personnel and resources? Could *terrorism* ever be justified as a means of overcoming oppression?

The burden of proof lies on those who would use physical violence to show why they are entitled to do so. The matter is serious, so—to put it colloquially—the arguments had better be good. As a means of waging political conflicts, political violence kills many, injures many more, and brings great damage to the physical and social environments. In what follows, I want to buttress the presumption against using physical violence by arguing along the following lines.

A. *The Intrinsic or Primary Effects of Physical Violence*
   1. Physical violence destroys or damages entities that have value.
   2. It is impossible to resist the impact of physical violence with human force.[15]
B. *The Immediate Consequences of Physical Violence in Political Conflicts*
   3. In conflict situations, physical violence tends to provoke or inspire further physical violence on the part of one's opponent.
   4. Victories won by physical violence are apt to be short lived.
   5. Damage to persons, resources, and relationships done in a conflict waged by physically violent means is difficult or impossible to repair.
C. *The Moral Corollaries of Physical Violence in the Context of Political Conflict*
   6. Persons who employ physical violence as a means of seeking victory in a political conflict are likely to desensitize

---

[15] What I mean by "human force" will be explained later.

and thus morally damage themselves in the course of doing so.

7. Agents of physical violence will communicate to others that they have been morally degraded by the means that they employ in quest of their goal.

8. A cause pursued by physically violent means will lose part or all of its moral credibility.

9. A cause pursued by physically violent means will be unattractive to many morally astute and sensitive people.

Such claims have been urged by Mohandas Gandhi, Martin Luther King, Jr., Desmond Tutu, Adam Michnik, Václav Havel, Gene Sharp, Peter Ackerman and Jack DuVall, to name just a few. They have featured in the planning of nonviolent social action in many parts of the world including China, the Philippines, Serbia, east-central Europe, the Middle East, and the United States.

I will consider the claims according in a logical order reflected in the grouping above. Claims 1 and 2, which constitute the first group, may be said to describe *intrinsic or primary effects* of physical violence; these effects exist simply in virtue of what physical violence is. Claims 3, 4, and 5, which constitute the second group, may be said describe *immediate consequences* of these primary effects. In the context of political conflicts, these are effects arising from the first effects and so common as to be nearly ubiquitous. These claims represent facts familiar to any observer of human history. Claims 6, 7, 8, and 9, which constitute the third group, may be said to be *moral corollaries* of the earlier claims. They describe the effects of using physical violence on the character and relationships of those who do it and others who will react to their activities. They presuppose a general presumption against the use of physical violence and a particular moral horror when it is used against our side.

A. The Intrinsic or Primary Effects of Physical Violence

One man I knew spoke of war as "body smashing," using deliberately pejorative language. His phrase had an obvious point: body smashing is a prominent feature of international and civil wars. People are blown up, burned, wounded, or maimed by bombs dropped from above. They are assaulted, beaten, abducted, tortured, or raped by enemies on the ground. They suffer terribly. In wars and other violent conflicts thousands of people lose their family, friends, possessions, livelihood, and lives. Killing is the most blatant and least reversible form of damage—a person who is killed cannot be brought back to life. The act cannot be undone and the damage is irreparable. Some of those injured by war recover only partially, with great difficulty— others not at all. We read sometimes of World War I veterans dying as centenarians, having suffered discomfort from war injuries over eighty years of remaining life. A moving description of a man severely handicapped by a war wound, a shot in the head, was offered by the Russian psychologist A. R. Luria in his book *The Man with a Shattered World*.[16] The injured man had perceptual and mental capacities that made even basic intellectual tasks enormously diffi- cult; he would live with his war injury for his remaining life. People who lose homes as a result of violent devastation are seriously dis- located and may become ill or even die as a result. Ordinary life does not go on in a plastic tent provided by the United Nations. Damage to some cultural and biological resources may be irreparable as well. And even reparable damage takes time and considerable financial resources to repair. These funds are not available for other worthy social purposes.

Even those who recover from physical injuries often suffer fear, anxiety, and lasting trauma as a result of the attacks. Families, friends, and communities incur losses from deaths, losses likely to be felt long after the violent conflict is over. The same may be said of many seri- ous injuries. Environmental damage resulting from war is harmful to animals and ecosystems, as well as to people affected by destruction, pollution, contamination, and the like. Violence to property may threaten health and well-being, as was illustrated with the destruction of sewage and water treatment facilities in the Gulf War of 1991. Tens of thousands of civilian deaths were later attributed to the damaging or destruction of those facilities. Property damage is by no means trivial in human lives. On January 22, 2003, the BBC International News showed Israeli tanks destroying some forty shops in a Palestinian territory. People had been warned to leave the area and the story did not report that anyone was killed. Nevertheless, television footage showed women crying desperately; these shops had supplied goods they needed. One could only imagine the distances—and checkpoints—these women might have to go through in order to feed and clothe their families.

---

[16] A. R. Luria, *The Man with a Shattered World*, repr. ed. (Cambridge, MA: Harvard University Press, 1987).

For terrorist violence, the same can be said, though the violence is usually on a smaller scale than the violence of war. A bomb in a night club or train station is highly disturbing; it may kill several people, damage shops, and affect the conduct of business. But with regard to scale, most terrorist attacks are limited in immediate impact when compared to the destruction caused by the aerial bombing of a bridge or city during war, or the suffering imposed on enemy personnel cruelly treated in a prison camp. The immediate and fundamental objection to the physical violence is the same in all these cases: this physical violence kills and hurts people and the resources they need and value. And it is objectionable for that reason. In short, physical violence is presumptively wrong because it damages and destroys people and resources, and in so doing, causes death, harm, and suffering.

One might ask in this context: what is so special about *physical violence*? Policies and practices that are not physically violent can also be profoundly hurtful to human beings. The nonviolent sanctions imposed after the 1991 Gulf War by the United Nations against Iraq are a case in point. No physical violence was involved in stopping the flow of many goods to Iraq; yet United Nations research indicated that one million or more deaths, nearly half of which were deaths of children, could be attributed to the operation of those sanctions. Operating over a long period of time, some "quiet violence" (or, as we might say, "passive violence") can be extraordinarily damaging. It can kill. Why, then, single out *physical violence* as the primary and sole focus for our concern?

To commence a response to this question, we may return to the other aspect of the definition of physical violence. Physical violence is a sudden and intense application of external physical force to persons, animals, or other valued entities so as to damage or destroy them. Force is carried forward strongly, intensely, suddenly—which is to say *violently*. A house that is blown up is destroyed by violence. A house that is taken apart, brick by brick, though also destroyed, is not destroyed by violence.[17] The point can seem frivolous: one might think that the *speed* of destruction in such a case is altogether irrelevant from a moral point of view.[18] Surely, one might insist, if it is wrong to destroy a house because someone needs to live in it, the wrongness of that destruction should not depend on whether it hap-

---

[17] This point is made by MacCallum, "What's Wrong with Violence?"

[18] Contrary to the present account, Steven Lee, in "Poverty and Violence," *Social Theory and Practice* 22 (1996): 67–82, argues that the lack of vigorous physical force as a feature of structural violence is not a morally relevant feature.

pens quickly or slowly. What, one might ask, is the morally significant difference between the situation of a woman whose house has been blown up and that of another whose house has been destroyed by slow dismantlement? In fact, there is an obvious response to this apparently strange question. The second woman can leave her house while its dismantlement is going on, so she and her family are not exposed to risk of injury or death as a result of a violent explosion. Furthermore, during the time that her house is being dismantled, she has opportunities to resist that process by discussion, argument, negotiation, organized protest, or legal action. That is to say, this person has opportunities to employ her own human deliberative capacities to resist the destruction of her house.

The *time frame* of the action gains moral relevance because of its bearing on opportunities for a *human response*. Immediate physical violence avoids our human capacities to deliberate, negotiate, and seek alternatives. By contrast, actions that are not physically violent may not be overwhelming in these ways.

To be sure, human beings are vulnerable to forms of treatment that do not involve physical violence. For good reason, we may fear many actions that do not involve the straightforward application of physical force: insulting comments, discriminatory or degrading treatment, damaging social policies, denial of resources and opportunities, and forced relocation are obvious examples. There are many ways of humiliating and injuring people, and we are all vulnerable to them. Apart from their damaging quality, what is special about physical violence is that it is so often literally impossible to resist. If a bomb lands in your locale and goes off without warning in your immediate vicinity, you can do nothing to prevent or limit death or injury. You are simply there and attacked—a vulnerable human being with a fragile body susceptible to gross physical injury. Whether you will experience such injury or not will be outside your control. A sudden physical attack is shocking, disturbing, perhaps fatal, often seriously damaging and difficult to repair, and, for many who survive it, profoundly disturbing to their fundamental sense of security and confidence in this world. In response to some physical attacks, people may be able to fight physically or negotiate to limit damage, but characteristically, that is not possible.[19]

---

[19] Consider, for example, a kidnapping victim who persuaded his abductors not to cut off his fingers because they could get more money for him if they could exchange him whole.

Vulnerability to damage from external forces inspires fear and anxiety on the part of nearly all human beings. When physical force is applied intensely, suddenly, and unpredictably—as is the case for most physical attacks—no such human response to them is possible. Thus the application of physical force is not only inhumane, but *inhuman*. Values, attitudes, interests, needs, feelings, and beliefs do not structure our response which—if it is possible at all—can only be an exchange of blow for blow, bomb for bomb. The physically violent qualities of an attack are morally relevant because they inhibit our abilities to respond in a human way while at the same time enhancing our sense of vulnerability and helplessness. The fear that we could be subject to physical violence at any given time will contribute enormously to our sense of anxiety and insecurity.

It is no accident that *security* is identified with the *physical security* of our bodies and the resources we need to support them. Our physical selves and resources are not all of our humanity and life, but they are its fundamental substructure. If a country is under threat of attack, people may seek to build bomb shelters and stockpile food. Nevertheless, if a bomb falls on them, they are purely and simply vulnerable. If militants threaten airports, office buildings, water, or food supplies, people begin to feel insecure in the conduct of their lives. What we fear in contexts of terrorism and war are violent attacks from agents with whom we cannot negotiate and to whom we can make no meaningful response. If it comes, physical violence is likely to be out of control and irresistible. In general, the more *violently* the attacks are conducted, the less amenable they will be to human intervention.

B. The Immediate Consequences of Physical Violence in Political Conflicts

Three points arise here: the strong tendency of physical violence to provoke responsive physical violence; the difficulty of repair and reconciliation with the opponent in the wake of physical attacks; and the probable short duration of any victory won by means involving physical violence.

The first point is the most basic. To state the matter in blunt and obvious language, people do not like to be physically attacked. When they are attacked, they are likely to become not only fearful, but deeply resentful. Physical violence feeds anger and hatred. If the attackers were not perceived as enemies before the attack, they will surely be so in its aftermath, and retaliation is likely to be the order of the day. Attacks will be feared and resented and that fact will bring forth an aggressive leadership with a strong tendency to respond to physical violence with more of the same. Any sympathizers one might have had on the other side of the conflict are likely to be alienated by the violence used against their group. If they can limit its damage by some physical response, they will do so. But whether or not any self-defense is possible, they are extremely likely to retaliate or seek revenge. And as a further response, they will build up the human and physical apparatus to deter further attacks. Efforts to defend against, retaliate against, and deter physical violence will almost certainly involve the use of physical violence against the attackers. These are the human responses that underlie the truism that violence provokes violence.

Suicide bombers blow themselves up in a nightclub, killing four and injuring twenty; government forces on the opposing side announce that they will retaliate harshly and do so by evicting families from fifty homes and taking ten young men into custody, where they are tortured; then more suicide bombers take action in response, killing six and injuring dozens at a busy market; in retaliation, government forces bomb the headquarters of a well-known opposition group, which in turn, results in further suicide bombings in retaliation.[20] Such stories are too painfully familiar to need repeating. It is a gross understatement to say at this point that the use of physical violence does not terminate a political conflict with a victory for one side. Rather, it invites more of the same as a response by those against whom it is used, an invitation accepted with vengeful enthusiasm in the delusory belief that suffering must be redressed by suffering and blood by blood.

Ted Honderich once said, "The proposition that violence does as a matter of fact promote progress toward freedom and equality in some circumstances can hardly be questioned." He added, "The nostrum that nothing is gained by violence does not survive a moment's reflection."[21] I beg to differ. In avoiding the moment of reflection,

---

[20] Readers will readily recognize the slightly abstracted scenario, which is based on relations between Palestinian suicide bombers and the military forces of the state of Israel in the fall of 2002 and the winter of 2003. I discuss revenge and retaliation in greater depth in chapters 1 and 2 of my *Forgiveness and Revenge* (London: Routledge, 2002).

[21] Ted Honderich, *Three Essays on Political Violence* (Oxford: Blackwell, 1976), 110.

Honderich seems not to have stopped to consider the profoundly important and virtually ubiquitous fact that political violence begets more of itself.

In many Hollywood Westerns, when cycles of violence occur, they end efficiently. This is art, not life, and tales have a form and a satisfying terminus. When a good guy, characteristically a John Wayne type, kills a bad guy, typically one with a look of evil about him, the good guy stands at the end holding his gun in triumph, or walks off proudly into the sunset. In these stories, conflicts between the bad guys and the good guys arise just because the bad guys are bad guys and are doing bad things and causing problems, while the good guys are simply good guys, and they can solve the problem by killing off the bad guys. That's the drama. Such stories represent physical violence in a positive light, as an efficient, necessary, and perfectly logical method of solving a problem: you kill the evil people.[22] Such fictional situations are grossly oversimplified, structured so as to validate the assumption that killing a few evil people can end a conflict and solve a problem. In the real world, people and groups are complicated, motives are mixed, situations ambiguous, and aftermaths highly messy. Serious political conflicts do not come into existence merely as a result of the actions of individuals. Individualistic narratives depicting the evil intentions and actions of Slobodan Milosevic, Saddam Hussein, Osama bin Laden (or—for that matter—George W. Bush) are grossly oversimplified. Histories, economics, contexts, relationships, and group dynamics profoundly affect the structure and responses to conflicts. Individual leaders could not do the things they do unless they had many thousands of supporters.

In the wake of political violence, there are not only lost lives and injured survivors but the families, friends, and cohorts of the people

---

Honderich's position in *After the Terror* (Edinburgh: University of Edinburgh Press, 2002) is substantially similar. He says there that terrorist violence is objectionable if it can serve no humanitarian purpose, and that was the case with the terrorist violence of September 11, 2001. If terrorist violence could serve a humanitarian purpose, in rectifying some of the horrifying inequality that exists in our world, then it would be justified. Honderich has claimed that that is the case for Palestinian suicide bombers, who are using terrorist violence to oppose an occupying power. This account has generated great controversy.

[22] In a conversation with peace advocates in January 2003, Canadian Alliance party MP Bob Anders referred repeatedly to the need to "whack" Saddam Hussein, according to my colleague Bev Delong, who talked to him at some length about Canadian foreign policy with regard to the issues between Iraq and the United States.

killed—people who are likely to be plenty mad at the attackers, think they have justice and even God Himself on their side, and do not hesitate to seek revenge in the aftermath. Given such realities, using physical violence will achieve a short-term solution at best. Reality is not the movies. Instead of ending, the story goes messily on. The idea that a victory can be achieved and imposed by physical violence and the story will end at that point is profoundly mistaken. This fundamental error is common enough to merit a special name. We can call it the John Wayne Fallacy. Or, if we wish to avoid insulting a man who did not, after all, write his own scripts, we can speak instead of the Fallacy of the Ending.

C. The Moral Corollaries

In itself, physical violence is not desirable and—with some qualifications—most people think of it that way and react accordingly to the agents of violence. Thus, violence tends to be a discrediting way of waging conflicts. The moral corollaries of resorting to physical violence arise because so many people value physical security and share a presumption against violence. We particularly resent it when violence is used against ourselves and our families and communities.

Persons who opt for physical violence in the conduct of a political conflict begin with (some) admirable and humane goals. This could be said of many in the French Revolution, of the Bolsheviks of 1917, the Chinese Communists in the thirties and forties, the Khmer Rouge, Peru's Shining Path guerrillas, and many other groups that, in the end, killed millions and perpetrated gross brutality and abuse. In the beginning many such revolutionaries had relatively benign intentions. Disturbed by social injustice and corrupt oligarchy, they wished to take power and use it to establish institutions more supportive of disadvantaged and marginalized peoples. That is to say, they began as persons sympathetic to injustice and human suffering, willing to dedicate their lives to the reform of an inequitable social and political situation. It is a notorious fact of history, however, that such humane instincts are severely jeopardized when these people become agents of physical violence, engaging in such activities as the smuggling of weapons, the harsh punishment of perceived "traitors," the intimidation of civilian populations, the planting or dropping of bombs, and the recruiting and training of young people in the arts of killing, including sometimes suicide as a means to do it. The polarization and confidence in the exclusive justice of one's own case creates a shift

from the premise that *some people deserve a better life* to the conclusion that *many others deserve no life at all.* There is a pervasive
tendency to be utterly convinced that we are right and have justice on
our side and are thus entitled to use whatever means are necessary to
pursue our goals. The same can be said of armies during wartime;
even those who profess allegiance to international legal standards of
just war violate them in the name of military necessity. Large-scale
deaths of civilians, rape, abuse, humiliation, and torture are common,
if not ubiquitous, characteristics of war, even as waged by states and
groups professing commitment to the Geneva Conventions and distinctions of just war theory.

The moral effects of committing oneself to violence are familiar
enough to be count as notorious. The history of violent struggle—
whether in the form of revolution, terrorism, or war—shows clearly
that many who resort to physical violence in a quest for justice
become desensitized to the realities of human suffering and the value
of human life. They may engage in a violent struggle as sympathizers
of the downtrodden, defenders of justice, or opponents of totalitari-
anism, and then become cruel killers and torturers. The use of physically violent methods against opponents degrades its agents,
lessening their sensitivity and capacities for sympathy and empathy,
and cultivating brutality and corruption.

Despite the qualifications noted earlier, there remains an important sense in which *the presumption against physical violence is
shared.* For that reason, persons who employ it as a response to conflict convey a highly negative message to the unaffiliated. To achieve
their goals, they are willing to kill, maim, and destroy; their actions
say this, and in a powerful way. Resulting as it does in death and
injury to others and brutality in themselves, physical violence will be
understood by vulnerable others as something fearful, meriting distrust. Any reflective person will find the implications of these means
difficult to reconcile with the idea that the ends in question are moral
goals such as justice and freedom. A movement endorsing physical
violence will seem more callous and hazardous, and less legitimate,
than one limiting itself to nonviolent methods. Not only are agents of
violence likely themselves to be corrupted by it, they will convey
aspects of that corruption to others. Violence tends, then, to be fundamentally discrediting for its agents.

A further moral corollary emerges when we consider the sorts of
persons who are likely to be or become adherents of a cause pursued
by violent means. Many sensitive and conscientious people will be

unwilling to join, while some of those attracted are likely to be callous to the point of criminal thuggery. For example, in Poland and Czechoslovakia, in the 1970s, those organizing in opposition to the governing communist regimes declared themselves to be *nonviolent* and interested in developing a more humane society respectful of human rights. As nonviolent movements, these movements attracted certain sorts of people. In Poland in the 1970s and 1980s, many oppositionists were highly religious Catholics inspired by the fact that the Pope was Polish; others were workers; still others, writers and intellectuals. Had the oppositionists used terrorist tactics, they would have no doubt attracted some adherents, but not the same ones.

The idea that physical violence corrupts and discredits its agents is admittedly more contestable in the context of state violence—especially that of a purportedly democratic state engaged a purportedly just war. Nearly all states maintain armies and weapons and are prepared to deploy physical force in situations of serious conflict with other states. Given the rather common assumption that war between states is a normal aspect of human history, governments can often plausibly represent themselves as using violence legitimately. It is often relatively easy to persuade people to support their own state in a war against outsiders, especially if that violence can be managed so as to make the other side the main recipient while one's own citizens remain relatively safe. Many people easily rally behind a leader in a context of war, especially when that leader can rhetorically depict an evil and dangerous enemy who is threatening their way of life. Far from being morally discrediting, the perception of a political leader in charge of a war may establish him as a strong person using the state's proud and strong military resources to protect the physical security of its citizens. Notoriously, this presumption may have highly positive effects on a leader's image and popularity. It may, for instance, work in his favor by establishing him as "strong" and "not a wimp." It would, then, be quite incorrect to claim that readiness to use physical force in international conflict will morally discredit a leader and a government in the eyes of its own people. The matter will look different to the other side and, in many cases, to the international community. A state that sees itself as strong and rightfully pursuing its own interests may appear to others to be an arrogant bully using its military force for selfish and unjust purposes.

The purported just cause and self-protection to which a country has committed itself often appear to be thinly disguised expressions of economic interest, and its military resources crude instruments of arrogant power. A state that readily resorts to physical violence to protect itself will convey to other states and to noncitizens a callous willingness to smash other people to protect the security of its own privilege. Moral credit may be lost abroad even when it is enhanced at home. The fearsome message that one is willing to kill, smash, and torture to protect oneself and pursue one's interests will not "win friends and influence people." Rather, it will inspire rage and resentment.

Concluding Comments

Rhetoric about physical violence being a last resort is common. What I am arguing here is that we should live up to our own rhetoric. I believe that the *last resort* idea is enormously important and should be taken with the utmost seriousness. The physical violence so often used in conducting political conflicts is damaging in itself and politically and ethically counterproductive in its effects. For these reasons a strong presumption against physical violence should always be a powerful factor in political reasoning. Whatever else human beings do in this world, we require our physical security as its necessary condition. In valuing that security, we are committed to a prima facie condemnation of physical violence as a primary threat to it. Any person or group who would use such violence as a means owes an account to the rest of humanity, an account demonstrating the legitimacy of his goals and the impossibility of achieving them in any other way.[23] When such arguments are put forth, they deserve intense scrutiny, for the resort to physical violence must, indeed, be a last resort. The burden of proof on those who would use violence as a means of engaging in conflict should be heavy indeed.

---

[23] Gerald MacCallum suggests in "Violence and Appeals to Conscience," in *Legislative Intent and Other Essays on Law, Politics, and Morality*, ed. Marcus G. Singer and Rex Martin (Madison: University of Wisconsin Press, 1993), that one's defense may come in some form other than that of an actual justification of resorting to violence. One might offer an *explanation* of why one was led to commit a violent act, show an *excuse* for committing it, offer an argument that it was *more or less all right*, under the circumstances, or show that it was the correct thing to do and he was *justified* in doing it. Differences in such accounts and arguments strike me as highly important;only the last should be referred to as a justification in the strict sense. But I cannot explore this topic further here.

Just War Theory and the War on Terrorism

| 7 |

Just War Theory, Legitimate Authority, and the "War" on Terror

LORRAINE BESSER-JONES

According to the most straightforward interpretation of traditional just war theory, there can be no such thing as a "war on terror," for wars can be fought only between states and certainly not between one state and an abstract entity. Nonetheless, the post-9/11 U.S.-led war on terror has been conducted in largely the same fashion as conventional wars, especially in its initial stages, and certainly *seems* to be a war. If traditional just war theory does not recognize the current war on terror to be an actual war, does this entail that there is something inherently wrong with the war on terror, or that there is something inherently wrong with just war theory? Those who endorse the view that there is something wrong with the war on terror face the urgent problem of explaining how a country is to respond to terrorist acts short of declaring a war on terror. Those who endorse the latter view, that there is something wrong with just war theory, run the danger of appearing to try to justify the immoral by rejecting the doctrine that declares it immoral.

If just war theory is truly antiquated and ill-equipped to address contemporary international politics, we should either dismiss it or completely overhaul it. But we must be careful not to jump to this conclusion too quickly. Simply because a doctrine does not legitimize a particular course of action does not mean it is outdated, so long as it can provide a convincing account of why we should not view that

I'd like to thank Colleen Murphy, Matthew N. Smith, and the audience at the "Understanding Terrorism" conference, especially Michael Baur and Trudy Govier, for their helpful comments on earlier versions of this chapter.

course of action as legitimate. In what follows I explore exactly what just war theory has to say about the war on terror, and in particular, look into the reasons underlying its requirement that wars must be fought between states. Perhaps unsurprisingly, I argue that just war theory must condemn the war on terror. Once we uncover the real reasons for this condemnation, however, we see that the reasons just war theory offers are both substantial and morally relevant. Just war theory is not an antiquated doctrine, although some of its more basic formulations might be.

There are two stages to my argument. The first stage, which comprises the bulk of my discussion, examines just war theory's requirement that wars must be fought between states—the requirement of legitimate authority. Here, I explore the two main ways to interpret this requirement and develop and defend my own interpretation, which is loosely based on Michael Walzer's view. With this understanding of the legitimate-authority requirement in hand, I then move to the second stage of my argument, where I apply it to a war on terror. Here I argue that the requirements of just war theory, and the legitimate-authority requirement in particular, must be applied bilaterally. I conclude by showing how, on the basis of this bilateral application, a so-called war on terror is not, in fact, a war and, if conducted as a war, will inevitably entail a violation of state rights.

Traditional just war theory is comprised of two sets of rules: the *jus ad bellum*—the rules guiding decisions of who can go to war and under what circumstances; and the *jus in bello*—the rules governing how to fight, once a war has already been declared. In this paper, I focus only on the *jus ad bellum*, and in particular on its legitimate-authority requirement. And while I will not here concentrate much on either the remaining *jus ad bellum* requirements (just cause, proportionality, right intention, and last resort), or the *jus in bello*, whose requirements include noncombatant immunity, military necessity, and proportionality, we should keep in mind that in order for a war to be just it must fulfill all of these requirements.

Central to the notion of *jus ad bellum* is the requirement that wars must be declared by and fought between authorities that are recognized in some sense as legitimate either in the international arena, or by the groups that they represent. This is the requirement of legitimate authority. It is the first requirement of the *jus ad bellum* and, I think, is the most essential. It is also, unfortunately, the most neglected. The requirement of legitimate authority distinguishes groups with belligerent status and the right to go to war from groups that are made up of criminals and aim only to create violence. When Timothy McVeigh bombed the federal building in Oklahoma City, the act of bombing may in itself have looked like an act of war: it was directed at a political target, it involved mass killing, and so on. The reason we do not think this bombing was an act of war is that McVeigh was acting as an individual (or with a group of individuals). Were it determined that he was an agent acting on behalf of a foreign state, then we most likely would have deemed the bombing an act of war and our response to it would have been different. The requirement of legitimate authority is essential to helping us make this distinction.

Coates brings up a similar example, writing about IRA prisoners' efforts to be recognized as having legitimate authority: "In defense of their special category (of claiming to have legitimate authority), the IRA prisoners in the Maze were prepared to commit collective suicide. What they were affirming was their right to war, so that their acts of killing could thereby be lifted out of the criminal category of common murder and into the lawful category of acts of war."[1]

The legitimate-authority requirement tells us how to classify groups, so that we know how to classify and respond to their actions. In so distinguishing these groups that have legitimate authority and the right to go to war from groups that lack legitimate authority, the legitimate-authority requirement sets up the playing field, as it were, and determines from the beginning when a war exists. In this respect it is distinctive from the other rules. The remaining *jus ad bellum* requirements (just cause, proportionality, right intention, and, on some accounts, last resort) are all requirements that help to determine whether or not a *war* is just; however, as Douglas Lackey aptly notes, "just war must, first of all, be war."[2] The requirement of legitimate authority is supposed to help us determine when we have a war, which the rest of the *jus ad bellum* and the *jus in bello* rules can then declare to be just or not.

Despite the centrality of the legitimate-authority requirement to just war theory, there is much debate and corresponding divergence over what entities count as having legitimate authority. This debate is of particular concern to the issue of terrorism, for whether or not a war on terror falls within the jurisdiction of just war theory depends

---

[1] A. J. Coates, *The Ethics of War* (New York: Manchester University Press, 1997), 123.

[2] Douglas Lackey, *The Ethics of War and Peace* (New Jersey: Prentice Hall Press, 1989), 29.

on whether a terrorist group can be a legitimate authority in the relevant sense. There are two broad approaches to determining legitimate authority: The first is to take a de facto approach and declare that groups that, in fact, have authority also have legitimate authority. An example of a de facto authority would be the Mafia. Members of the Mafia take charge of certain communities, and members of these communities recognize them as being in charge—as having power over them, regardless of whether or not this authority is legally recognized or morally justified. The second way of interpreting the legitimate-authority requirement is to take a de jure approach. The de jure approach focuses on whether or not de facto authorities are, in fact, "legitimate" in its robust sense. In order for an entity to have de jure authority, it is not enough that they have power over a certain group. Their power must be justified, either on legal or moral grounds. These approaches lead to different interpretations of whether or not terrorist groups can have legitimate authority. After reviewing defenses of both approaches, I will argue that a de jure approach best satisfies the needs and purposes of a just war theory and, moreover, that the de jure interpretation must be grounded in a theory of state rights, although sometimes we must use a de facto theory of state rights to ground it. The implications of this discussion for our evaluation of a war on terror are twofold: First, we will see that terrorist groups lack legitimate authority; and second, we will see exactly why this lack makes a war on terror impermissible: because conducting a war on terror entails an unjustifiable violation of state rights.

Lackey presents the most straightforward de facto interpretation of the legitimate-authority requirement. In deriving his interpretation, he looks first to the definition of a war, which he takes to be "a controlled use of force, undertaken by persons organized in a functioning chain of command . . . directed to an identifiable political result," where "an identifiable political result is some change in a government's policy, some alteration in a form of government, or some extension or limitation of the scope of its authority."[3] From this definition of war, Lackey's interpretation of the legitimate-authority requirement, what he terms the "competent authority" requirement, easily follows: to have belligerent status, a group must have a chain of command and some political orientation. If a group fulfills these two requirements, then its acts are acts of war, as opposed to acts of criminal violence.

---

[3] Lackey, *Ethics of War and Peace*, 30.

Lackey's conception of legitimate authority allows for many non-state groups to be recognized as having legitimate authority. Under Lackey's conception, acts performed by rebels and revolutionaries are acts of war; indeed, Lackey thinks it a merit of his approach that such groups can be granted belligerent status regardless of whether they are associated with a particular territory—something with which states are inherently associated. It also follows from Lackey's interpretation that terrorist groups can have legitimate authority, so long as there exist the requisite chain of command and political purpose—requirements that many terrorist groups satisfy.

The upshot of Lackey's de facto interpretation is that any group that can organize itself with a political purpose in mind can have belligerent status, thereby transforming acts of violence from crimes into acts of war (although not necessarily *just* acts of war). Many have argued that this interpretation is too lenient and fails to preserve the spirit of just war theory, which was meant to separate and define acts of war as something inherently distinct from criminal violence.[4] On Lackey's account, any group that has the ability to organize, as long as they have political purposes in mind, can commit an act of war. It is indeed a de facto approach to the concept of legitimate authority: if there is authority, then it is legitimate.

This is a far cry from the original intent of just war theorists such as Aquinas, who sought from the very beginning to distinguish groups with legitimate authority from mere private individuals, who, on Aquinas's account, regardless of their purposes, did not have the right to go to war. This basic thought guides the legitimate-authority requirement, although in contemporary society it becomes substantially more difficult to instantiate, as there are numerous cases of "private" individuals who have conducted wars that many think are legitimate instances of war—revolutionary wars, for one, are wars conducted by "private" persons. It is instances like these that lead Lackey to his minimal interpretation of the authority requirement; however, it seems that Lackey has gone too far in trying to include nonstate groups. In an effort to recognize nonstate groups as having legitimate authority, Lackey ends up with a conception of authority that amounts to self-authorization and thereby loses the normative force that lies at the core of just war theory. There must be a better way to understand legitimate authority.

---

[4] See, for example, Coates, *Ethics of War*, 126.

A de jure approach towards interpreting legitimate authority looks more promising, at the very least because it captures the regulative ideals of the *jus ad bellum* rules of just war theory. A de jure approach takes seriously the "legitimate" aspect of the authority requirement and looks past the existence of de facto authority (whether it be Lackey's interpretation, or simply a state-recognized authority) in an effort to determine whether or not a given entity has the authority to engage in an act of war. It is an open question on this approach whether or not states have legitimate authority, and whether or not a nonstate could have legitimate authority. The deciding factors, and in particular, the question of whether the deciding factors are legal, moral, or some combination of both, are relative to the particular interpretations of the approach. As we will see, the crucial question that defenders of this approach must answer is not, as it was for Lackey, whether or not a group could commit what looks like an act of war, but rather whether or not a given entity has the authority to declare belligerent status and to subject its members to the repercussions that result from acts of war.

A. J. Coates presents a thorough defense of the de jure approach, grounded in the idea of legal justification. He argues that only states that govern through the rule of law can have legitimate authority. According to Coates, a state's legitimate authority must possess both *external* and *internal* authority. External authority involves (1) being a member of an international community; and (2) acting consistently for the international common good. The general idea underlying this external-authority requirement is that wars are fought within the public sphere and between public parties. As such, Coates argues that in order for an act of violence to be an act of war and authoritative, it must be conducted by a state defending its publicly recognized interests: "In order to be authoritative the defense of [a state's] 'particular' right must constitute at the same time an upholding of the rule of international law and of the shared values in which the common good of the international community consists. Without such simultaneous justification the state has no right to war, although of course its power may enable it to wage 'war' regardless."[5]

In addition to externally recognized authority, Coates believes that legitimate authorities must also have internal authority. A state has internal authority when it is "properly public and legal" that is, when it has been legally instituted and is run through a rule of law. The

---

[5] Coates, *Ethics of War*, 128.

United States government provides a nice model of a state with internal authority: it was legally instituted through the constitution, and, to the extent to which its legal actions reflect the constitution; it is run through a rule of law. This requirement of internal authority rules out forms of governments whose "exercise of force is wholly without public sanction or authority," for example, those that systematically oppress their citizens.[6]

On Coates's account, being a state is a necessary yet not sufficient condition for attaining legitimate authority; it is possible for states to lose their claim to authority. This happens when a state fails to act for the good of the international community, when a state misuses its authority internally, or when the state's power was attained through unjust means, and thus was not legally instituted. The problem with Coates's account is that it is too exclusionary. His legitimate-authority requirement excludes many states that we ordinarily think of as having legitimate authority from having legitimate authority. It would also deny that many historical wars were wars at all. The American Revolution, for example, could not have been a literal war on this interpretation, for Americans (1) lacked a legally recognized government that could even be a candidate for having internal authority; and (2) seemed to be challenging the international order and thus apparently lacked external authority as well.

Moreover, if in order to have legitimate authority a state must be acting for the sake of the international community, then states that threaten the international community lack belligerent status and, if they do commit violence, it is criminal violence, rather than war. By tying legitimate authority to legal foundations, Coates's conception, I think, takes the de jure approach too far and ends up granting legitimate authority only to those states whose *cause* is legal and just (that is, whose purpose in using force is to uphold international values). This move, however, conflates the requirement of legitimate authority with the requirement of just cause. We see this conflation in the following passage where, arguing explicitly against the de facto approach endorsed by Lackey, Coates writes:

> When an individual state acts ostensibly on its own behalf, if it acts in defense of its legitimate interests or in vindication of its rights, it acts at the same time as the agent and representative of the international community. In order to be authoritative the defense of its "particular" right

---

[6] Coates, *Ethics of War*, 128

must constitute at the same time an upholding of the rule of international law and of the shared values in which the common good of the international community consists. Without such simultaneous justification the state has no right to war, though of course its power may enable it to wage "war" regardless.[7]

This claim, that authority is derived ultimately from the international community, is grounded in Coates's belief that acts of war must be seen in legal terms as acts that are carried out in "defense of the international order";[8] presumably, acts carried out that are not in defense of the international order, or are explicitly against international order, are not acts of war.

Surely this cannot be right. An act of war need not be in defense of the international order; if this were the case then acts of war would only be unilateral, as presumably, in any given conflict, only one side can be fighting in defense of the international order.[9] We need to distinguish between a just act of war, and an act of war itself; Coates's requirement of external authority does not make this distinction and so ends up declaring war only when we have a just war.

Is there a better interpretation that maintains the regulative force of the requirement that de facto approaches seem unable to do, yet nonetheless does not make Coates's mistake of placing too much regulative force on the conception of legitimate authority? I think there is and that the way to develop such an interpretation is to look at why the legitimate-authority requirement is a morally important part of the *jus ad bellum* conditions.

From the outset we have seen that the *jus ad bellum* and, in particular, the legitimate-authority requirement, is set up to define acts of war, as opposed to acts of criminal violence. Just war theorists accept the reality of war, and try to define acceptable conduct within it in an attempt to limit the atrocities committed in the name of war. The *jus ad bellum* works to regulate the decision to go to war and, ideally, ensures that wars are fought for just causes—only when war is a last resort and the expected damage of war is proportional to the expected benefits, and that the decision to go to war is made by some-

---

[7] Coates, *Ethics of War*, 128

[8] Coates, *Ethics of War*, 127.

[9] Although this point can be debated. Coates himself believes that just cause must be interpreted on the assumption that two sides can be just. On this account, which is controversial, two sides can have just cause to go to war and so two sides could have legitimate authority.

one with the authority to do so. One of the reasons why it is important that wars involve groups with the authority to go to war is because wars inherently involve and affect the people represented by the group. When the United States decides to go to war, it does so with the authority of the people, knowing that it is these actual people (as opposed to some abstract entity of the "United States") whose lives will be affected by the war. The danger that arises when a group lacking authority goes to war is that it puts people's lives on the line, without having the authority to do so. This is why violence conducted by a group that lacks authority, or directed towards such a group, is criminal violence, rather than an act of war.

A defensible interpretation of the legitimate-authority requirement thus must take as central the internal politics of an entity, and, most importantly, whether or not a given entity has been allotted authority over the whole. Such an interpretation requires more than Lackey's chain of command and political purpose; yet, on the other hand, it must recognize that nonstates could have legitimate authority, thus accommodating the possibility that revolutionary groups could declare war. To develop this interpretation, I first look at the role that the legitimate-authority requirement plays within the just war theory tradition, arguing that any interpretation of legitimate authority must cohere with the basic motivations underlying just war theory itself. I then go on to defend an interpretation of legitimate authority loosely based on Walzer's conception of state rights. I argue that the most plausible way to understand legitimate authority is within the context of state rights.

The Roots of Just War Theory: Self-Defense

We have seen already that the goal of just war theory is to establish guidelines that constrain acts of violence; when these guidelines are followed, we have a war—ideally a just war—as opposed to mere criminal violence. This distinction is a morally important one, as most agree that, under certain circumstances, war is justifiable, whereas criminal violence is never justifiable. One way of understanding the purpose of just war theory is to see it as helping people, states, and so on, to make this distinction—to determine when violence is justifiable, and then, to see what sorts of acts are justifiable once the violence has been defined as a war.

The general model that just war theory assumes for determining justifiable violence at the level of states or political groups is that of the aggressor-defender. This model is made explicit in the traditional (yet increasingly controversial) interpretation of the just cause requirement: that the only just cause to go to war is in defense against an act of aggression. This aggressor-defender paradigm has its roots in individual cases of self-defense. Just as we think cases of individual violence are justifiable in situations of self-defense, the so-called domestic analogy holds that incidences of group/state violence are also justifiable in situations of self-defense. In order to understand fully when acts of group/state violence fall under the aggressor-defender paradigm of self-defense, we must first focus on the individual level and look at what justifies violence between individuals.

Most agree that when an individual acts in self-defense, she is justified in her actions—even if those actions would be considered criminal or morally reprehensible under other circumstances. Exactly what are the circumstances, though, that make this sort of violence justifiable? Presumably, the individual must be acting in defense of something—most frequently, in defense of some right that the aggressor has violated. The most common right that "justifies" an act of self-defense is that of bodily integrity. When an aggressor attacks a person, she violates her victim's right to bodily integrity and, in most circumstances, we think the victim is justified in fighting back against the aggressor. Another right that warrants self-defense is that of private property—when an aggressor enters into one's house with intent to do harm, the owner of that house is justified in using force against that aggressor.

One feature of an act of self-defense, then, is that there is one party—the aggressor—who violates the right of another. However, rights violation alone does not justify acts of defensive violence. That is, though a party's established rights may have been transgressed, this alone is not enough to justify an act of violence. In order for violent retaliation to be justifiable, it stands to reason that we must know something more about the *aggressor*. For example, we must know that the aggressor was acting on her own accord. She was not being forced by someone else to violate another's rights, nor was she inadvertently doing so. In cases where acts of self-defense are truly warranted and so justifiable, the aggressor must have been committing the act of aggression based on her own free will and thereby forfeiting one or more of *her* rights.

This claim may come as a surprise to many who feel that acts of self-defense are justifiable *whenever* one's rights are violated, so long as the act of self-defense is somehow proportional to the violation.

While this may be true when the act of self-defense is a *preventive* one that, for example, saves one's life in the face of an attack, the situation changes when we consider acts of self-defense on a more retributive level, which is the level on which just war theory primarily draws. Just war theory is not interested primarily in preventive self-defense, but rather in defense against an attack that has already been committed.[10]

To see how the conditions change on this level, consider a typical case of "justifiable" self-defense. Without being provoked, Jack hits Matt in the nose. Let us call this scenario case A. Most people would think that Matt was justified in fighting back, for Jack has transgressed Matt's right to bodily integrity. The situation changes remarkably, however, if we learn that an enemy of Matt's, who has threatened the life of Jack's son unless Jack starts a fight with Matt, has taken Jack's son hostage. In this case (call it case B), it seems that Matt would not be justified in fighting back—as long as he knew that Jack's actions were, in fact, not his own. *If Matt knew that Jack had been forced to hit him,* then it is reasonable to conclude that were Matt to go ahead and fight back anyway, Matt's act of violence would not be justifiable.

What exactly has changed between these two scenarios? In both cases, Jack has violated Matt's rights. In case A, we think that Matt could justifiably act in self-defense, yet in case B, we would hesitate to call any retribution by Matt against Jack justifiable. The morally relevant difference between these two instances is this: in case A Jack knowingly chooses to violate Matt's rights and, in doing so, implicitly forfeits his own rights against Matt. In case B, Jack does not forfeit his own rights against Matt, for he did not freely decide to violate Matt's rights. In choosing to commit violence against another, one opens oneself to harm, and puts one's life on the line. This is why we think acts of self-defense are justifiable; they are not justifiable simply because one party's rights have been transgressed, but additionally, because the aggressor forfeits her own rights through her aggressive action.

---

[10] The contrast between retributive and preventive self-defense is not one that easily fits onto the level of states. In saying that state defensive actions are retributive, my point is not that they are made solely with the intent to punish, but simply that they are made after an offensive attack has already occurred. In this sense they are not preventive, because the attack has already occurred, although theoretically they are meant to prevent further attacks.

To draw an analogy from individual cases of self-defense to
group cases of self-defense, then, two conditions must hold. First,
we must establish the rights of *each* party involved. Second, we
must establish that there is one party whose rights are violated, and
another party whose rights are forfeited. It is on the basis of these
conditions, modeled through the aggressor-defender paradigm, that
the *jus ad bellum* requirements find their footing; by bringing the
aggressor-defender paradigm to the foreground, we can reach a better understanding of the importance and nature of the legitimate-
authority requirement.

The reason why it is important that the aggressor knowingly
choose to transgress another's rights is because in doing so, the
aggressor forfeits her rights and puts her life on the line. As we move
from the individual to the group level, this requirement becomes even
more important. When a state attacks another state, the aggressing
state forfeits its rights, just as an individual aggressor forfeits her
rights. In forfeiting its rights, however, a state in effect forfeits the
rights of each of its individual members who stand to be impacted by
the defending state's act of self-defense. While it is tempting to think
that when a state goes to war, its actions only affect its soldiers, this
is simply not true, given the overwhelmingly large number of civilian
casualties incurred during wartime. This is why it is so essential to
just war theory that states or groups have legitimate authority—
because when a state or group involves itself in a war, be it as an
aggressor or defender, its actions inevitably affect the people who
comprise the group. It is the people's lives that are at stake, and the
people's rights that are forfeited when an aggressor attacks another
group or state. When the aggressor has legitimate authority, then this
rights forfeiture is voluntary, in the sense that Jack voluntarily hits
Matt in case A; however, when an aggressor lacks legitimate authority, then that aggressor does not forfeit the rights of its members
(technically, the aggressor has no members whose rights it can forfeit), and so we have a situation similar to case B, where Jack has
been forced to hit Matt, and so has not forfeited his rights. The
aggressor may have forfeited her individual rights, but she has not
forfeited the rights of those with whom she is associated or those that
surround her.

As war and violence are essentially matters of rights violation,
legitimate authority must essentially be a matter of having rights. The
two rights distinctive of states are the right to territorial integrity, and

the right to political sovereignty.[11] These are the rights over which wars are fought; these are the rights that, to a certain degree, are forfeited when a state attacks another. These rights are unique in that they belong to abstract entities, yet their violations and forfeitures are felt by the individuals who comprise the group or state. States thus must derive rights essentially from their members and, given what is at stake when a state either fights in defense of those rights, or forfeits those rights, a state will have the de jure legitimate authority to make these sorts of decisions only when its members grant it de jure legitimate authority through the transference of their rights. This is how we should understand legitimate authority, as having everything to do with the possession of rights, and very little to do with chain of command, political purpose, or even possession of a just cause. These features are all secondary to the question of whether or not a state has the de jure legitimate authority to put its members' rights at risk.

In order to determine whether a particular group has legitimate authority, we must determine whether or not it has been granted the rights in question (political sovereignty and territorial integrity) by its members. There are several different accounts of how we should go about doing this; one that I find most compelling is Michael Walzer's theory of state rights. His theory of state rights draws loosely on the social contract tradition, according to which members "contract" and agree to transfer their rights to the state. Yet, rather than positing the unrealistic existence of actual contracts and transfers, Walzer instead appeals to the development of a common life as representative of forming a contract. People develop a common life through the shared experiences and cooperative ventures that evolve inevitably among people living together, and states derive their rights to the extent that they provide them with this common life and protect them in it. This protection involves not only protecting people in their basic individual rights, but also in "their shared life and liberty [and] the independent community they have made, for which individuals are sometimes sacrificed."[12] When a state provides and protects this common life, it attains moral standing: "The moral standing of any particular state depends upon the reality of the common life it protects and the extent to which the sacrifices required by that protection

---

[11] For simplicity's sake, I will now refer to the groups in questions as "states"; yet my use of the term is meant to apply to any entity capable of having these sorts of rights.

[12] Michael Walzer, *Just and Unjust Wars* (New York: Basic Books, 1992), 54.

are willingly accepted and thought worthwhile. If no common life exists, or if the state doesn't defend the common life that does exist, its own defense may have no moral justification."[13]

Essential to Walzer's account is that members of a particular group identify with the group with which they live, see their participation in the group as something worthwhile, and see that state as being the entity that will protect that shared life. It is through this identification that groups/states derive their rights.[14]

Walzer's theory of state rights lays the foundation for a morally grounded de jure interpretation of legitimate authority. It is relatively easy to see how an entity that enables this conception of a common life and thus enjoys state rights also has the legitimate authority to put its member's lives at risk through endangering those rights. When a state has rights, it has them in virtue of providing a service for its members, and in exchange, its members authorize the state to act on their behalf.

I think Walzer's interpretation sets an ideal of legitimate authority that states should try to approximate. In particular, I hope to have shown that this interpretation of the legitimate-authority interpretation is the one that best fits the requirements and purpose of just war theory. It allows for the possibility that some states could lack moral standing, through failing to provide for and protect the common life, and presumably it allows for the possibility that some nonstates could have moral standing, thus allowing for the possibility that certain revolutionary groups could have legitimate authority. For example, on Walzer's account the African National Congress plausibly had moral standing and legitimate authority, even during the time of white minority rule in South Africa. However, his conception of the moral foundation of state rights is one that is too idealistic to serve as a plausible and realistic requirement for an entity's having legitimate authority. On Walzer's account, too few states would end up having legitimate authority and this implication leads to very counterintuitive results. What we need, then, is an interpretation that preserves the spirit of Walzer's morally grounded de jure approach, yet nonetheless lowers the standard for what counts as granting state rights.

---

[13] Walzer, *Just and Unjust Wars*, 54.

[14] One advantage of this account of state rights is that it allows for the possibility that nonstates could have "state rights," so long as they fulfill the requirements of the common life.

Walzer's most important insight is the idea that essential to a state is the common life. This is what binds people together and what warrants their inclusion in the entity of the "state." This is also what leads us to think they are somehow accountable for their government's action, and allows us to think that, on some level, their rights are forfeited when their leaders commit aggressive acts. The existence of a common life—be it glued together by mutual respect, or by the happenstance of living and working together—that is somehow regulated or protected by a governing body is, I think, enough to grant that governing body state rights and give that body legitimate authority.

Why is the common life so important for the question of whether or not a governing body has legitimate authority? One reason is that the presence of a common life is a sign that the people have deferred to the power to the governing body. This does not mean that they have actively consented to the authority of the government; nor does it mean that they see their government as having legitimate authority over them. What it means is that, in virtue of being involved in a common life that exists under the power of a governing entity, people grant that entity authority.

Trudy Govier writes, "A person can have power only if other people are prepared to defer to him or her."[15] No matter how tyrannical a dictator, he will only have power to the extent that people around him defer to that power. This was one of Gandhi's most fundamental messages: to end domination, people need to resist the power that dominates them. They need to stop cooperating with the power, and stop seeing that power as an authority. Only when people resist the power of another, will that person cease to have power over them. When people continue to live and exist as subjects to an authority, they are granting that authority power over them. Being part of a common life made possible and/or governed by a given entity thus amounts to granting that entity authority.

This interpretation of legitimate authority is de jure in spirit, yet because it severely weakens the moral foundation of state rights, is not far from a de facto interpretation. Regardless of where it falls on the scale of robust legitimacy, it reflects the moral purpose of the legitimate-authority requirement while nonetheless maintaining a realistic grasp on contemporary politics, where very often we have states whose rulers are there by force, not by right.

---

[15] Trudy Govier, *A Delicate Balance* (Boulder, CO: Westview Press 2003), chap. 6.

War on Terror

This interpretation of legitimate authority helps us to determine whether or not terrorist groups have legitimate authority and so are proper initiators or subjects of war. The deciding factor is whether or not terrorist groups can have the rights to political sovereignty and territorial integrity, and the test at hand is whether or not they provide for, and protect their members in having, a common life, understood in a morally unloaded way to include, for example, dictatorships.

While it is certainly the case that terrorists groups enable cooperative ventures and appear to enjoy a degree of political sovereignty, they are not candidates for having the full state rights of both political sovereignty and territorial integrity, as most terrorist groups fail to occupy a unified territory that is essential to the development of a common life. The common life essential to the granting of state rights involves people living together, working together, fighting together, reconciling together and, importantly, making sacrifices together. By living in a society, people essentially agree to restrict their behavior in ways necessary to enable society to function smoothly. This agreement, be it implicit or explicit, forced or unforced, is what grants states the authority to govern, and is what grants them the moral standing to defend their rights. It is essential to this picture of the common life, and the resulting conceptions of legitimate authority, that there be a particular territory inhabited by members of the group in question. Without a particular territory gluing its members together, they would fail to develop the common life from which a state derives its rights.

The inhabitance of territory is also important for more practical reasons. Wars are always fought within a given territory and territories always belong (or are at least inhabited by) some group. If a given group, say a terrorist group, lacks a territory that is in some sense their own, any wars with which they are involved will put *another group's* territory at risk, as well as the lives of the people who inhabit that territory.

Territorial occupation is thus essential to the concept of legitimate authority and state rights. Absent common territory, groups are simply that: mere groups. They can be held together by common political bonds, as the group of Republicans is, or they can be held together by certain hero worship, as a group of Elvis impersonators are. What makes a particular group a "state" with state rights is partly that they occupy a particular territory. As terrorist groups typically lack a unified, central territory to call their own, they lack the moral standing of a state. Because they lack moral standing, they lack state rights, and so lack legitimate authority.

Groups that are candidates for having legitimate authority, on the other hand, are groups that (1) occupy a particular territory, thus allowing for the development of a common life; and (2) in some sense "govern" or lead the people that have formed the common life. On this reading, almost all states will have legitimate authority and some, but certainly not all, nonstates will have legitimate authority. Revolutionary groups may have legitimate authority; groups trying to secede from their original state may have legitimate authority. Yet, again, most—if not all—terrorist groups will not have legitimate authority.

This claim is not a unique one; many have argued that terrorists lack legitimate authority, and thus acts of terrorism are not appropriately called acts of war. What is unique about this understanding of what exactly terrorist groups lack is the implication it has for a war on terror. As I will now argue, when acts of large-scale, state-sponsored violence are carried out against terrorist groups, they (1) are not acts of war; and (2) essentially involve the violation of another state's rights to political sovereignty and territorial integrity.

The first thing we need to realize is that legitimate authority, and indeed all of the *jus ad bellum* conditions, are requirements that apply bilaterally, to both sides of a conflict. The distinction is important especially for consideration of a war on terror, although it is one that easily gets lost in discussions of just war theory. The *jus ad bellum* requirements are most often viewed *from the point of view of an entity* deciding to go to war. In this regard, the requirements give an entity a checklist to determine whether its proposed actions are just. Do they have the legitimate authority to go to war? Do they have just cause? Is this their last resort? And so on. While this is the typical application of the *jus ad bellum*, we must also recognize that *both sides* of a dispute are also subject to the *jus ad bellum* requirements. In particular, we must recognize that, in order to have a war, we must have two legitimate authorities. We do not have a war, not even an unjust war, when one legitimate authority attacks random and unassociated civilians; the fact that one party may have legitimate authority does not make all of its actions acts of war. As we know well, states can commit crimes and violence against certain parties, and commit acts of war against other parties. What makes the latter acts of war is that they are committed against entities considered to have legitimate authority.

In order to decide whether a war on terror is, in fact, a war recognized as such by just war theory, it is not enough to decide whether one entity has legitimate authority. We must look at both sides, and ensure that both sides have legitimate authority. What we see when we do so is that a so-called war against terror is not a war.

To show that acts of violence against terrorist organizations are not justifiable acts of war because terrorist groups lack legitimate authority, we need only to revisit our discussion of self-defense and the aggressor-defender paradigm. We have seen that there are two conditions that must hold in order for an act to be an act of self-defense. First, there must be two parties with rights. Second, there must be one party whose rights have been transgressed, and one party whose rights have been forfeited. In a situation where a terrorist group attacks a state, the state's rights have been transgressed; however, the terrorist group has not forfeited its rights in the relevant sense.

The first worry is that the terrorist group lacks the appropriate rights in question (territorial integrity and political sovereignty) and so cannot forfeit rights it does not have. Certainly a terrorist group has forfeited individual rights to life and liberty; however, they have not forfeited state rights of territorial integrity and political sovereignty. This makes the situation importantly different from a case where a state attacks another state, and calls for a different sort of response than a simple case of self-defense. While large-scale violence may be a justifiable and appropriate response against a state that has forfeited its right to political sovereignty and territorial integrity, it is not likewise appropriate against individuals, regardless of the nature of their crime. Were such large-scale violence to occur, it would not be a justifiable act of war, primarily because it is conducted against a group that lacks legitimate authority.

This brings us to the second concern, one about what actually happens when a state brings large-scale violence against individuals in the name of "war." It is the nature of large-scale violence that it is aimed not at individuals, but rather at groups, and in particular, groups that inevitably occupy a certain territory and that are governed by a particular government. These groups are the ones affected by acts of large-scale violence. This, after all, is why it is so important that states have legitimate authority—for it is their member's lives that they stand to put at risk through their actions. A unique situation arises when the target of large-scale violence is not a state, representing its citizens, but is rather a group of terrorist individuals who happen to be living in a particular state. What ends up happening is that the state and its members inevitably become the target of the large-scale violence simply because certain individuals are inhabiting their territory. As it is the terrorists who have forfeited their individual rights, and not the states who have forfeited their state rights, such acts of large-scale violence constitute acts of unprovoked aggression and as such violate the just war requirements.

The U.S.-led war on terror provides a clear example of the repercussions of conducting a war on terror. Most agree that Al Qaeda, despite having a clear chain of command and political purpose, nonetheless lacks the rights to territorial integrity and political sovereignty essential to having legitimate authority. And while Al Qaeda certainly violated the United States' rights on September 11, 2001, retributive acts of large-scale violence made by the U.S. are not justifiable as acts of war, for Al Qaeda is simply a group of individuals, not a state. The individual members of Al Qaeda feasibly have forfeited their individual rights; however, they have not forfeited the rights of Afghans, simply because their leader happens to inhabit Afghanistan. This is especially true, as not a single Afghan has been named by the FBI to be involved in the September 11 attacks.

In bringing large-scale violence, and aerial bombings in particular, against Al Qaeda, the U.S. has, in effect, declared war against Afghanistan. And along with war comes the inevitable civilian casualties. An estimated 3,767 Afghani civilians died in the first two months of the U.S.-led war on individual members of Al Qaeda.[16] The U.S. tries to justify these civilian casualties through their appeal to the self-defensive war on terror; however, the war on terror is neither a war, nor justifiable. Rather, it amounts to an unprovoked attack on Afghanistan and a violation of their rights to political sovereignty and territorial integrity.[17]

---

[16] See Marc Herold, "A Dossier on Civilian Victims of United States' Aerial Bombing of Afghanistan," in *September 11 and the U.S. War: Behind the Curtain of Smoke*, ed. Roger Burbach and Ben Clarke (San Francisco: Freedom Voices Press, 2002).

[17] This situation is complicated by the fact that the existing government at the time of the first attacks on Afghanistan was a systematically oppressive one and an attack on the Taliban government may have been warranted on humanitarian grounds (as I tend to think it was). My point here is that the attack on Afghanistan was not justifiable as a war on terror. This holds true, I think, regardless of the fact that the Taliban refused to turn over Osama bin Laden. Such a refusal does not constitute an attack against the United States, which is the justification necessary to warrant the attacks.

Conclusion

I hope to have shown that just war theory has some important insights into the war on terror, and that, rather than being an antiquated theory, the requirements of just war theory, when properly interpreted, are ones that have strong foundations and should be looked to for guidance even when, and especially when, we are faced with new circumstances that appear to go beyond the scope of just war theory. I especially hope to have shown that the requirement of legitimate authority is of particular importance, even though it is perhaps the most neglected requirement of the *jus ad bellum*.

The requirement of legitimate authority traditionally has been seen from the point of view of the aggressor, rather than the target of that aggression, and many people tend to think that as long as a state is conducting large-scale violence, then it is an act of war. By understanding the potential dangers of this assumption, we will better be able to limit and regulate acts of large-scale violence, and, in particular, we will be able to determine when such violence is justifiable and appropriate. Large-scale violence is not a justifiable response to terrorist attacks. Rather, because terrorists groups lack legitimate authority, the appropriate response is to persecute terrorists as individuals.

We must start to think of the "war on terror" only in figurative terms; for it is not a literal war and should not be conducted as such. Rather, we should think of the war on terror as being akin to the war on drugs. We should hunt down terrorists the way we hunt down drug lords; we should track terrorist money the way we track drug money; we should arrest terrorists and their associates the way we arrest drug dealers and users. The war on drugs is the appropriate model for our response to terrorism, not a literal war against a state.

| 8 |

Moral Justification for Violent Responses to Terrorism

BRETT KESSLER

> A war to protect other human beings against tyrannical injustice; a war to give victory to their own ideas of right and good, and which is their own war, carried on for an honest purpose by their free choice— is often the means of their regeneration.

—John Stuart Mill

Introduction

The attacks of 9/11 and subsequent U.S.-led military action have, in many ways, redefined the world in which we live. Most people now know that international terrorism and responses to it have become a permanent fixture in our world, changing the shape of our future through dramatic foreign policy shifts and a position called preemption.[1] The questions are obvious. How are we to understand our radically different world? How do we make sense of terrorism and the

---

The ideas expressed in this paper are the author's alone and are not necessarily representative of those of the U.S. government, the Department of Defense, the U.S. Army, or the United States Military Academy.

[1] I am making a clear distinction up front between domestic terrorism and international terrorism, a distinction based simply on the idea of boundaries, the arbitrary though often contested lines we draw on a map. Terrorist activities directed from the top down, or what we might call State Terrorism, are cases of domestic terrorism. Likewise, terrorist activities directed from the bottom up, directed at the government from the people governed, are cases of domestic terrorism. International terrorism as I understand it is directed outward, directed towards people or a government outside national boundaries, within the international arena.

responses to it? Is the use of organized armed force in a fight against international terrorism morally legitimate? This paper is an attempt to answer some of the questions international terrorism generates through a reexamination of international terrorism and modern just war theory.

Following a brief explication of the assumptions I've made to establish a starting point for this examination, I will argue that international terrorism is illegitimate violence of a *particular* sort that can be resisted in a *particular* way. More specifically, international terrorism is violence that follows from a disregard for our shared humanity and the rights that shared humanity generates. International terrorists intentionally target the innocent, and the intentional killing of the innocent for its own sake or as a means to an end is always murder.

In response to international terrorism, just war theory's criteria of *jus ad bellum*—if understood in only the modern or what I call "strong" sense—would render a war on terrorism unjust. Understood in the strong sense, *jus ad bellum* has six independently necessary criteria for just recourse to war. The problem is that all six criteria can never be satisfied. The six independently necessary criteria would render *all* wars unjust: past, present, and future. I submit, however, that the strong sense of *jus ad bellum* is not the way the theory ought to work, because there certainly seem to be cases when the use of armed force is justified. For example, most everyone would accept that the struggle against Nazi Germany's conquests and acts of genocide was a just war. To make sense of this from within the framework of just war theory, I will suggest a different sense of *jus ad bellum* that will capture the same concerns and criteria as the strong sense, but will do so in a way that will allow us to use the theory to make the distinctions between what seem to be cases of genuinely just and unjust uses of force.

Finally, seeing that the theory places things in the categories in which we think they ought to be, the theory applied to the world we live in yields the conclusion that international terrorism can be responded to in a *particular* way. Because there is no equivalent to a police force in the international area, and because of the particular sort of illegitimate violence that international terrorism is—a total disregard for our shared humanity and the rules of justice our humanity lays down—we can justify the use of organized armed force as the *particular* response to international terrorism. As long as the violent response to international terrorism satisfies the criteria of *jus ad bellum* I've suggested and holds a respect for shared humanity and the rights humanity generates—demonstrated in the adherence to the rules of *jus in bello*—then we can morally justify what will be the controlled application of violence in response to international terrorism.

Assumptions

Given the constraints a chapter of this length imposes, I can't reasonably argue for all the claims necessary to start the argument where I'd like to start it. So, before moving on to my argument let me put the assumptions I've made up front. First, the ancient notion of "the natural law," or the idea of a common law that is in accordance with nature, independent of community or contract, is correct.[2] A significant part of what it means to be a human being is to have the capacity for rationality, a capacity universal among men and women that transcends boundaries, a capacity that itself lays down the rules of justice that govern the relationship between men and nations, even in a time of war. Cicero states:

> There is a true law, a right reason, conformable to nature, universal, unchangeable, eternal, whose commands urge us to duty, and whose prohibitions restrain us from evil. . . . This law cannot be contradicted by any other law, and is not liable either to derogation or abrogation. Neither the senate nor the people can give us any dispensation for not obeying this universal law of justice. . . . It is not one thing at Rome and another at Athens; one thing to-day and another to-morrow; but in all times and nations this universal law must for ever reign, eternal and imperishable. . . . He who obeys it not, flies from himself, and does violence to the very nature of man.[3]

The implication of this assumption about universal laws of nature and the capacity for rationality is that the criteria for the determinations we will soon make about legitimate or illegitimate violence apply to everyone. It isn't the case that only the winners in a fight have to follow the rules, or that the rules apply only to this or that

---

[2] All that is really needed to get this argument off the ground is an objective standard of morality. This can of course be had from a Kantian perspective, a divine command perspective, some versions of a virtue ethics perspective, even the rule versions of utilitarianism. I defend a natural law perspective elsewhere, but from any of these approaches, the arguments will look almost the same.

[3] From *The Political Works of Marcus Tullius Cicero: Comprising his Treatise on the Commonwealth; and his Treatise on the Laws*, trans. Francis Barham (London: Edmund Spettigue, 1841–42), vol. 1, http://oll.libertyfund.org/Texts/Cicero0070/PoliticalWorks/0044-1_Bk.html#hd_lf044.1.head.018.

group because of some status as a nation or non-nation. The judgments we make about permitting or condemning violence are based, first, on the notion that the rules apply to everyone in virtue of being human.

The second assumption is that we all have an equal right to life, a right and an assumption that follows readily from the first. Our rational capacity as humans lays down the rules of justice which govern everyone equally, rules of justice first articulated as rights; chiefly among them the right to life. The third assumption follows from the second and is simply that rights generate obligations. In this case, the right to life generates for others a negative obligation to not take life and a positive obligation to protect life. However, while I more or less agree with Peter Singer's general principle about obligations to assist—"If it is in our power to prevent something very bad happening, without thereby sacrificing anything of comparable moral significance, we ought to do it"—I am only concerned with the *can* that Singer's ought presupposes.[4] I will not assume that we *have* to do something to protect the right to life, only that we *can*, that we are justified in doing so.[5]

So how will these assumptions help us begin to make sense of terrorism and responses to it? What follows from these assumptions? I suggest that these assumptions serve as an anchor point for our understanding of both international terrorism and responses to it. First, there is a distinction to be made between legitimate and illegitimate violence, and from our assumptions it will be clear that terrorism is illegitimate violence which can be legitimately resisted. Second, in the debate about how to respond to international terrorism, our assumptions serve as the foundation for a theory whose widely recognized maxims not only prescribe when the use of armed force is appropriate, but also provide a framework for evaluating action within the conduct of war to determine what is and what is not morally acceptable behavior. In other words—and this is significant—the same reasons we use to condemn international terrorism will justify armed force in response to international terrorism and will then set limits on how that armed force is used.

---

[4] Peter Singer, "Rich and Poor," in *Morality and Moral Controversies*, ed. John Arthur (New York: Prentice Hall, 1999), 275.

[5] While this is an equivocation on "can," it seems to work. Singer means it in the sense of "is able" (ought implies can), I mean to use it in the sense of "is morally permitted." Yet, ought implies can in this sense as well. My thanks to colleague Dr. Richard Schoonhoven for pointing this out.

Violence and Terrorism

I need, at this point, to make a distinction between what seem to be different types of violence, namely legitimate violence and illegitimate violence. It seems that the intuition we draw on when making judgments about violence lies in the relationship between the violence and the rules that apply to all people. Generally speaking, violence meant to protect, preserve, or enforce the rights that the common law of nature establishes can be legitimate violence. This distinction coupled with the third assumption about protecting rights is easy to see in our everyday thinking. For example, we grant police officers moral permission to use force in the apprehension of criminals; we accept arguments of violence in the name of self-defense, perhaps resisting a mugger or even coming to the aid of a woman fighting off a would-be rapist. Further, notice that it is for the same reason that we condemn the violence of the criminal and of the would-be rapist—violating *human rights*—we justify violence against the criminals and would-be rapists—protecting *human rights*.[6] As can be seen from the distinction between legitimate and illegitimate violence and the connection between the violence and the foundational notions of rights that follow from our assumption of universal rules of justice as part of the human condition, illegitimate violence can be legitimately resisted.

At this point someone might suggest that I've just assumed almost the entire argument. All that remains is to make some claim about terrorism as illegitimate violence, a claim with which most would agree, and the conclusion that terrorism can be legitimately resisted simply follows. True enough. Most people already accept that terrorism can be legitimately resisted. I am primarily concerned, however, with *how* we resist terrorism, namely with further violence. How we respond to terrorism is going to depend, in part, on the sort of violence that terrorism is. So, while most people accept that terrorism is illegitimate violence, and that illegitimate violence can be legitimately resisted, I want to say that terrorism is illegitimate violence of a *particular* sort that can be resisted in a *particular* way, namely with the violence of armed force. The particular sort of illegitimate violence that international terrorism is will become clearer through an examination of the fundamental reasons we condemn terrorism.

---

[6] Of course, this would only apply to cases where crimes are committed against other people.

Within the framework of illegitimate violence, there is yet another distinction to be made. Namely, I suggest a difference between illegitimate violent acts that can be acts of terrorism and illegitimate violent acts that are not, a suggestion that also seems to capture the way we already think. For example, a bank robber who screams and yells, threatens the customers and bank tellers and even fires his weapon is engaged in illegitimate violence but not terrorism. Likewise, a murder that follows from a domestic dispute is illegitimate violence but not terrorism. I want to defend the position that international terrorism is best understood as the calculated employment or threat of a particular sort of illegitimate violence by individuals or subnational groups, primarily directed toward noncombatants, to further a particular goal or set of goals within the international arena. What seems to be a significant element in judging whether certain acts are acts of terrorism or not is contained in my language of illegitimate violence. Labeling an act "a particular sort of illegitimate violence" seems to depend, first and foremost, on whether there is regard or disregard for what I have called our basic humanity, what Cicero called the "natural law." In the case of what we want to call terrorist acts, there is a disregard that dismisses or operates outside the framework of laws our shared humanity generates, something quite different than just breaking the laws.

Imagine that you are sitting in a stadium somewhere watching a football game between two rival teams, X and Y. By the third quarter team X is losing miserably and starts cheating. Elbows are flying and facemasks are grabbed each time the referees aren't looking. Now consider what we might say of team X, if during the opening ceremonies they rumbled onto the field with bulldozers and dump trucks intending to crush, maim and kill their opponents. While we want to condemn team X's third quarter cheating, we probably want to say more about their use of construction equipment on the field. While we call cheating of the first sort illegitimate and are not surprised when the penalties are assessed, driving dozers onto the field is illegitimate in a different way.[7] The third quarter cheaters were "in the game" so to speak, meaning that they looked and acted like a football team, a team governed by rules, who for whatever reason decided to

---

[7] It is also important to note that the same penalties the referees assess for cheating in the first example won't work in the case of the bulldozers and dump trucks. A different sort of response is required to stop the construction equipment, a particular response based on the nature of the illegitimate violence.

break the rules for some advantage. Our team with construction equipment, on the other hand, either failed to recognize that football was a rule governed activity or dismissed the structure of the activity altogether.[8] Their actions represented illegitimacy of a particular sort; they didn't try to get away with not following the rules, they demonstrated a blatant disregard for the rules from the outset.

The same distinction can be made between the illegitimate violence the bank robber engaged in and the illegitimate violence that Palestinian suicide bombers or Al Qaeda members engage in, violence that completely disregards the rules of justice our humanity establishes. The bank robber's target was the bank, or at least the money in the bank. Terrorists, on the other hand, target people, people who should not be targets and are, on any conception of the word, innocent. International terrorists intentionally target and kill the innocent to further their political or religious goals. Further, as far as the modern international terrorists are concerned, the more death and destruction the better. Terrorism is the sort of illegitimate violence that dismisses the framework of laws our universal capacity for rationality lays down as rights. Violence pursued without regard to our humanity, without regard to the universal nature of human reason that defines us is illegitimate in this particular way. This, I suggest, is precisely why most people regard the intentional targeting or killing of innocent people to be, at least, instances of illegitimate violence. I want to suggest something a bit stronger, namely that the intentional killing of as many innocent people as possible, the killing of innocent people without a regard for their humanity that would require considerations to minimize casualties rather than maximize them, is illegitimate in a particular and terrible way.

A possible concern at this point might be that my distinctions do not allow for the difference between international terrorism and murder. As I've constructed the sort of illegitimate violence that terrorism is, it applies equally to a Jeffrey Dahmer case and even cases of ordinary murder, meaning that either these are cases of terrorism or that

---

[8] I will suggest though not argue for the claim that anyone who knows even the slightest thing about football recognizes that it is a rule-governed activity, and while the myriad of particular rules might not be known, bulldozers and dump trucks are clearly outside the rule set. It follows, then, that the rules have been dismissed rather than not recognized. In the same way, because we all know at least the slightest thing about being human, we recognize immediately that our relationships with other humans are rule-governed activities. While we may not know all of the particular rules, we can immediately recognize that some things fall outside the rule set.

the distinctions are inaccurate. In response, let us first be clear what kind of murder we are talking about. It seems that we can rule out crimes of passion or anger, acts of violence for which we apply and often accept "not guilty by reason of temporary insanity" claims. While these are still, in every way, cases of illegitimate violence, premeditated murder seems worse.

What remains of the objection, then, are cases of premeditated murder; the calculated, planned, and often rehearsed killing of innocent people. Earlier, I said that international terrorists intentionally target the innocent, and the intentional killing of the innocent for its own sake or as a means to an end is always murder. The difference, then, between a terrorist whose actions are murder and these other cases of premeditated murder necessarily lies in the motives because the violence is of precisely the same sort. International terrorism always has either a political or religious motivation as one of its distinguishing characteristics. So, the violence terrorists perpetrate that follows a disregard for the rules of justice is the same sort of violence other calculating murderers employ. However, there is no equivocation, for when the motives for the murder are considered, it is clear that terrorism is illegitimate violence of a particular sort, but illegitimate violence of the same particular sort is not always terrorism.

The position I've laid out has, in other contexts, been associated with natural law and Kantian traditions.[9] Because of the assumptions about natural rights and the defense of rights we started with, we were able to conclude that the intentional killing of as many innocent people as possible is morally impermissible, illegitimate in a particular way. So, since illegitimate violence can be legitimately resisted, and international terrorism is illegitimate violence, then international terrorism can be legitimately resisted. Further, since international terrorism is illegitimate violence of a particular sort—a dismissal of the rule set that governs human behavior—we can respond to terrorism in a particular way, a way necessary to stop the murder. But is the use of armed force in response to international terrorism justified? It seems to me that we can justify the use of armed force, but we must first have evaluation criteria to make sure the fight itself is justified and that the conduct within the fight is justified. As Frey and Morris suggest, "Just as natural law and Kantian moral theories constrain our behavior and limit the means we may

---

[9] R. G. Frey and Christopher W. Morris, eds., *Violence, Terrorism and Justice* (New York: Cambridge University Press, 1991), 5.

use in the pursuit of political ends, so they constrain our responses to terrorists."[10] This is the same significant idea I previously mentioned; namely that for the same reasons we condemn terrorism we justify the use of force against it. Further, the same justifications will also constrain how the force against terrorism is used. This is the second thing that follows from our beginning assumptions; a theory whose widely recognized maxims prescribe when the use of armed force is appropriate and provide a framework for evaluating action within the conduct of war.

In a fashion similar to Cicero, seventeenth-century jurist and humanist Hugo Grotius, often referred to as the father of international law, grounds his ideas of justice in war on the natural law, on human reason. Grotius thinks that the precepts of the just war tradition exist independently of recognized legal systems, that they are there to be discovered and applied by all nations, independent of a nation's particular laws or customs. For Cicero and Grotius, our rationality, or capacity for rationality, is what governs our interactions with others; it is what defines our humanity even in a time of war. In other words, the foundation of what is known as the just war tradition is recognition of the same assumptions we made in the beginning. The just war tradition is an attempt to recognize and codify the laws and rules of human interaction our shared humanity generates. Operating from within the requirements of the just war tradition recognizes and respects human reason and our humanity. Violence that recognizes and regards this foundation of the just war tradition, violence that does not disregard our humanity, can, in some cases, be legitimate.

The Just War Tradition

You don't know the horrible aspects of war. I've been through two wars and I know. I've seen cities and homes in ashes. I've seen thousands of men lying on the ground, their dead faces looking up at the skies. I tell you, war is hell.[11]

—General William T. Sherman

The most often used framework for the moral evaluation of war is what has become known as the just war tradition. Maxims have been

---

[10] Frey and Morris, *Violence, Terrorism and Justice*, 6.
[11] General William T. Sherman in a speech at the 1880 Ohio State Fair, Fifth Michigan Regiment Band website, www.mi5th.org/warishell.htm.

developed that not only prescribe when war is appropriate, morally acceptable, or even necessary, but also provide a framework for evaluating action within the conduct of war to determine what is and what is not morally acceptable behavior. These maxims have influenced and formed what has been called the War Convention, "the set of articulated norms, customs, professional codes, legal precepts, religious and philosophical principles, and reciprocal arrangements that shape our judgment . . . of the ethics of war and peace."[12] The fundamental concepts that support the maxims of the just war tradition are by no means modern conceptions. Some of the roots of the just war tradition can be traced as far back as the Roman Empire and the soldier's code to fight and die with honor. The just war tradition has been developed and shaped by religious and secular thinkers alike, such that most modern conceptions of just war theory are rooted in a historical tradition formed by experience and reflection, and influenced by international law, traditional notions of chivalry, and battlefield lessons.

The first part of the just war tradition, first by virtue of the determination of "going to war" occurring prior to "conducting the war," is called *jus ad bellum*. It specifies conditions that must be met for a permissible recourse to war. Most modern just war theorists contend that for a resort to war to be justified, a state must satisfy each of the following six requirements: (1) just cause, (2) right intention, (3) proper authority and public declaration, (4) last resort, (5) probability of success, and (6) macroproportionality (total cost of war vs. total benefit realized from winning the war).[13] The problem is that if each of these requirements is independently necessary, all wars are rendered unjust and the just defense of a nation becomes impossible. It seems to me that rarely if ever can all six requirements be met. Questions about last resort, proper authority, and probability of success, in particular, enter the discussion at several points and put pressure on the thesis that those requirements are necessary for a war to be just, and thus call into question the traditional just war doctrine. At the same time, it is generally agreed that the use of armed force is in some cases legitimate, for instance, in the Allied fight against Nazism in World War II. The problem, then, is to reconcile the sorts of condi-

---

[12] Michael Walzer, *Just and Unjust Wars: A Moral Argument with Historical Illustrations*, 2nd ed. (New York: Basic Books, 1992), 44.
[13] Brian Orend, *Michael Walzer on War & Justice* (Montreal: McGill-Queen's University Press, 2000), 87.

tions laid down in the just war tradition with uncontroversial cases of the morally legitimate use of armed force.

A better way to think about the *jus ad bellum* conditions, one that facilitates a clearer understanding of the relationship between the conditions themselves, is to return to the conceptions of just war from antiquity and, in the process, consider how some of the more modern conditions might relate. The first person to establish a rather theological doctrine toward justice in war was St. Augustine who, around the turn of the fifth century, posited several general principles.

First, a proper authority, that is, a prince in Augustine's time, must declare a war. Second, the war must have both a just cause and a right intention. Augustine's examples of a just cause for war, apart from a Divine command, include only an injustice or wrong caused by the enemy. What exactly qualifies as an injustice or wrong remains unclear, although Augustine thinks an enemy's refusal to restore property unjustly stolen to be a sufficient just cause of war. As to a right intention, Augustine clearly holds that war is *only a means of restoring order and of achieving peace*. Augustine considers two other factors to be essential for the justice of war, namely that the war should be necessary and that it should be carried out with mercy.[14]

By the early 1300s, significant social and political change had taken place. The fall of the Roman Empire under Charlemagne saw the rise to power of numerous dukes, barons, and counts, and a feudal system that contributed to conflicts between these power holders and those that opposed them. With Rome gone, there was no higher authority to which an appeal could be made. Almost any injury received was deemed sufficient to warrant war. It is interesting to notice that the arguments St. Thomas Aquinas posited in the mid-1300s about the justice of war did not significantly diverge from the work of Augustine written hundreds of years earlier. Aquinas accepted the autonomy of the many petty princes as a natural condition. Those who opposed this multiplicity of autonomy thought that the power to declare and wage war could be held only by the pope or the "emperor." On this opposing view, only the emperor or pope could authorize war against "infidels or against subjects and subordinates who had broken some internal law of the 'State.'"[15] However, those who accepted the autonomy of the numerous princes, like Aquinas, and those who

---

[14] Joan D. Tooke, *The Just War in Aquinas and Grotius* (London: SPCK, 1965), 11–12.

[15] Tooke, *The Just War*, 16.

thought authority to wage war rested only with the pope or emperor did make an exception; namely, "A war of self-defence and the killing of . . . those who had given refuge to criminals [is] thought permissible even without the authority of emperor or pope."[16]

What Aquinas himself thinks about the conditions for a just war is evident in his responses to several different objections to legitimate war.[17] The first two objections Aquinas responds to hold that war is always sinful. In the first objection, because punishment is only inflicted for sin, and the Lord threatens punishment on those who wage war—"All that take the sword shall perish with the sword"—all wars are sinful. In the second objection, whatever is contrary to a Divine precept is a sin, for according to the scriptures, "But I say to you not to resist evil"; "Not revenging yourselves, my dearly beloved, but give place unto wrath." Therefore, all war is always sinful. In response, Aquinas first offers the general idea that the scriptures do not expressly forbid soldiering. For example, Aquinas's response to the second objection is a general recapitulation of Augustine's idea that military service is not expressly forbidden in the scriptures. Aquinas, following Augustine, contends that if the Christian religion forbade war altogether, the Gospel would have commanded soldiers to lay down their arms and give up soldiering. But they were told by John the Baptist to be content with their pay. Since John the Baptist told them to be content with their pay, he did not forbid soldiering. In a specific response to the first objection, Aquinas contends that to take the sword means only to take it unlawfully, but that using the sword at the behest of an appropriate authority is not sinful. From this response, we begin to see the conditions that Aquinas thought necessary for a justified war; in this case, the paramount requirement for proper authority. Aquinas continues to claim that the proper authority to wage war must be exercised only for a good reason, or sufficient cause, namely, "A just war is wont to be described as one that avenges wrongs, when a nation or State has to be punished for refusing to make amends for the wrongs inflicted by its subjects, or to restore what it has seized unjustly."[18] The right intention of a war is to bring about what Aquinas calls "the common good" or the good of the com-

---

[16] Tooke, *The Just War*, 16.

[17] Tooke, *The Just War*, 36.

[18] This quotation, credited to St. Augustine, appears in St. Thomas Aquinas's *Summa Theologica* in the second part of book 2 (Benziger Bros., 1947). It is his response to question 40, about fighting only for a just cause. Online at www.ccel.org, http://www.ccel.org/a/aquinas/summa/SS/SS040.html.

munity. This is strikingly similar to Augustine's "right intention" to bring about peace.

Aquinas holds that three main conditions must be met for a war to be just: right authority, sufficient cause, and right intention. Further, and perhaps the reason Aquinas's thought on war is often considered the foundation of the just war tradition, Aquinas's considerations about war go beyond the justice of the war, *qua* war, to consider a particular action conducted in the course of a war, namely ambushes.[19] In considering whether ambushes are just actions in war, Aquinas is one of the first to consider just actions in the conduct of war separate from considerations of justice for the war itself, distinctions now commonly referred to as justice for war, or *jus ad bellum*, and justice in war, or *jus in bello*.[20]

To return to Grotius for a moment, recall that he is renowned for his contribution to international law. Grotius wrote extensively about the right of nations to use force as necessary for the cause of self-defense. Grotius, whose work is considered to have "secularized" the just war arguments of Aquinas, held three basic criteria for a just war: "(1) the danger faced by the nation is immediate; (2) the force used is necessary to adequately defend the nation's interests; and (3) the use of force is proportionate to the threatened danger."[21] Again, Grotius grounded his ideas of justice in war on the natural law, on human reason, much like Cicero almost 1500 years earlier. A result of this view is the idea that the precepts of the just war tradition exist independently of recognized legal systems and that they are there to be discovered and applied by all nations, independent of their own laws or customs. Grotius hoped to persuade the world, a world of developing nation states like England, France, and Spain, that there are indeed

---

[19] Aquinas considers whether it is a just action to lay in ambush for your enemy, given that an ambush involves deceit. In his argument, Aquinas draws a distinction between deliberate deceit, such as lying or breaking a promise, and deceit through silence, i.e., concealing intentions from your neighbors. Aquinas condemns deliberate deceit outright, believing that we have a duty to preserve the rights of others, even our enemies. However, preserving the rights of the enemy does not require that one divulge the intent to attack or the plan to attack. In fact, one interpretation of Aquinas's writing suggests that he thought it important for soldiers to become proficient in the art of concealing their purposes from the enemy. See Aquinas's response to question 40 in *Summa Theologica*, book 2, part 2.

[20] Though it seems to be some hint of the *jus in bello* in Augustine's argument that a war should be carried out with mercy.

[21] Tooke, *The Just War*, 76.

such independent rules governing warfare, therefore preventing war and loss of life. From Grotius's work, the tradition of just war changed little until the mid-1800s when Daniel Webster, the secretary of state in the relatively young United States of America, acknowledged the legitimacy of the precepts in the just war tradition. Throughout the remainder of the nineteenth and early twentieth centuries, the precepts of the just war tradition were codified in treaties such as the Hague Convention and two particular documents that followed WWII: the charter for the Nuremberg war crimes trials and the United Nations charter.

So, through a return to the foundations of the just war traditions it seems that the quintessential aspects of a just war necessarily included Aquinas's three conditions—proper authority, sufficient (just) cause, and right intention. So, I suggest that the just war tradition be understood and applied in accordance with Aquinas's three necessary requirements: proper authority, just cause, and right intention, and that the more modern "requirements" like probability of success, macroproportionality, and last resort are subcategories that, for the most part, are not independently necessary but function as a weighted average. What we mean by the just cause requirement is the substance of the just cause, the probability of success, whether or not recourse to war is the last resort, and making sure that the benefits of winning the war outweigh the costs of fighting the war (macroproportionality). Each of these subcategories, save the substance of the just cause, is not independently necessary but can lend strength to or detract from the substance of the just cause. Further, each of Aquinas's three conditions has subcategories. For example, what we mean by proper authority for war is a legitimate and competent authority to declare it, a legitimate process to arrive at the decision to declare it, and a formal declaration of it. What we mean by right intent is that peace is the ultimate objective and armed force is used only in pursuit of the just cause. In each of these cases, the subcategories taken together serve as a weighted average that can either fail to satisfy the requirement, satisfy the requirement, or exceed the requirement, lending further strength to the overall just cause. A concern might be raised that by reducing the necessary requirements for a just war from six to three, something might be lost. However, I suggest instead that something is gained, namely the ability of the just war tradition to actually make significant distinctions between truly just and unjust wars and, further, make distinctions among just wars based on the strength of the just cause.

The first criterion to be satisfied for a just recourse to war is proper authority. The proper authority requirement insists that a state may go to war only if appropriate and competent authorities make the decision for war, arrive at the decision through adherence to the proper process, and make the decision public to citizens of the state and enemy state(s). This is the positive requirement of proper authority in modern just war theory. However, we must not lose sight of the fact that for Aquinas, proper authority functioned in a negative way, forbidding certain people from declaring a war. That only appropriate authorities can declare war is important for Aquinas because his belief is that individuals may not declare war, that individuals have recourse to the higher authorities of the state. The thought is that the sovereign authorities of the state have no recourse to a higher authority and can therefore legitimately declare war (other conditions having been met). As the conditions in the world have changed significantly since the time of Aquinas, this condition is often challenged. For example, there may often be disputes as to the constitutional competence of a public official or even a segment of the government that participates in the decision process. Further, wars that are categorized as civil wars or wars of revolution, wars that we intuitively want to call just (the American Revolution, for example), have historically been initiated by persons and/or organizations claiming revolutionary rights. Nonetheless, the requirement for proper authority to declare war has remained a condition of the just war tradition since the mid-1300s. The second and third tenets of the proper authority condition, proper process and public declaration, seem inexorably linked. Most states in the world today have specific constitutional provisions for declaring war on another state. If a public official or a department of the government involved in the process violates the constitutional provisions, then the requirement for proper authority might not be met. For example, many critics of the Vietnam War base their claims of the illegality of the war on President Johnson's failure to seek a formal declaration of war from Congress.

The requirement of a just cause for recourse to war is certainly the most contentious of the *jus ad bellum* considerations. Aquinas thinks that a just cause is one that avenges some wrong, punishes a nation or state for failing to make amends for a wrong committed, or restores what was unjustly taken.[22] The substance of the just cause must be "serious and weighty" to overcome the presumption against killing

---

[22] Aquinas, *Summa Theologica*, book 2, part 2, response to question 40.

in war.[23] It is in this regard that the substance of the just cause is the only one of the subcategories of just cause that is an independently necessary condition for a just recourse to war. The idea of the substance of the just cause acknowledges that not to kill, even in war, is a duty, but that it is a duty in conflict with some other overriding duty. Examples of what the overriding duty might be are to protect the innocent from unjust attack, to restore rights wrongfully denied, and to re-establish a just order.[24] One advantage of evaluating the substance of just cause is the inevitability and necessity of some sort of comparative analysis of the characteristics of the parties involved in the conflict. This is an advantage that is either not terribly clear or altogether absent in other conceptions of the just war tradition. The comparative analysis of the parties, then, along with consideration of the act or grievance that spurred the consideration for war in the first place, becomes the substance of the just cause. Further, because the analysis of the parties involved will be different depending on their nature and the sort of violence they perpetrate, and because the nature of the act or grievance also varies, the strength of substance of the just cause, while necessary, will also vary.

In the classical just war tradition, offensive use of armed force is permitted to protect vital rights that are threatened unjustly or perhaps previously injured. Therefore, the classic tradition of justice in war holds that offensive wars to enforce justice for oneself are permissible. However, the idea of a permissible offensive war has lost its popularity since the early twentieth century and in fact, the embodiment of the idea that the only just war is a war of defense is captured in modern international law, namely the Charter of the United Nations.[25] What remains is the fact that, according to the classic just war tradition, in contrast to modern international law, offensive wars to pursue justice for oneself remain an option, but a war of vindictive justice, "wherein the belligerent fights against error and evil as a matter of

---

[23] William V. O'Brien, *The Conduct of Just and Limited War* (New York: Praeger Publishers, 1981), 20.

[24] O'Brien, *Conduct of Just and Limited War*, 20.

[25] Article 2(4) of the UN charter says, "All members shall refrain in their international relations from the threat or use of force against the territorial integrity or political independence of any state, or in any other manner inconsistent with the Purposes of the United Nations." Further, article 51 in chapter VII of the charter begins, "Nothing in the present Charter shall impair the inherent right of individual or collective self-defense if an armed attack occurs against a Member of the United Nations."

principle and not of necessity is no longer condoned by just-war doctrine."[26] Modern international law generally embodies what is often referred to as the "no first strike rule." In other words, according to the classic just war tradition, the offensive use of armed force in the pursuit of justice is legitimate, but according to modern international law and the modern just war theory, it is not.

The problem is that that there are occasions when initiating offensive action, "striking first," is indeed legitimate and perhaps even morally obligatory. For example, we might say, in hindsight, that given the conditions at the time of the U.S. Civil War and the atrocities of slavery specifically, the Union could have legitimately initiated the war on the Confederacy rather than waiting for the attack on Fort Sumter in 1861. Given the constraints of modern international law and modern just war theory, the use of armed force that seems offensive in nature is deemed legitimate with appeals to self-defense in one form or another. These operations are clearly offensive operations justified as self-defense. Understanding Aquinas's requirement of sufficient cause in the manner I suggest, namely, a duty that is serious and weighty enough to overcome the presumption against killing in war, allows us to accommodate the rare occasions when the genuinely offensive use of armed force is legitimate. That the *substance* of the just cause be serious and weighty enough for recourse to war is the first subcategory of just cause and the only one that *is* independently necessary. Any war that fails to meet this requirement is unjust.

The second subcategory of sufficient (just) cause is proportionality between the just ends and the means pursued to achieve those ends, what has been called macroproportionality. Proportionality, in the simplest of terms, is nothing more than a measurement of cost versus benefit with the "macro" meaning calculating the total costs of fighting the war, totaling the benefits realized by winning the war, and comparing the two. Only when the benefits outweigh or are at least equal to (in some cases) the costs of engaging in the war is the war considered just. However, measuring proportionality is never that simple. Because of the problematic nature of measuring the costs of war, whether it should be measured in terms of human lives lost, in terms of property damaged or destroyed, in terms of the potential for future aggression or any other abstract measurement, the calculus involved makes the proportionality requirement highly contentious.

---

[26] O'Brien, *Conduct of Just and Limited War*, 22.

As O'Brien notes, "The process of weighing probable good against probable evil is extremely complex. The balance sheet of good and evil must be estimated for each belligerent. Additionally, there should be a balancing of effects on individual third parties and on the international common good. . . . Manifestly, the task of performing this calculus effectively is an awesome one. But even its successful completion does not fully satisfy the demands of the just-war condition of just cause."[27]

The principle of proportionality, as I understand it, includes at least two requirements: (1) the calculated probable good that will result from a war in pursuit of a just cause must outweigh the calculated probable evil that the war will produce; and (2) the calculation must include all belligerents, any neutrals that are affected, and the international community, and must be periodically reevaluated throughout the war.[28]

The third subcategory of sufficient (just) cause is the probability of success. The aim of this criterion is to restrict the use of armed force in futile action. However, even if the chance of victory is low for a particular nation resisting unjust aggression, they still have a legitimate right to resist. To claim that they must acquiesce in the face of unjust aggression simply because the odds of victory are not on their side is to deny them the sovereignty and autonomy that guarantee the right of self-defense in the first place. Most modern just war theorists rightfully hold that the probability of success principle can be waived in a war of self-defense, particularly if there is a great threat to fundamental values and continued existence.[29] If the probability of success requirement can be waived, then it isn't a necessary requirement, but merely a condition that, if met, lends additional strength to the supported requirement of sufficient cause.

The last of the subcategories of just cause is the principle of last resort. In order for war to qualify as a just war under this condition, sufficient other, presumably nonviolent measures must have been taken and proved ineffective, leaving the resort to war as the last available option. Certainly, the intention behind the formation of the United Nations was to create the means for peace that would replace quick recourse to war. For example, the preamble of the UN Charter says, "We . . . determined to establish conditions under which justice and

---

[27] O'Brien, *Conduct of Just and Limited War*, 27.
[28] O'Brien, *Conduct of Just and Limited War*, 28.
[29] O'Brien, *Conduct of Just and Limited War*, 31.

respect for the obligations arising from treaties and other sources of international law can be maintained, and . . . for these ends, to employ international machinery for the promotion of economic and social advancement of all peoples." [30] Modern theorists suggest that the existence of the UN, and the methods of dispute resolution available through the "machinery" provided by the UN, have resulted in a general rule of thumb among statesmen and lawyers of international law that if a state fails to exhaust all available peaceful remedies before engaging in war, it is an unjust aggressor. [31] As we have seen, current international law and modern just war theory hold that aggressive or offensive wars are essentially unjust; therefore a war that is not the "last resort" is unjust. There are, however, a few problems with the last resort principle. Walzer claims that the last resort can either never be reached: that there can always be another diplomatic measure to be taken, or that even if it could be reached, a state would never know it had done so. [32] Walzer still adheres to the principle of last resort, but gives it a slightly different connotation: "It is only normative lastness which we can require. . . . States must have explored all *reasonable* and *plausible* avenues prior to launching armed force." [33]

The appropriate or "right" intention for war, since its presentation by Aquinas, has been to achieve peace. Walzer's consideration of the principle of right intention places it in the mix of motives, moral and nonmoral, for conducting war, but one that must necessarily be present for the war to be considered just. It is rather unclear whether the motive of right intention needs to be at the forefront of motives for a war to be just, but it must be present. The right orientation toward just cause is a necessary condition for just recourse to war. [34] We can unpack the requirement of right intention into at least two separate elements. First, the right intention limits those who engage in a just war to the just cause. In other words, right intention means that pursuit of a just cause cannot be turned into a pursuit of other causes. Second, right intention requires those engaged in war to keep in mind the ultimate object of the war: a just and lasting peace. An implication in the second element of right intention is that those engaged in war cannot translate their anger toward belligerents fighting against

---

[30] Charter of the United Nations, preamble.
[31] O'Brien, *Conduct of Just and Limited War*, 31.
[32] Walzer, *Just and Unjust Wars*, xiv.
[33] Walzer, *Just and Unjust Wars*, 84 (emphasis added).
[34] Orend, *Walzer on War*, 94.

them into prohibited behavior that runs contrary to right intention.[35] For example, the isolated incidents of American soldiers removing ears and fingers from wounded and killed combatants in Vietnam, a result of understandable but ill-placed hatred, are human rights violations that fail to satisfy the second element of the principle of right intention.

While an argument could be made for Aquinas's consideration of just actions *in* war—his response to the question of whether conducting an ambush in war is a sin, for example—the *jus in bello* principles of the just war tradition appeared only late in the tradition's development and now include prescriptions for conduct in war drawn from modern international law. The first and perhaps most important underlying principle of *jus in bello* requirements for a just war is the requirement for war to be limited. Unlimited wars are always unjust.[36] Based on that foundation, the modern *jus in bello* principles include three limitations of the conduct of war. The first limitation on the conduct of war is the principle of proportionality, in this case microproportionality, requiring proportionality between the military means used to achieve particular military ends.[37] The second limitation on the conduct of war is the principle of discrimination, prohibiting direct, intentional attacks on noncombatants and nonmilitary targets. Within the context of discrimination, two further considerations that appear are the doctrine of double effect and the "due care" principle. The third limitation on the conduct of war is a category of restrictions that includes prohibitions of means that are by definition disproportionate and cannot be used, even if they meet the requirement of discrimination. These restrictions are often divided into categories called means *mala in se,* or means evil in themselves, and means *mala prohibita*, or means prohibited in and of themselves, means that some modern theorists refer to as acts or weapons that shock the moral conscience of humankind.[38] Other than to suggest that the rules of *jus in bello* derive from the same foundational assumptions of human rights that articulate the rules of justice that our shared rational capacity makes universal, my understanding is the same as modern theorists. The requirements of *jus in bello* must be satisfied for specific wartime conduct to be legitimate.

---

[35] O'Brien, *Conduct of Just and Limited War*, 34.

[36] O'Brien, *Conduct of Just and Limited War*, 38.

[37] Orend, *Walzer on War*, 121–24.

[38] Orend, *Walzer on War*, 124.

In sum, Aquinas thinks the three conditions of proper authority, sufficient cause, and right intention must be met for a war to be just. Modern just war theorists suggest further *jus ad bellum* principles such as the probability of success, last resort, and proportionality. As I have presented the just war tradition, however, the principles of last resort, probability of success, and macroproportionality are subcategories of Aquinas's condition of sufficient cause. There is a significant philosophical implication of this formulation. To say that there are six independent *jus ad bellum* principles that must each be met for a war to be just is to say that each of the six is a necessary condition for a just war. Any war that did not meet each of the criteria would be deemed unjust. Understanding the principles of last resort, probability of success, and macroproportionality as subcategories of sufficient cause, however, means that sufficient cause is something like a weighted average of the subcategories, that the conditions that constitute sufficient cause might not in themselves be necessary as long as the cumulative average renders the judgment that the sufficient cause has been met. What this allows for is the strength of one subcategory to offset, to some degree, deficiencies in another category.[39]

So, the just war tradition recognizes the moral reality of war and wartime behavior and offers a possible analysis, the most commonly accepted analysis, of the application of moral principles toward the use of armed force and the specific conduct of members of the armed forces. Modern just war theory is neither specifically theological nor secular, neither specifically utilitarian (measuring costs vs. benefits) nor constrained by duties and rights. The just war tradition and modern just war theory have a rich and long history, touch the foundations for different ethical theories, and include some of the ideals of chivalry, soldierly honor, Christian and secular principals, and even lessons learned from the history of warfare itself. Most importantly, if understood correctly, the just war tradition, as Grotius envisioned it, is anchored to the rights that follow from rules of justice established by our shared humanity.

---

[39] This is clearly something Walzer would deny. He contends, for example, that there cannot be a sliding scale of just cause, that the strength of a just cause cannot make a difference in the way one fights (Walzer, *Just and Unjust Wars*, 228–32). However, I am not suggesting a sliding scale that allows for relaxing the *jus in bello* requirements based on the strength of sufficient cause, a *jus ad bellum* requirement. I only suggest that within the requirements *of jus ad bellum*, the requirements of last resort, macroproportionality, and probability of success might not be individually necessary, or at least the strength of one might offset the weakness of another.

We ought to be concerned about justice and warfare because there is currently a war going on. We, as a nation, are using our armed forces in a faraway land and people are dying. It certainly seems to me that the nature of this war is different from any other war, the conduct in this war has been and will continue to be different from that in any other war, the enemy we face in this war is different from that in any other war, and the outcome of this war will most likely be different from that of any other war. With all the differences, can the just war tradition do any work for determining the justice of our cause? Can the tradition make any prescriptions for the wartime conduct in this very different war? I believe it can do work and that it can make prescriptions. Because the criteria used to condemn the criminal or would-be rapist in one of my first examples are the very same criteria used to justify violence directed towards the criminal or would-be rapist, the same criteria used to condemn international terrorism can and must be used to justify violence directed towards international terrorists. One question remains: Can we justify violence as the particular way to respond to terrorism? I've argued thus far that terrorism is illegitimate violence of a particular sort that can be resisted in a particular way. But why suppose that the particular way to respond to international terrorism is with the use of armed force?

First, recall that I am not arguing that we have to respond with violence, only that we can; that the use of armed force in response to terrorism *can* be justified. Second, given the way the world is constructed, the use of armed force is often the only way to respond to international terrorism. The structure of our international arena is such that crimes, acts of war, acts of terrorism, and any violations of international law, for that matter, are difficult if not impossible to enforce without the use of the armed force of one country or another. There is no such thing as an international police force analogous to a police officer apprehending a criminal in the domestic analogy I used earlier. So, military force in response to international terrorism, if a response is to be made, is often the only and therefore necessary option. The complete idea, then, is that because international terrorism is a particular sort of illegitimate violence that occurs within the international arena constructed as it is, and because illegitimate violence can be legitimately resisted, a military response to international terrorism can be legitimate as long as the decision to use military force and the force itself does not dismiss the universal rules of interaction that our shared humanity generates.

Preemptive Strikes and Targeted Killing

| 9 |

The Moral Consequences of Preemptive Strikes and Preventive War

RICHARD C. ANDERSON

It has now been several years since the infamous terrorist attacks of 9/11, while the War on Terrorism has raged on for nearly as long. Ever since the attacks, American politicians have suggested that the War on Terrorism is a new type of war, presenting unique threats and unparalleled challenges. In response, many have suggested that we should redefine the criteria used to justify the use of military force. Politicians have reconsidered the doctrines of deterrence and containment, while "preemption" has become the new buzzword describing our proposed tactics for engaging terrorist threats. Our preference for an active defense is surely warranted; however, the proposed use of preemptive strikes seems to blur the traditional line between legitimate and illegitimate first strikes.

In this essay, I will examine recent just war theory perspectives regarding preemptive strikes and preventive war. I will focus primarily on Michael Walzer's account of just war theory, which is based on the principle of inalienable human rights. My purpose is not to criticize, or support, any current policy or operation. Instead, my enterprise is applied ethics—in this case, the application of an accepted just war theory to the conditions present ever since the first plane hit the World Trade Center on 9/11/01. Even though our enemy has demonstrated a willingness to engage in terrorist actions, I will argue that the war on terrorism must be fought within the constraints of just

The views expressed in this article are those of the author and do not reflect the official policy or position of the United States Military Academy, the Department of the Army, the Department of Defense, or the U.S. government.

war theory in order for the United States to maintain its legitimacy as the standard-bearer of international law.

Throughout the months following the attacks of 9/11, it seemed that administration officials were presenting new policy initiatives at virtually every public appearance. While delivering the commencement address to the 2002 graduates of West Point, President Bush made the case for significant changes in United States foreign policy; not only in how we perceive our enemies, but also in how we will react to the threats they impose. President Bush went on to clarify these changes:

> For much of the last century, America's defense relied on the Cold War doctrines of deterrence and containment. In some cases, those strategies still apply. But new threats also require new thinking. Deterrence—the promise of massive retaliation against nations—means nothing against shadowy terrorist networks with no nation or citizens to defend. Containment is not possible when unbalanced dictators with weapons of mass destruction can deliver those weapons on missiles or secretly provide them to terrorist allies.[1]

In response to these "new threats," President Bush proposed a dynamic shift in our strategic mission to maintain the peace and security for our nation:

> We cannot defend America and our friends by hoping for the best. We cannot put our faith in the word of tyrants, who solemnly sign non-proliferation treaties, and then systematically break them. If we wait for threats to fully materialize, we will have waited too long. Homeland defense and missile defense are part of stronger security, and they're essential priorities for America. Yet the war on terror will not be won on the defensive. We must take the battle to the enemy, disrupt his plans, and confront the worst threats *before they emerge*. In the world we have entered, the only path to safety is the path of action. And this nation will act.[2]

President Bush's remarks that day were more than just encouraging words to the newest batch of U.S. Army junior leaders. The

---

[1] "President Bush Delivers Graduation Speech at West Point: Remarks by the President at 2002 Graduation Exercise of the United States Military Academy, West Point, New York," June 1, 2002, http://www.whitehouse.gov/news/releases/2002/06/20020601-3.html.

[2] "President Bush Delivers Graduation Speech"; emphasis is mine.

remarks signaled a dynamic change in our nation's traditional stance regarding preemption and the justified use of force, while also displaying our newfound distrust in diplomatic solutions for the problems that the world's tyrannical regimes present to our nation.

As a confirmation of this new stance regarding preemption, Vice President Cheney recalled the words of Henry Kissinger in a moving speech to the VFW's national convention in August of 2002:

> "The imminence of proliferation of weapons of mass destruction, the huge dangers it involves, the rejection of a viable inspection system, and the demonstrated hostility of Saddam Hussein combine to produce an imperative for preemptive action."[3] If the United States could have preempted 9/11, we would have, no question. Should we be able to prevent another, much more devastating attack, we will, no question. This nation will not live at the mercy of terrorists or terror regimes.[4]

While the Vice President's statement may seem reasonable in post-9/11 America, in many countries around the world his remarks were ill received. Given the unforeseen destruction resulting from the terrorists' actions, a preemptive strike against Al Qaeda prior to the 9/11 attacks would certainly have seemed warranted. Yet, the notion of striking first, before a threat actually materializes, appears to contradict the accepted tenets of just war theory. Prior to 9/11, America seemed committed to the just war theory motto, "Nothing but aggression can justify war,"[5] since it had not landed the first blow in any recent major conflict. However, the current preference for preemptive action against countries opposing the United States indicates a willingness to deviate from the motto.

Is such a willingness to deviate really warranted? Has the world changed so radically that our policies of deterrence and containment have outlived their usefulness? Clearly, the terrorist actions on 9/11 yielded unprecedented destruction, while also exposing the inherent weakness of our national air-travel system and our vulnerability to clandestine operations within our open society. Nevertheless,

---

[3] Henry Kissinger, quoted by Vice President Richard Cheney, in "Vice President Speaks at VFW 103rd National Convention," August 26, 2002, The Official Site of Veterans of Foreign Wars of the United States, http://www.vfw.org/conv103/vpspeech.htm, accessed August 28, 2002.

[4] Vice President Richard Cheney, "Vice President Speaks at VFW 103rd National Convention," August 26, 2002.

[5] Michael Walzer, *Just and Unjust Wars*, 3rd ed. (New York: Basic Books, 2000), 62.

although the tactics of terrorist organizations surely present new challenges for our nation's security establishment, these actions do not seem to warrant the forsaking of our traditional predisposition towards restraint when considering the use of force in the international arena. The doctrines of deterrence, containment, and military restraint have enabled the United States to maintain the moral high ground during most of our military conflicts throughout the twentieth century. These doctrines were shaped by our nation embracing the tenets of just war theory, while also respecting the international society of states made manifest by the creation of the United Nations from the ashes of World War II.

There are many theories prescribing the conditions that must be met before any use of force by one nation against another is justified. In his seminal work, *Just and Unjust Wars*, Michael Walzer argues for a comprehensive just war theory based upon the inalienable rights of individuals (or human rights) and how those rights should affect our judgments regarding *jus ad bellum* (justice of war) and *jus in bello* (justice in war). His theory is unique in that it does not rely on the traditional just war theory criteria of just cause, proper authority, right intention, reasonable chance of success, proportionality of ends, and last resort. Instead, Walzer proposes that the recognition of inalienable human rights yields a comprehensive theory to shape our moral judgments regarding war.

According to Walzer, the rights of individual states are derived from their representative nature resulting from the "coming together" of a people within any given territory.[6] Since every person is endowed with the inalienable rights of life and liberty, states are formed to protect and represent citizens' rights in the world community. In this sense, the rights of any state are derived from the recognition of the individual citizens' rights that the state represents. This distinction forms the basis for Walzer's "Legalist Paradigm," which recognizes the inherent rights of individual states to their own territorial integrity and political sovereignty.

When the rights of a state are violated, we call it an act of "aggression." The state that violates the rights of another is deemed an "aggressor," guilty of the single "crime of war" that one state can

---

[6] Walzer, *Just and Unjust Wars*, 57. Walzer suggests that this "coming together" also forms the basis for a rights-based social contract theory. Although Walzer's theory is not dependent on social contract theory, clearly the relationship between citizen and state that he describes fits within the Lockean perspective.

commit against another.[7] Therefore, Walzer's just war theory limits the morally justified use of force primarily to those occasions when an aggressor state violates the rights of another, such as a war of self-defense. However, Walzer realizes that requiring states to wait until they are militarily attacked before they can take action is too restrictive and could even result in the complete destruction of states *before* they have a chance to defend themselves. He proposes that states need not wait until an enemy attack is imminent, since this would require that states wait until they are actually going to be attacked. Instead, Walzer states that "the line between legitimate and illegitimate first strikes is not going to be drawn at the point of imminent attack but at the point of sufficient threat."[8] Walzer defines "sufficient threats" as those that present a "manifest intent to injure, a degree of active preparation that makes that intent a positive danger, and a general situation in which waiting, or doing anything other than fighting, greatly magnifies the risk."[9]

By recognizing the moral justification of striking first in the face of imminent attacks *and* sufficient threats, Walzer clarifies his notion of aggression to include not only actual violations of a state's rights, but also the threatened violation of those rights. What is crucial for Walzer is that the threats must be manifested through the clear intentions and actions of an aggressor state, not just the potential for action. In this sense, states are justified in protecting the rights of their citizens through preemptive strikes when they know that their rights are in jeopardy, and failure to act would place the territorial integrity or political sovereignty of the state at greater risk.

However, Walzer is very careful not to open the doorway to legitimate first strikes too wide. He clearly admonishes the doctrine of "preventive war," which attempts to justify fighting earlier rather than later. Preventive wars are usually fought out of fear and distrust of another country, rather than out of defense against aggression. Instead of waiting for threats to *actually* materialize, states fight preventive wars to engage enemies before they actually obtain the capability for aggressive action.

Generally, states fight preventive wars in order to maintain the "balance of power" that appears threatened by the growing power of a rival state. The arguments for preventive war are rather simple and

---

[7] Walzer, *Just and Unjust Wars*, 51.
[8] Walzer, *Just and Unjust Wars*, 81.
[9] Walzer, *Just and Unjust Wars*, 81.

rely on common utilitarian calculations used to justify the needs of the many over the needs of the few. The proponents of preventive wars suggest that the overall loss of life and destruction of property would be less if they strike earlier, rather than waiting for the threatening country to fully develop its capabilities. Although there may be many pragmatic arguments for the doctrine of preventive war, virtually every variation of just war theory has traditionally condemned such doctrines, labeling nations that engage in preventive wars as aggressors themselves.

When analyzed within the context of Walzer's just war theory, President Bush's statements regarding preemptive strikes during his West Point address seem to suggest a preference for preventive war rather than preemptive strikes, since the goal of the action he describes aims at engaging threats *before* they actually emerge. For this reason, the doctrine of "preemption," as described by President Bush, would be better understood as a doctrine of prevention, thereby bringing the moral consequences of the doctrine into question. According to Walzer's just war theory, if a country, or a terrorist organization, were to pose *sufficient* threats to our nation, then preemptive strikes would certainly be warranted. However, if the goal is to destroy our enemies *before* they materially threaten us, then striking first would constitute an act of aggression.

The moral quandary resulting from our proposed use of preventive war stems from the premises underlying Walzer's just war theory. Walzer has provided us with a just war theory built upon the premise that all persons possess inalienable human rights. How or why people possess these rights does not really matter to our understanding of the theory. Instead, what matters is that we recognize that all people are entitled to the same rights regardless of what country they live in, or what type of political system they happen to be part of. In this sense, the human rights of an American citizen are equal to the human rights of an Iranian, Syrian, or North Korean citizen, even though the current political regime in those countries may not recognize the rights of their own citizens. The recognition of inalienable human rights has tremendous consequences for any just war theory because it entails an equal consideration for both "friendly" and "enemy" noncombatant citizens. The United States made this recognition formally in "The National Security Strategy of the United States," which states: "In the twenty first century, only nations that share a commitment to protecting basic human rights and guaranteeing political and economic freedom will be able to unleash the potential of their people and assure their future prosperity. . . . Freedom is the non-negotiable demand for human dignity; the birthright of every person—in every civilization."[10]

Since it has become a matter of the United States' national security policy that we recognize human rights and dignity, it is even more important that we effectively honor them throughout the world. In order to honor the human rights and dignity of all people, we should not engage in a policy that directly places those rights in jeopardy, which is exactly what the preventive war doctrine does.

The proposed preventive war doctrine of the United States does not cohere with Walzer's doctrine of human rights because it necessarily places the rights of some people above those of others. For instance, in any preventive war, the attacking country necessarily violates the rights of the defending country, since the attack comes before the defender has actually materially threatened anyone. In this case, the threat merely perceived or imagined by the aggressor provides the catalyst for military action, instead of sufficient threats by one nation against another. Since the defender against a preventive attack has not sufficiently threatened anyone, the responsibility for the lives lost, and the individual rights violated, falls directly on the aggressor nation. Therefore, if the United States is going to be the champion of human rights and dignity, as our national security policy suggests, it is crucial that we do not violate the rights of others in the process.

Given that all people everywhere possess the same human rights, how active should the United States be in securing and protecting those rights? Many politicians argued that the threats posed by Saddam Hussein warranted not only preventive war, but also a forced "regime change" due to the Saddam's human rights violations. However, does the quest for universal freedom entail that some people must make the ultimate sacrifice in order to secure the rights of others? Here I am not referring to the sacrifices made by soldiers defending the rights of others; instead, I mean the rights of citizens living in countries ruled by tyrannical regimes. Once again, I turn to the "National Security Strategy" for guidance on the matter. The policy states, "The United States should be realistic about its ability to help those who are unwilling or unready to help themselves. Where and when people are ready to do their part, we will be willing to move decisively."[11]

---

[10] "The National Security Strategy of the United States," September 2002, http://www.whitehouse.gov/nsc/nss.html.

[11] "The National Security Strategy of the United States."

This readiness to help those who are willing to help themselves is certainly commendable and is reminiscent of John Stuart Mill's doctrine of "self-help."[12] Mill's doctrine proposed that people essentially get the government that they deserve, and that people living under tyrannical regimes will continue to do so until they were willing to engage in the "arduous struggle" for freedom themselves. What is crucial for the doctrine of self-help is that the rights of citizens to effectively *remain* oppressed must be respected until they are willing to make the necessary sacrifices themselves. According to Walzer, except in cases of enslavement or massacre (when the notion of arduous struggle would seem impossible), a state's sovereignty must be respected in order to protect the individual rights of its citizens. Otherwise, any forced liberation would certainly violate both the rights of individual citizens, as well as the rights of the state that oppresses them. Although this may seem somewhat demanding for those oppressed by tyrannical regimes, as well as those who wish to liberate them, it is important to remember that the price of freedom is sometimes very high. Therefore, in order for a people to truly be free, they must take the first steps towards freedom themselves. Once they have taken these steps, any lives lost, or rights violated, will be the result of their own free choice.

By engaging in preventive wars, even if those wars were fought to "liberate" people, the United States would violate the very rights of the people that we seek to protect. Given that there are numerous tyrannical regimes around the world, we must restrain ourselves from embarking on a crusade to liberate oppressed peoples, especially if that means deciding their fate for them. As Walzer suggests, "Only domestic tyrants are safe, for it is not our purpose in international society (nor, Mill argues, is it possible) to establish liberal or democratic communities, but only independent ones."[13] However, once a people have demonstrated their representative nature, and their willingness to fight for their own rights, Walzer argues that we could intervene in their struggle in order to put freedom within their own reach. For example, the "no-fly" zones in Iraq imposed by the United Nations in order to protect the Kurdish people living within Iraqi bor-

---

[12] John Stuart Mill, "A Few Words on Non-Intervention," in *Dissertations and Discussions* (New York, 1873), III, 238–63. Walzer makes use of this reference in *Just and Unjust Wars,* chapter 6, to describe and apply Mill's doctrine of self-help as criteria to consider before any military intervention becomes morally acceptable.

[13] Walzer, *Just and Unjust Wars*, 94.

ders were viewed as a "just" intervention. Even though the United Nations intervened on behalf of the Kurds, the goal was not to fight the Kurd's battles. Instead, the United Nations only provided a safe haven from the threat of Iraqi aggression.

In order for the United States to retain moral clarity regarding just war theory, we must remember what constitutes aggression and what does not. The attacks of 9/11 clearly violated the rights of American territorial integrity as well as the individual rights of those lost at the World Trade Center, the Pentagon, and United Airlines flight 93. According to the vast majority of just war theorists, the American response to this aggressive act was swift and justified. By targeting members of the Al Qaeda organization and the Taliban government of Afghanistan (which enabled Al Qaeda's training, planning, and coordination for the 9/11 attacks), America fought a war of self-defense against an aggressor. Although Al Qaeda was not a state, the organization qualified as a viable aggressor due to its organizational structure and its representative nature for the political goals of a radicalized Islamic group. Although the Taliban government did not directly attack the United States, its harboring of Osama bin Laden clearly placed Afghanistan into the position of aiding and abetting an aggressor. Clearly, these actions precipitated the justified use of force against Al Qaeda and the Taliban. However, now that the Taliban is ineffectual, and Al Qaeda seems to have lost its foothold in Afghanistan, America has turned its attention toward groups whose direct connection to 9/11 seems somewhat questionable.

The central issue facing the United States today is how we will respond to the various threats of the post-9/11 world. In order to retain the moral advantage offered by adherence to just war theory, we must not act militarily against merely perceived or imagined threats. This could lead us into wars that should not be fought, against "enemies" that may not deserve the full wrath of the most powerful nation on earth. In order to maintain the moral justification for our response to the 9/11 attacks, and the threats of the post-9/11 world, we must remain committed to our pre-9/11 understanding of just war theory. Although we should certainly reevaluate our security posture, and our political and economic relationships with certain countries, we should not change our moral perspectives regarding the difference between just and unjust wars. If we maintain that human rights and dignity are universally inalienable, then we should not violate the rights of some in order to secure the rights of others; nor should we

violate the rights of nations *before* they actually threaten us. By clarifying our understanding of what constitutes a justified preemption,
the United States should be able to refrain from preventive wars and
the inherent violation of rights those wars entail.

| 10 |

Targeted Killing

DANIEL STATMAN

Introduction

The threat of terror has found the West widely unprepared. The standard means of waging war are irrelevant to contending with this threat; tanks, jets, and submarines are helpful when confronting other tanks, jets, and submarines, but not for hijackers carrying knives or terrorists wearing explosive belts. The standard means of fighting crime also seem unaccommodating in the face of this threat; the chances of Interpol capturing bin Laden and his followers and bringing them to justice are remote, as are the chances of the Israeli police arresting and trying the leaders of Hamas and Islamic Jihad. Hence, to effectively stop terror, the West must seek a different model, not the model of conventional war with its machines and tools, nor that of the police and court activities conducted against ordinary criminals. Rather, the wars against terror must adopt methods that are less common, or altogether uncommon, in conventional wars. One such method, whose legitimacy I wish to defend here, is that of targeted killing.

In choosing the term "targeted killing" rather than "assassination," I have sought to avoid the negative moral connotation that is almost inherent in the latter. If the argument of this chapter is sound, then not all acts of assassination are morally wrong or, alternatively, not all acts of targeted killing are assassinations. Prior to September 11, 2001, Israel was the only country openly employing this tactic in its

This essay was previously published in *Theoretical Inquiries in Law* 5, no. 1 (2004): 179–98. Reprinted by permission.

fight against terror, and it was strongly condemned for doing so by most of the international community, including the U.S. But since the September 11 attacks, the U.S. itself has adopted this policy in its war against Al Qaeda. In November 2002, an American Predator unmanned aerial vehicle targeted and killed an Al Qaeda activist in Yemen[1] using a technique similar to that used by the Israeli army against Hamas or Islamic Jihad activists. Furthermore, in December 2002, *The New York Times* reported that "the CIA is authorized to kill individuals described as 'terrorist leaders' on a list approved by the White House."[2] However, some commentators continue to believe that there is a moral difference between the Israeli and the American positions, and I will address their argument later on.

The main thesis of this essay is that acceptance of the legitimacy of the killing and destruction in a conventional war necessarily entails accepting the legitimacy of targeted killings in the war against terror. In other words, a principled objection to targeted killings necessarily entails a pacifist approach to conventional war. I present this thesis and defend it in section I. In section II, I explore the possibility of justifying targeted killings on the basis of retribution, which, I argue, might play a more significant role in this context than usually assumed. Section III rejects a sophisticated philosophical argument against targeted killings, namely, that based on the alleged problematic implications of "named killing" for war ethics. In section IV, I turn to the effectiveness of targeted killings and, in section V, analyze the moral status of targeted killings in the context of conventional war. The final section summarizes the conclusions of the discussion regarding the legitimacy of targeted killing.

I. Morality and War

I mentioned at the outset two general models for dealing with threats to vital interests: the war model and the nonwar (i.e., criminal law and individual self-defense) model. In war, goes the common wisdom, soldiers of all sides are permitted to kill any soldier of the adversary, unless the latter surrenders or in limited exceptional circumstances. This permission to kill is not contingent on establishing that the sol-

---

[1] Walter Pincus, "U.S. Strike Kills Six in Al Qaeda; Missile Fired by Predator Drone; Key Figure in Yemen Among Dead," *Washington Post*, November 5, 2002, A1.
[2] "C.I.A. Expands Authority To Kill Qaeda Leaders," *New York Times*, December 15, 2002, A2.

dier being killed poses any significant threat to the other side or, even assuming that he does pose such a threat, that he is morally responsible for doing so. Moreover, under the principle of *jus ad bellum*, states are not required to establish the imperativeness of the interests threatened in order to justify going to war. Usually a violation of territorial sovereignty will be considered just cause for going to war, a *casus belli*, even if the consequences of that violation for human lives and dignity might be relatively insignificant. Many believe that the British attack on the Falkland Islands was not only legally justified but also morally justified, despite the fact that the Argentinean invasion most likely would not have led to the killing of British citizens or acts of oppression. Thus: (1) states can go to war for the sake of formal sovereignty with no need to show that, beyond that formal sovereignty, any vital interests are in clear and imminent danger, and (2) once they actually do wage war, they can kill any enemy soldier, regardless of the personal danger posed by or responsibility of those being killed. Following McMahan, I shall call this view the "Orthodox View." [3]

Things are, of course, totally different, both morally and legally, in the context of the relations between individuals under criminal law and accepted rules of self-defense. To kill in self-defense, one is required to verify that the perceived attacker poses a clear and imminent danger to one's vital interests and that the attacker bears responsibility for this danger. And of course with respect to punishment, it can be imposed only after establishing beyond reasonable doubt that the accused committed the alleged crime with the required *mens rea*.

It is truly puzzling that most people who endorse the strongest restrictions on killing in self-defense and the most stringent procedures and application of criminal law, often including an objection to capital punishment, subscribe to the Orthodox View with regard to the morality and legality of killing in the context of war. What is puzzling is that not only do they accept this view, but they do so with almost no reservation and with no awareness of the tension that exists between the blanket license to kill (enemy soldiers) in war and the strict limitations on killing in a nonwar context. This seems another instance of the human ability to compartmentalize, a capacity that is probably advantageous from an evolutionary point of view, but still startling whenever we face it. I am referring to the cognitive ability to

---

[3] Jeff McMahan, "Innocence, Self-Defense, and Killing in War," *Journal of Political Philosophy* 2, no. 3 (September 1994): 193–221.

allocate different judgments to the different "compartments" within which we function: home, work, politics, and so forth. Thus, people generally fail to notice the moral problem with many instances of killings in war even when they are fierce objectors to the death penalty, because they view the situation of war as different from the nonwar context. They see war as constituting a separate sphere with its own set of rules, which are, after all, almost universally accepted. Jurists are especially vulnerable to this kind of thinking, because since international law recognizes the legitimacy of large-scale killing in war (of soldiers), it fosters the line of thought that wars are simply different than regular conflicts between individuals and are governed by different rules.

Let me leave the psychology of these conflicting attitudes to others and focus instead on the relevant normative issues. The contention that war *qua* war is simply "different" and, hence, governed by a different set of rules is merely a sophisticated (albeit more moderate) version of the realist view, according to which *Inter arma silent leges* (In time of war the laws are silent). We need to understand why this is so, how it is that human life, held so sacred in domestic law, is held in such light regard by the laws of war. Killing in war can be justified only on the basis of the same fundamental principles that guide relations between individuals outside the sphere of war. If these principles fail to provide the justification for killing in war, then the Orthodox View can be maintained only at the cost of inconsistency and with the aid of psychological mechanisms such as compartmentalization and self-deception.

Discussing the tenability of the Orthodox View is far beyond the scope of the present paper. It is, however, crucial to note that most philosophers who have addressed this topic over the last two decades have taken for granted what may be called the unity of our moral and legal thought—that is, that the same general justifications for killing people in nonwar situations must apply to war situations as well. This assumption has led some philosophers to call into question the validity of the Orthodox View and to suggest that some modifications are, in any event, warranted. I will offer two examples of such modifications, one relating to *jus ad bellum*, the other to *jus in bello*.

The first example is in the context of the previously mentioned Falkland Islands War. The common view holds that the Argentinean invasion of the Falkland Islands was a *casus belli*; hence the U.K. was morally and legally justified in going to war. Yet, according to Richard Norman, the war was unjustified as it was waged for the sake of formal sovereignty alone.[4] Just as in the case of individual self-defense, the mere formal violation of rights (for example, property rights) is not sufficient to justify killing another human being. Violation of territorial sovereignty can justify going to war only if it threatens substantive values such as life, dignity, or the survival of a culture and, of course, when there is no other way of protecting such values. Thus, the common view regarding the conditions that justify going to war tends to be overly lax.

The second example is the stance taken by Jeff McMahan. Arguing against the Orthodox View, he defends what he calls the "Moral View," under which a combatant's moral innocence or guilt is determined, in part, by whether or not he is fighting in a just war. If his war is unjust and if he is not forced to take part in it, he cannot claim a moral right to kill enemy soldiers on the basis of self-defense.[5] This conclusion, which makes a lot of moral sense, runs counter to a widespread convention of *jus in bello*, namely, that all combatants are "morally equal."

These two examples illustrate what happens to the ethics of war once one takes seriously the requirement to square the moral rules concerning war with those regulating relations in nonwar situations. If the moral rationale for going to war is self-defense, then the same conditions that govern self-defense on the individual level must do so at the level of nations too, in particular: (1) the rule that what is defended is either one's life or something close to it in value and (2) the rule that the attacker's responsibility is highly relevant in making him the object of killing in self-defense.

With this brief introduction in mind, we can now move to wars against terror.[6] Let me start by asking, What entitles the U.S. to define its campaign against Al Qaeda as war, with the loosening of various moral prohibitions implied by such a definition, rather than as a police enforcement action aimed at bringing a group of criminals to justice? The answer here—as with conventional war—lies in: (a) the gravity of the threat posed by Al Qaeda and (b) the impracticality of coping with this threat by conventional law-enforcing institutions and

---

[4] Richard Norman, *Ethics, Killing and War* (New York: Cambridge University Press, 1995), 156–58.

[5] McMahan, "Innocence, Self-Defense, and Killing," 172–73.

[6] I say "wars against terror" rather than "the war against terror" because I see no reason to regard the various actual or potential wars against terror as part of one big war against one defined enemy.

methods. The threat posed by Al Qaeda to the U.S. is enormous. It is not only a threat to the lives of thousands of people, Americans and others, but also the threat of the terrorizing results of such mass killing on the entire country in terms of the economy and the quality of day-to-day life. A war of terror does not mean that all citizens are under actual attack all the time, but that such attacks are frequent enough and devastating enough to make life unbearable. As Hobbes observed, being in a state of war does not mean that there are battles all the time, but, rather, a miserable condition in which "there is no place for industry; because the fruit thereof is uncertain: and consequently no culture of the earth; no navigation, nor use of the commodities that might be imported by sea . . . no account of time; no arts; no letters; no society; and which is worst of all, continual fear, and danger of violent death; and the life of man, solitary, poor, nasty, brutish, and short."[7]

Clearly enough, condition (1) applies *a fortiori* to the situation to which Israel is subject in what the Palestinians call the *Alaqsa Intifada,* whose main characteristic is almost daily attempts at murdering Jews across Israel, in buses, restaurants, nightclubs, universities, wherever possible. If ever there could be a *casus belli* on grounds of self-defense, it is such a terror campaign launched against a country or some other collective. From a moral point of view, the values under threat in such cases are far more important than those involved in cases of a mere formal violation of sovereignty, which, under the common view, justify waging war. To make the point as clear as possible, if the United Kingdom was morally justified in waging war to regain control over the Falkland Islands when there was no threat to the lives of British citizens and no significant threat to their security or economy, then surely the U.S. is morally justified in going to war against bin Laden to prevent another attack against it, an attack that could cause the loss of many innocent lives and have catastrophic effects on the life of the nation. And if the U.S. is justified in going to war after only one (awful) day of terror, Israel certainly has the right to do so after so many dark days of terror.

The second condition mentioned above for regarding a situation as war rather than as a law-enforcement operation—namely, the impracticality of coping with the threat by means of conventional law-

---

[7] Thomas Hobbes, *Leviathan*, ed. J. C. A. Gaskin (New York: Oxford University Press, 1998), pt. 1, chap. 13, p. 84. (Originally published in 1651).

enforcing institutions and methods—is met in the case of the U.S. campaign against Al Qaeda as well as in the case of the Israeli struggle with the Palestinian terror organizations. The proposition that Al Qaeda members could be prevented from carrying out further terror attacks by issuing an arrest order to the governments harboring them, is, at best, naïve, and the same is true with regard to the thousands of Palestinians involved in planning and executing murderous actions in Israel. Things might have been different had the Palestinian Authority and its police cooperated with Israel in capturing the criminals and bringing them to justice. But this, of course, is pure wishful thinking. The Palestinian Authority not only refrained from arresting terrorists and, in general, from taking action against terror; it actually supported it in various ways.[8]

If we are to accept that the struggle against Al Qaeda and, likewise, that against the Palestinian armed organizations can be described as war, it follows that just as the U.S. can use lethal means to kill Al Qaeda members, so too can Israel do so to kill Hamas or Tanzim members—just like in conventional war. Yet, while in conventional wars, enemy combatants are identified by their uniform and are located in camps, bases, and bunkers separate from the civilian population, in wars of terror, the fighters hide amongst the civilian population, which shelters them and supports them by various means. Hence, the latter wars do not take the conventional form of soldiers from one side of the conflict fighting directly against soldiers from the other side in an open space—in trenches, in the air, or at sea, remote from civilian life. Indeed, they take a rather different form. If we are to continue to adhere to the fundamental idea of just war theory, namely, that wars are fought between combatants only and should avoid targeting noncombatants, we must conclude that in wars against terror, too, the combatants of the terrorized country may direct their weapons only at members and activists in the terror organizations against which they are fighting.

To complete the analogy between conventional wars and wars against terror, we can assume that just as all soldiers (but only soldiers) are legitimate targets in the former, regardless of their individual roles, the threat they pose as individuals, or their personal responsibility in the waging or conducting of the war, so in the latter

---

[8] For the deep involvement of the Palestinian Authority in terror, see, e.g., Ronen Bergman, *Authority Given* (Yedioth Aharonot Books, 2002). (In Hebrew.)

all members of the relevant terror organizations are legitimate targets and can be killed by the terrorized side on the basis of the latter's right to self-defense. Moreover, members of terrorist organizations bear far greater moral responsibility for their actions than soldiers in conventional wars, because many of the latter are conscripts forced to participate in the war, whereas joining a terror organization is usually a more voluntary act.

The problem, of course, is that terrorists do not come out into the open to fight against the armed forces of the other side, but, rather, hide among the civilian population and use the homes of families and friends as bases in planning and executing their attacks. But the fact that civilians are the shield behind which terrorists hide should not be grounds for granting the latter some sort of immunity from attack. If they use their homes as terror bases, they cannot claim that these bases must be regarded as innocent civilian buildings. If soldiers in a conventional war hide in a residential building and shoot through its windows at enemy soldiers, there is no dispute that the latter are justified in using snipers to target and kill the former. Thus, if in a war against terror, terrorists establish their base in a residential area from which they launch murderous attacks (dispatching suicide terrorists or firing artillery), the other side is justified in using snipers, helicopters, and other methods to target and kill the terrorists.

Targeted killing, then, emerges as the most natural manifestation of *jus in bello* in wars on terror, for under *jus in bello*, even if a war is unjust, it should be directed (to as great an extent as possible) only at combatants. This implies that wars against terror should be directed (to as great an extent as possible) only at terrorists. However, unlike enemy soldiers in conventional wars, terrorists are embedded in civilian populations and can be hit only (or mainly) in their homes, cars, and so forth. Thus, targeted killing is the most natural application of the principles of *jus in bello* in wars against terror.[9]

---

[9] Some critics totally deny the fundamental distinction made by "just war theory" and international law between combatants and noncombatants and, hence, see nothing wrong in principle with acts of terrorism. A notorious example is Ted Honderich, who explicitly states that "the Palestinians have exercised a moral right in their terrorism against the Israelis . . . those who have killed themselves in the cause of their people have indeed sanctified themselves." *After the Terror* (Edinburgh: Edinburgh University Press, 2002), 151. Obviously, if indiscriminate killing of children is a legitimate means of achieving political aims, then targeting killing is even more so. Hence, we cannot morally object to targeted killing on the grounds that it constitutes an illegitimate means *of warfare*. Views such as Honderich's thus *reduce* the arguments available to opponents of targeted killing.

The moral legitimacy of targeted killing becomes even clearer when compared to the alternative means of fighting terror—that is, the massive invasion of the community that shelters and supports the terrorists in an attempt to catch or kill the terrorists and destroy their infrastructure. This mode of operation was adopted, for example, by the U.S. and Britain in Afghanistan and by Israel in its "Operation Defensive Shield" carried out after the terrorist Passover massacre in March 2002. While many claim this method to be morally preferable to targeted killing—probably because it bears more of a resemblance to "real" war—I believe the opposite to be true. First, invading a civilian area inevitably leads to the deaths and injury of far more people, mostly innocent people, than does careful use of targeted killing. Second, such actions bring death, misery, and destruction to people who are only minimally involved (if at all) in, or responsible for, terror or military attacks, whereas with targeted killing, collateral damage is significantly reduced (though not prevented altogether). Hence, targeted killing is the preferable method not only because, on a utilitarian calculation, it saves lives—a very weighty moral consideration—but also because it is more commensurate with a fundamental condition of justified self-defense, namely, that those killed are responsible for the threat posed. Members of Hamas in Gaza are far more responsible for the threat of terror to Israel than their nonactivist neighbors are; hence it is preferable from a moral standpoint to target the former directly rather than invade Gaza and inevitably cause great injury to the latter and to the general population.

Let me press this last point a bit further. Suppose that the Palestinian Authority were to formally declare war on Israel by all means available. Suppose further that in the wake of this declaration, Israel were to face a wave of terror identical to that it faced in the months preceding Operation Defensive Shield. Surely no one would question Israel's right to wage war in return, that is, to invade the Gaza Strip and the West Bank and fight against its enemy, though such an operation would claim the lives of many people bearing no, or only minimal, responsibility for the terror wreaked on Israel. How could such an operation be considered morally justified, yet the measure of killing fewer people and only those more active in and responsible for the terror (namely, targeted killing) be less justified or even unjustified?

To conclude, it is my claim that there is a profound inconsistency in, on the one hand, accepting the legitimacy of killing in conventional war but, on the other, making a moral objection to targeted killing in wars against terror. If, as Georg Nolte emphasizes, "the right to life must be protected most strictly,"[10] it is, indeed, understandable that he would have qualms with regard to the killing of terrorist leaders or activists. However, it is then puzzling how he can accept large-scale killing in a war of human beings, that is, soldiers (e.g., in Afghanistan[11]), whose personal responsibility for the waging of the war and whose direct threat to the other side are, at best, uncertain.

II. Targeted Killing and Retribution

In a recent article on targeted killing, Steven David argues that the best moral justification for Israel's policy of targeted killing is retribution.[12] The argument is a simple and straightforward one: Those people targeted committed terrible crimes. Evildoers deserve to suffer in response and in a way suited to their crimes. Palestinian terrorists with blood on their hands therefore deserve death, the ultimate punishment for their crimes. Hence, the targeted killing of these terrorists is justified.

One could object to this argument by claiming that acts of retribution can be imposed only by a court of justice, within whose authority it is to punish and only after establishing the relevant facts of the case and the blameworthiness of the defendant. Retribution cannot be imposed by private individuals, nor by governments, but only by legal institutions.

But this objection must be wrong. First, for those who accept the idea of retribution,[13] the legal institution of punishment is the best means of achieving it, but not a necessary condition for its possibility. For retribution to apply, evildoers need to suffer, and this can be

---

[10] Georg Nolte, "Preventive Use of Force and Preventive Killings: Moves into a Different Legal Order," *Theoretical Inquiries in Law* 5, no. 1 (2004).

[11] See Nolte, "Preventative Use of Force," 9–10. Nolte concedes that "Taliban and Al Qaida fighters could be killed by U.S. and other troops in Afghanistan as long as the United States was exercising its right of self-defence against organized and identified resistance in Afghanistan." Yet that this was a case of exercising the right of self-defense is exactly what needs to be established, and in any case, it does not imply that each individual Taliban fighter was a legitimate target.

[12] Steven R. David, "Fatal Choices: Israel's Policy of Targeted Killing," *Ethics & International Affairs* 17, no. 1 (Spring 2003): 1–25.

[13] Needless to say, not everybody does. See, e.g., David Dolinko, "Three Mistakes of Retributivism," *UCLA Law Review* 39 (1992): 1623–57.

imposed by God, by nature—or by some human being. No doubt there are powerful social and moral reasons for making the courts the only body that administers retribution in society, but these reasons bear no relevance to the justification of retribution per se, which, in principle, can be achieved outside the courtroom too. In the case of terrorists, the problem that arises is that retribution through the legal system is not an option with regard to most of them, because the countries that harbor them hardly ever bring them to trial within their territories, nor do they extradite them to be tried in a foreign domestic or international court. Since in such cases, retribution through the legal system is unfeasible, and if we take seriously the idea that evildoers deserve punishment, the inevitable conclusion is that retribution can, or must,[14] be imposed by some other entity, such as the army of the injured country.

Second, the role of courts in establishing the facts of the matter and the blameworthiness of the alleged criminal seems less significant in the context of terrorists because many of them are only too happy to admit their participation in the relevant crimes or their active membership and roles in the relevant organizations.

In conventional wars, when the enemy upholds the conventions of war, retribution is irrelevant with regard to individual soldiers, and hence self-defense provides the only framework for justifying killing them. In wars against terror, retribution offers a justificatory framework that complements and bolsters the self-defense justification. Thus, killing enemy combatants in wars on terror—namely, activists in the terror organizations—is, if anything, more, and not less, justified than killing enemy combatants in conventional wars.

In the next section, I discuss a philosophical argument against targeted killing developed by Michael Gross.[15] After showing that it is unconvincing, I return, in section IV, to questions of effectiveness.

---

[14] I wish to take a neutral stance between the "hard" and "soft" views of retributivism. Under the former view, we have a moral duty to impose upon evildoers what they deserve, while under the latter, we are merely allowed to do so. For the purpose of the present argument, the weaker version is sufficient, because my central aim is to show that targeted killing is morally acceptable, not that it is morally mandatory.

[15] Michael Gross, "Fighting by Other Means in the Mideast: A Critical Analysis of Israel's Assassination Policy," *Political Studies* 51, no. 2 (June 2003): 350–68; Michael Gross, "Assassination: Killing in the Shadow of Self-Defense," in *War and Virtual War: The Challenges to Communities*, ed. J. Irwin (Amsterdam: Rodopi, 2004).

III. The Argument against "Named Killing"

According to Michael Gross, the blanket license to kill soldiers in conventional war, even though they might be innocent both materially and morally, is deeply puzzling. The only way to justify this (albeit vaguely) is by considering soldiers on both sides not as individuals, but as agents of their respective polities. Judged as individuals, most soldiers would be morally exempt from being killed by the enemy, but judged as agents of a collective, they would lose this immunity and become (morally) legitimate targets. For this reason, anonymity is so imperative to justifying killing enemy soldiers in war: the license to kill soldiers from the other side rests precisely on the fact that their personal merits or demerits are ignored, that they are seen merely as the enemy. The problem with targeted killing is that it does not meet this condition, thereby undermining *the very justification for killing in war*. This violation of the anonymity condition in targeted killing is termed by Gross "named killing."

This is an original argument against targeted killing, albeit, in my opinion, an unsuccessful one, in two aspects.[16] To begin with, the argument sets out with a very permissive moral premise (i.e., that all soldiers can [morally] be killed in war, regardless of their individual innocence or blameworthiness) and ends with a very restrictive conclusion (i.e., that even soldiers who are definitely not innocent [either morally or materially] are illegitimate targets for killing). This move seems odd, if not paradoxical. The source of the problem lies in the collectivist solution to the problem of killing in war. If the ordinary notion of self-defense fails to provide justification for most killings in war, then the conclusion must be that these killings are morally unjustified and, hence, war in general is morally unjustified. It is of no help to *choose* to relate to the people killed in war as agents of a collective rather than as individuals, as their moral dignity is not contingent on how anybody arbitrarily chooses to relate to them.

My second point concerns Gross's proposition that regarding soldiers merely as agents of their polities requires a veiling of their individual identities, a veil supposedly lifted by named killing. Yet, targeting perpetrators of terror is not killing them by *name*, but by *role*. To kill by name is to kill somebody simply because he is who he is, regardless of any contingent features he possesses or actions he

---

[16] For a wider criticism of Gross's position, see my "The Morality of Assassination: A Reply to Gross," *Political Studies* 51 (2003): 775–79.

has committed. This type of killing is, indeed, deeply problematic from a moral point of view. But targeting soldiers in war is not of this kind. It is connected to the special role the targets play in the war or, more precisely, to the special threat they pose to the other side. In other words, even if soldiers are only agents of some collective, some agents might be more important than others in carrying out the policy or ideology of that collective. Targeting such agents rather than others expresses no "personal" grievance against them, but is simply recognition of their special excellence in executing their role as agents.

What emerges from these two points of criticism is a view that is opposite to that propounded by Gross, one that must be credited to Richard Norman.[17] Under Norman's view, what is wrong with killing human beings is the failure to respect them as individuals, "and the killing even of combatants in war is most often a depersonalized killing which reduces individual human beings to the status of 'the enemy.'"[18] In line with this view, it seems to me that far from being "morally abhorrent," as Gross seems to believe, targeted killing expresses the appropriate respect for human life during wartime. With targeted killings, human beings are killed not simply because they are "the enemy," but because they bear special responsibility or play a special role in the enemy's aggression. This is particularly true in wars against terrorism, where those targeted are usually personally responsible for atrocities committed against the lives of innocent civilians.

IV. The Effectiveness Argument against Targeted Killing

A further argument against targeted killing in war is that even if the killing is role-based and not name-based, it can be said to violate a fundamental condition of *jus in bello*, namely, that of effectiveness. Killing in self-defense is justified only if—among other conditions— it achieves its primary objective, which is defense. If the killing increases the threat and danger to the side carrying it out, it is unjustified from both a moral and pragmatic perspective. Many argue that this is precisely the problem with targeted killing. Its cost is too high, it is argued, as it is usually followed by waves of terrorist attacks and it tends to escalate the conflict; moreover, in general, targeted killing

---

[17] Norman, *Ethics, Killing and War.*
[18] Norman, *Ethics, Killing and War,* 188.

does not succeed in deterring potential terrorists who, in any event, are willing to sacrifice their lives for what they regard as a sacred cause.

Note that this argument is not necessarily founded on strictly utilitarian premises. From a utilitarian point of view, we can conceive of a situation in which killing in self-defense decreases the overall utility rather than increases it, for example, when one has to kill five culpable attackers in order to save one's life. The justification for killing in self-defense rests on notions such as responsibility, blame, desert, and rights, not on the notion of utility. But, nonetheless, the justification for acts carried out in self-defense is contingent, among other things, on the effectiveness of those acts. If A wants to prevent B from doing X to her but shooting B will not accomplish that goal, then shooting B cannot be justified on grounds of self-defense. In other words, effectiveness is a constraint on the right to self-defense in general and on the right to use targeted killing for self-defense in particular. Does targeted killing meet this condition? Let me make the following comments in response.

First, in the war against terror, just as in the war against the mafia, what counts are the long-term results, not the immediate ones. In the short run, acts of revenge might follow the killing of terrorists, but in the long run, there is good reason to believe that such killings will weaken the terror organizations, generate demoralization among their members, force them to restrict their movements, and so on. The personal charisma and professional skills of the leaders and key figures of certain organizations are crucial to the success of their organizations, something that is especially true with regard to terror organizations that operate underground with no clear institutional structure. It is reasonable to assume that killing such individuals will gradually make it more difficult for the terror machinery to function.[19]

Second, there is some room for skepticism about the assessments regarding the ineffectiveness of targeted killing when one compares them with similar assessments made vis-à-vis the use of other measures, which have proved to be false or, at least, questionable. I refer to the general claim made repeatedly that terror cannot be fought by military means and, more particularly, to the widespread view that a massive military operation in the West Bank would fail to reduce terror directed against Israeli civilians. Yet, the fact is that Operation

---

[19] My view on this point concurs with that taken by Steven David, "Fatal Choices."

Defensive Shield significantly weakened the ability of the Palestinian terror organizations to carry out murderous attacks. Though the war against Palestinian terror is far from over and though dozens of Israelis have been murdered since the invasion of the Palestinian cities in the operation, the situation is much better at the time this article goes to press than it was in March 2002, when Israel was facing two to three terrorist attacks a day, resulting in the deaths of more than a hundred Israelis in one month. In retrospect, it seems that many of the predictions about the ineffectiveness of the measures taken against terror during that time were premature.

Third, while I do not deny the importance of effectiveness as a justificatory condition for self-defense, I think that wars against terror should not be subject to a much stricter application of this condition than conventional wars. In the latter, there is only a general requirement that there be "a reasonable hope of success,"[20] with no need to establish the effectiveness of every military action taken during wartime, even though such actions bring about the deaths of hundreds, even thousands, of human beings. In retrospect, it is sometimes possible to determine that some actions were of little or no effect, while others were essential for victory, yet rarely will we hear condemnation of these ineffective actions on moral grounds. If, as claimed above, wars against terror follow the same moral logic as that of conventional wars, one cannot require that the effectiveness of every action carried out in the former be established beyond any reasonable doubt for it to be granted moral license.

Unfortunately, recent history provides us with examples of conventional wars with dubious effectiveness that have, nonetheless, been accepted as legitimate, even after the fact. Georg Nolte, for example, who strongly objects to the method of targeted killing, seems to think that the American-British war in (or against) Afghanistan was morally justified.[21] But to judge by the murderous actions of Al Qaeda that took place after that war, especially in Bali and Mombassa, Al Qaeda is still alive and kicking and still poses an enormous threat to the free world. Accepting the legitimacy of the Afghanistan war in spite of its very limited effectiveness (if any) in destroying the Al Qaeda organization is not consistent with endorsement of a strict condition of effectiveness regarding each instance of targeted killing.

---

[20] See, e.g., Norman, *Ethics, Killing and War*, 118.
[21] Nolte, "Preventive Use of Force," at section 6.3.1.

If my argument up to this point has been successful, targeted killing is a legitimate method in the fight against terror. Yet curiously, while some accept this conclusion with respect to the struggle against Al Qaeda, they reject it with respect to the Israeli struggle against Hamas and Islamic Jihad. Such a distinction was made by the *Washington Post* after the American targeted killing of an Al Qaeda activist in Yemen, arguing that what makes the Al Qaeda case unique is that the organization lacks affiliation to any national cause, has no leaders to speak of, and does not seek any political compromise or accommodation.[22] I will address briefly each of these considerations.

First, the nature of the cause prompting the acts of the aggressive group or "affiliated" therewith is, in itself, morally irrelevant, just as it is irrelevant in individual cases of self-defense. The cause might be national, as in the case of the Tanzim organization, religious, as in the case of Al Qaeda, national and religious, as in the case of Hamas, or of some other nature altogether, such as social justice. Similarly in individual self-defense, the threat might originate in greed, sexual desire, racial hatred, or a host of other problematic motivations. What is relevant for questions of self-defense is not the cause of the aggression but its gravity and immediacy, as well as the responsibility of the aggressor. In these respects, no real difference exists between Al Qaeda and Hamas.

Second, that Al Qaeda has no apparent leaders also bears no moral significance in and of itself. The relevant issue is not whether the leaders are military or political, but whether or not they can be persuaded to stop terror by diplomatic, nonviolent methods. Which brings us to the third issue, namely, the claim that Al Qaeda, allegedly unlike Hamas, does not seek compromise or accommodation. The issue of compromise and accommodation is always tricky in the context of self-defense, because most aggressors would be only too happy to compromise with their victims rather than use violence to achieve their goals. The robber would gladly relinquish part of his loot if he could be spared the need to use his gun, and the sexual attacker would usually refrain from using violence against his victim if she were to agree to voluntary sexual relations. Similarly, aggressive countries certainly would be happy to compromise on some part of their demands, say, ten percent of the disputed territory, if they could get the remaining ninety percent without opposition. I would expect that even bin Laden would be willing to enter into some kind

---

[22] "A Strike in Yemen," editorial, *Washington Post*, November 6, 2002, A20.

of dialogue with the U.S. if the U.S. were to stop all support for Israel and to take measures to reduce American presence and influence in Muslim countries, for example. Hamas would also undoubtedly be willing to make some compromises if Israel were to withdraw to the pre-1967 borders, grant a right of return to all Palestinian refugees, and agree to forego the Jewish nature of the State of Israel.

In all these cases, the question is not whether the aggressor's demands could be accommodated without the use of force, but whether such accommodation would be morally acceptable—and the answer seems to be in the negative. Yielding to Hamas in order to prevent their murderous attacks is no more acceptable than yielding to bin Laden. Hence in both cases, the victims of the aggression have the right to kill their aggressors in self-defense.

V. Targeted Killing in Conventional Wars

The argument developed thus far, especially my critical discussion of Gross, seems to lead to the conclusion that targeted killing is morally acceptable not only in wars against terror but also in conventional wars. This conclusion might seem hard to swallow, as targeted killing, or assassination, as it is referred to in the latter context, is often considered illegitimate.[23] Some clarification is in order regarding the possible uses of the notion of targeted killing in conventional wars.

Let us begin with the example of attacks aimed at killing or injuring particular individuals, such as an enemy chief of staff or the commander of a brigade, by targeting their offices or their (military) vehicles. Gross might object to such attacks as prohibited cases of named killing, but I doubt whether many scholars or jurists would join him in this view. Attacks on enemy headquarters are very common in all wars, and if the senior officers are known to be present, such actions are even more welcome. Indeed, once the argument from named killing is rejected, it is hard to reject such targeting of military leaders, carried out by jets, artillery, or special task forces.

But let us now consider a slightly different case, where the enemy chief of staff is not targeted while riding in his armored car or while sitting in his headquarters, but while on a vacation with his family. A sniper manages to get close enough to the hotel they are staying at

---

[23] As Gross points out, American military regulations often ban assassination *as a measure*, by its very nature conceived of as an act of treachery or perfidy. See the references he mentions in "Assassination."

and shoots the chief of staff, or a soldier dressed as a waiter poisons him while he is eating dinner. Is such killing morally acceptable? While we do feel some initial revulsion toward it (especially if it is *our* chief of staff who has been targeted), it is not easy to explain why killing an enemy officer in a hotel would not be morally legitimate, but killing him on the way to his office or in his office would be. The problem is that it is morally justified for Q to kill P in self-defense only because P poses a serious threat to Q that cannot be neutralized in any other way. But if this is the case, why should P's location be relevant to the question of whether or not he can justifiably be killed? It would be relevant if self-defense were allowed only in cases of a direct and imminent threat. But in war, much broader, blanket license to kill the enemy is granted: soldiers and officers can be killed while asleep, while doing office work, or while out on maneuvers. There is most decidedly no requirement to refrain from shooting at enemy soldiers until ascertaining that they are about to strike and hence must be stopped. With respect to high-ranking officers, this point is even clearer, as they can rarely be said to pose any immediate danger. If a chief of staff is targeted while in his office, the justification for this killing will rest not on the need to prevent any immediate danger emanating from him, but, rather, with the aim of weakening the enemy. But if so, then—to return to our original question—why would it be legitimate to kill him at his office, but not at his home or in a hotel on a family vacation?

From a moral standpoint, the distinction does, indeed, appear shaky. A change in one's location (from office to home or from headquarters to a hotel) cannot provide moral immunity from attack to a person who might otherwise be killed in self-defense, assuming—I emphasize again—that the permission to kill him does not rest on his posing an immediate threat. This, however, does not mean that the distinction is of no moral significance. Many rules of war are no more than mere conventions that contribute to reducing the killing, the harm, and the destruction of war. Such conventions help to confine wars to bearable limits and to prevent them from deteriorating into total chaos. In this vein, a rule against targeting officers or soldiers at home or on vacation can be seen as a convention aimed at the reduction of pain and death and at enabling the civilian population to conduct more or less normal lives without fear of bullets and bombs in residential areas (even if directed at soldiers only).

Needless to say, like all conventions, the moral force of this convention is contingent on its being followed by all sides. Hence if one side violates the convention, the other is no longer committed to adhering to it. In this regard, rules based on a convention differ from rules founded on strict moral grounds, which are obligatory regardless of what the other side does. Since the killing of children is subject to such a strict moral prohibition, it is forbidden even if the enemy takes such a horrendous course of action. But killing officers in their homes (during war) is not, in itself, morally worse than killing them in their headquarters; therefore, if one of the sides violates this convention, it loses its moral force.

This discussion of targeted killing in conventional wars helps to reinforce the conclusions reached earlier about targeted killing in wars against terror. My claim was that from a moral perspective, terrorists cannot claim immunity to being targeted. To this one might respond by claiming that even if a prohibition against targeted killing is not intrinsically valid, it might still be a useful convention and, as such, ought to be followed. Conventions, however, require mutuality; otherwise the side adhering to them would simply be yielding to the side that refuses to follow them. Since groups like Al Qaeda, the Tanzim, and Hamas have no regard whatsoever for the conventions of war, the party fighting against them is released from these conventions too, though not from strict moral rules of conduct.

Summary and Conclusions

The purpose of this paper is to provide a philosophical defense of targeted killing in wars against terror. It argues that if one accepts the moral legitimacy of the large-scale killing of combatants in conventional wars, one cannot object on moral grounds to the targeted killing of members of terrorist organizations in wars against terror. If one rejects this legitimacy, one must object to all killing in war, targeted and nontargeted alike, and thus not support the view, which is criticized here, that targeted killing is particularly disturbing from a moral point of view.

Defining a conflict as war, with the moral license to kill entailed thereby, is not an arbitrary decision. It has to do with the gravity of the threat to the vital interests of a given community and the absence of any other option for this community to defend itself against this threat. Under this understanding, certain conventional wars, such as the Falkland Islands War, do not justify the above license to kill, whereas certain unconventional wars, such as that waged against Al Qaeda, do. Moreover, the perception of a conflict as war and the legitimacy of using lethal measures in that conflict do not depend on the nature of the aggressor's motivation, be it national, religious, or otherwise, unless that motivation happens to affect the severity of the threat or the availability of nonwar methods for coping with it.

Regarding the effectiveness of targeted killing in wars against terror, here, too, we can draw an analogy to conventional wars. Fighting armies do their best to choose effective measures, that is, measures that will contribute to the defeat of their enemy. But very rarely will they be criticized, prospectively or retrospectively, on the grounds that ineffective actions caused the unnecessary deaths of enemy soldiers. Applied to targeted killing, this means that its effectiveness should concern us morally no more than the effectiveness of methods used or actions taken in conventional wars. At any rate, in most cases and in the long run, there is no convincing evidence that targeted killing is an ineffective means in fighting terror.

Finally, objectors to targeted killing (and to other antiterrorism methods) often warn of overestimating the danger posed by terror and of hastening to use violent solutions instead of seeking a peacefully diplomatic solution. They urge the attacked country or collective to "understand" the roots of terror, implying that once these roots are understood and dealt with in a peaceful and constructive manner, the terror will vanish with no need for war. There is something to be said for these warnings. Yet, just as there is a danger of overestimating threats of terror, there is also a danger of underestimating them. Just as there is a danger of overlooking possible peaceful solutions and rushing to use force, there is also a danger of over-delaying the use of force due to false hopes for peaceful avenues. The atrocities in the former Yugoslavia in the 1990s provide us with a painful reminder of the toll in innocent lives that hesitation to use force to counter aggression can take.[24] The argument developed in this paper contends that with organizations such as Al Qaeda and Hamas, the danger of over-delaying the use of force is more alarming than the prospect of missing out on peaceful solutions. Those who hold the opposite view and are more optimistic about human nature than I am are, of course, to be respected. But—one last time—I think their view applies, a fortiori, to conventional wars too.

---

[24] See, for example, Jonathon Glover, *Humanity: A Moral History of the Twentieth Century* (New Haven, CT: Yale University Press, 2001), 133–40, who argues that "the UN would have been more effective from the start if it had come closer to wielding Leviathan's power."

Terrorists: Enemy Combatants or Criminals?

| 11 |

Legitimate Combatancy, POW Status, and Terrorism

MICHAEL W. BROUGH

Before the war on terrorism, wars seemed simpler, at least in one respect: we could tell the combatants from the noncombatants. Of course, this historical appearance is only a product of short memory, for history bulges with examples of obscure combatancy. At one time, warriors made no such distinction, and, when a particular nation became the enemy, its *people* became the enemy as well (even when instantiated as the aged, the infirm, or the infant). As the just war tradition developed, thinkers sharpened the combatant-noncombatant distinction and eventually accorded special rights to the combatant, including the right of potential POW status. When states warred with other states, most questions about potential POW status were relatively unproblematic.[1] Now that September 11, 2001, has symbolically, if not actually, catapulted the world into an age of terrorism, the category of potential POW requires careful reexamination in light of new complexity.

The views expressed in this article are those of the author and do not reflect the official policy or position of the United States Military Academy, the Department of the Army, the Department of Defense, or the U.S. government.

[1] Which is not to say that there were not questions: There was debate over the status of Otto Skorzeny's Nazi commandos, the black pajama-clad Viet Cong in the U.S. action in Vietnam, and U2 pilot Gary Powers. Still, who deserved POW status typically seemed an unnecessary question since most situations manifested moral clarity. Whether individual soldiers or their states discerned this, or tried to, is completely another question. Unfortunately, examples of those who denied POW status to those who unambiguously deserved it are plentiful.

The situations are confusing, the responses confused. Some examples: On January 31, 2003, "shoe bomber" Richard Reid, who sought to detonate explosives on a commercial transatlantic jet, was sentenced to three life terms in prison. During the trial, he characterized his struggle as a war against the United States. District Judge William G. Young vitiated Reid: "You are not an enemy combatant. You are a terrorist. You are not a soldier in any war. You are a terrorist . . . to call you a soldier gives you far too much stature."[2] American treatment of "dirty bomb" suspect Jose Padilla has been bewilderingly different. FBI agents seized Padilla for planning to detonate a radioactive bomb in the U.S., and he was spirited to a military confinement facility in South Carolina. According to the *New York Times*, Justice Department officials "justified his detention by saying he is considered to be an *enemy* combatant."[3]

The depth of moral quandary is manifested in the words we use to discuss the issues. The Bush administration has famously labeled enemy soldiers captured in recent combat operations "detainees" or "unlawful combatants," though it has gradually both relaxed its standards for granting POW[4] status and admitted that the treatment of non-POW detainees would probably be identical to that of POWs. Proclaiming a "war on terrorism" further clouds the issues of this struggle, for war connotes a violent struggle between parties—a struggle wherein soldiers can kill with moral legitimacy and judicial impunity. A state of war implies that combatants are on equal moral footing, even though their governments and leaders might not be. But it is not clear whether the U.S. is at war in the literal sense.[5] If this is merely war in metaphor (as in American wars on poverty, illiteracy, and drugs), then war rhetoric turns largely flat, and a more precise term for the conflict against terrorists might more appropriately be "police action."

---

[2] "Reid at Sentencing: 'I am at War with Your Country,'" *Los Angeles Times*, January 31, 2003, A20.

[3] David Johnston, "F.B.I. Talked of Following Bomb Suspect Before Arrest," *New York Times*, June 13, 2002, A32 (emphasis mine).

[4] I will use the term prisoner of war (abbreviated POW) because this is the term used by the Geneva Convention (III) Relative to the Treatment of Prisoners of War; August 12, 1949. The term is synonymous with the term EPW (Enemy Prisoner of War).

[5] Although others have also made the point, Marc O. Hedahl's paper ("Stop Calling It the War on Terrorism: An Argument for Moral Clarity," Joint Services Conference on Professional Ethics, Springfield, VA, January 30, 2003) has been very helpful to me in demonstrating the deleterious exercise of language in the "war on terrorism."

In this paper, I will explore a limited portion of the confusion, seeking to develop a concept of legitimate fighting organization that will aid us in assaying groups that inflict violence for political reasons. The question of an organization's legitimate combatancy[6] is an important one, for moral culpability of its members rests on the issue, as does the *post bellum* treatment of the captured: whether to punish, rehabilitate, or repatriate individual fighters depends a great deal on the legitimate combatancy of their fighting organizations. I hope to, in the end, deliver a concept of legitimate fighting organization that takes into account both the just war tradition and pragmatic concerns—a concept that will help to answer the question of which fighters, in a time of terrorism, should qualify for POW status when captured, and which should better be regarded as criminals.

Assumptions

At the outset, I will reveal three key assumptions that serve as a foundation for my argument. While disavowal of these might very well result in rejecting my theory, I think these are widely granted premises that support much of modern just war theory. First, I will assume a rights-based foundation for the war convention. This does not mean, of course, that other concerns are never considered; cogent arguments have been made for utilitarianism[7] and natural law[8] as substantive bases for it. Still, it seems that rights talk has colored most recent just war thought,[9] and it has been convincingly argued, too, that the war convention generally accords with a theory of rights better

---

[6] I have decided upon the term *legitimate combatancy* to distinguish my meaning from another, *lawful* (or, more commonly since U.S. actions in Afghanistan, *unlawful*) *combatancy*. In the past year, *unlawful combatant* has suffered as a term that has been forced to do more than its share of heavy lifting in the endeavor to clarify issues, yet has been supplied with little (with respect to definition) to sustain it.

[7] See, e.g., R. B. Brandt, "Utilitarianism and the Rules of War," *Philosophy and Public Affairs* 1, no. 2 (winter 1975): 145–65; and N. Fotion and G. Elfstrom, *Military Ethics: Guidelines for Peace and War* (Boston: Routledge & Kegan Paul, 1986).

[8] See, e.g., James Turner Johnson, "Natural Law as a Language for the Ethics of War," in *Just War Tradition and the Restraint of War* (Princeton, NJ: Princeton University Press, 1981), 85–118.

[9] Most notably Michael Walzer's seminal *Just and Unjust Wars*, 3rd ed. (New York: Basic Books, 2000).

than any other ethical theory.[10] That is, it seems that there is good reason to use it, and it seems, too, that it is already what we do in fact
use.

Second, I will assume a *jus ad bellum/jus in bello* distinction that
considers the two areas logically separate. The result, for my purposes, is the moral equality of soldiers. The *jus ad bellum* wrongness
of a combatant's cause does not permeate his moral status: his country's aggression does not taint his personal morality, and he bears no
guilt for it. My third assumption stems from the second: that the rules
we (as moral investigators) decide on are ones that we will embrace
in all instances and on all occasions. Like the rules of a game, the
rules of war are useful only when the players obey them. As in a
game, adherence to the laws of war will sometimes be clearly deleterious to the actor's cause. We should frame our discussion with this
principle in mind: that accepting a rule signals our willingness to
apply the rule both to ourselves and to the enemy, both when it is
advantageous to us and when it is not.[11]

There are arguments to be made against these assumptions. Some
have already been made. I do not attempt here to refute such arguments, but instead say that if the reader finds these three assumptions
convincing, perhaps he will find force in my argument.

The Codified War Convention Today

War ethics prefers a binary approach to combatancy: either one is a
combatant, or one is not. Although there are instances when one may
cross over between the two realms, there is no interstice, and there are
good practical as well as moral reasons for continuing the delineation.[12] The question of whether a fighter is a potential POW is, to

---

[10] See Anthony Hartle, "Humanitarianism and the Laws of War," *Philosophy* 61
(January 1986): 109–15.

[11] We should be wary of making too much of the game resemblance, but this point
seems right. Arthur C. Danto is correct when he says the war-game analogy "is dangerous but instructive." "On Moral Codes and Modern War," in *War, Morality, and
the Military Profession*, ed. Malham M. Wakin (Boulder, CO: Westview Press, 1979),
479–80.

[12] Notice that the endeavor here will not be to discover which individual combatants are lawful (and therefore deserving of potential POW status), but to discover
which groups of combatants are lawful, thus earning potential POW status for their
constituents.

large extent, intertwined with the matter of legitimate combatancy, so to explore one is to explore both.

Current war convention relevant to POWs is largely recorded in the Geneva Convention III Relative to the Treatment of Prisoners of War (August 12, 1949). According to that document, fighters can become POWs when they become *hors de combat* through surrender, sickness, or injury. The Detaining Power must respect and protect POWs, and the Geneva Convention (GC) commits Detaining Powers to furnishing sufficient medical care, hygiene, food and water, wages, and opportunities for recreation. The GC ostensibly seeks to separate POWs from their combatancy—to exclude them from the fight in a humane manner, regardless of their causes—and to recognize their rights as humans. The GC allows a Detaining Power to punish POWs only for actions that are punishable for the Power's own soldiers, as well. Since no state would punish its soldiers for killing its enemies, POWs are legally immune from the legitimate killing of enemy soldiers they performed in the course of armed combat. It is this immunity, even in imprisonment, that poet Lincoln Kirstein seems to describe in these lines:

> In scarecrow coat, in bandage soiled,
> > Crusty with bearded grime,
> To well-washed warders claim to be
> > Confederates in crime,
> Whom crime abandoned on the spot
> > Once having used their knives,
> Then freed them to captivity
> > Whereby they saved their lives.[13]

Even in light of the difficulties POWs will encounter, the benefits of POW status are significant. This immunity the GC grants POWs contrasts starkly with the alternative. Captured combatants who are not POWs are devoid of GC protection, and they are at the mercy of the Detaining Power. The Detaining Power may agree to treat the captives as if they were POWs (as President Bush declared he would do for Afghan detainees), but they are not bound by international agreement to do so, and a Detaining Power may instead

---

[13] Lincoln Kirstein, "P.O.W.," in *The Poems of Lincoln Kirstein* (New York: Anthenum, 1987), 244.

prosecute the captives for their crimes. But which fighters are potential POWs? Article 4, in particular, concerns who is included in the
set:

A. Prisoners of war, in the sense of the present Convention, are persons
    belonging to one of the following categories, who have fallen into the
    power of the enemy:

    (1) Members of the armed forces of a Party to the conflict, as well
        as members of militias or volunteer corps forming part of such
        armed forces.
    (2) Members of other militias and members of other volunteer corps,
        including those of organized resistance movements, belonging to
        a Party to the conflict and operating in or outside their own terri-
        tory, even if this territory is occupied, provided that such militias
        or volunteer corps, including such organized resistance move-
        ments, fulfill the following conditions: (a) that of being com-
        manded by a person responsible for his subordinates; (b) that of
        having a fixed distinctive sign recognizable at a distance; (c) that
        of carrying arms openly; (d) that of conducting their operations
        in accordance with the laws and customs of war.
    (3) Members of regular armed forces who profess allegiance to a
        government or an authority not recognized by the Detaining
        Power.[14]

These first three categories are the ones that will be most germane
to my discussion. The others (not quoted) deal with accompanying
civilians, civilian crews of air and watercraft, and participants in a
levée en masse.

It is worth noting that the Convention is binding only when the
belligerents are parties to it or when the belligerents accept its terms.
The Geneva Convention does not appear to bind a belligerent nation
when it is engaged in conflict with a nation (or other collection of
individuals) that is not a party to the Convention and rejects its provisions. Regardless, there is a feeling that we as combatants are
bound not just by what our opponents do, so that if they break the
rules, we can, too. If there is really a moral truth about the matter,
then it seems we should make significant efforts and bear some costs
to do right, even when the enemy refuses to.

---

[14] Geneva Convention III Relative to the Treatment of Prisoners of War, August 12,
1949, The Avalon Project at Yale Law School, http://www.yale.edu/lawweb/avalon/
lawofwar/geneva03.htm.

There are two intuitions at work here. The first recognizes the importance of a morality that takes as its foundation more than the conduct of surrounding actors (such that my prohibition against murder remains in place only as long as no one attempts to murder me). There are at least some moral rules that bind regardless of how one (individual or state) is treated: the proscription of torture is a good example, and proscriptions against the cruel and unusual punishment of criminals (even the perpetrators of hideous crimes) reflect the intuition.

The second emphasizes individual rights. Even though a combatant fights for an authority that refuses the war convention and its *jus in bello* rules, he is not personally responsible for that refusal, and since he, typically, has had little say in the deliberate decision making, it is misleading to say that the refusal is his. Guilt only adheres when he is guilty of personal infractions of the war convention. To abrogate the Geneva Convention for these enemy soldiers, solely because their political authority rejects the war convention and prior to establishing the personal culpability of each, is to punish the potentially innocent.

The war convention seeks to stem unnecessary violence (or at least to protect human rights in the midst of widespread violence), and it governs more than simply declared war between the regular forces of recognized nations. Certainly, the war convention pertains in undeclared international conflict (as in Vietnam and Korea) and in some intranational conflicts, as well. But all aspects of the war convention may not apply in all cases of conflict, and POW status may remain dormant in some instances of interpersonal or international violence. There are those who perpetrate violence who ought not to be insulated from repercussions by POW status, and I think examining those categories of combatants may be helpful in determining the limits of POW status. Common intuitions deny POW status to some combatants, and these commonly agreed upon categories will clarify our ideas about legitimate combatancy.

In considering the problem of legitimate combatancy for violent organizations, I will seek to propose three conditions a belligerent fighting group must meet in order to deserve potential POW status. All bona fide members of the group should, I think, be considered potential POWs prima facie, even though subsequent investigation may discover war crimes that make trial and punishment justified. The three conditions, which I will consider in turn, are military command structure, observance of the war convention, and representativeness.

Military Command Structure

Martin van Creveld offers two responsibilities of command in his seminal *Command in War*. The first is logistical; more to our point, the second concerns enabling "the army to carry out its proper mission, which is to inflict the maximum amount of death and destruction on the enemy within the shortest possible period of time and at minimum loss to itself."[15]

As many other military ethicists would, I disagree with van Creveld about what the army's "proper mission" is—generally speaking, it is not inflicting death and destruction, although that may be the means required to attain the end. I instead prefer a definition that emphasizes the end of a better peace, and neither death nor destruction is its necessary component. In fact, the just peace achieved without violence is to be desired over the just peace won through battle. The victorious military is, to my mind, not just the one that emerges triumphant in war; even more, it is the military that through its capabilities dissuades potential aggressors. With that in mind, van Creveld is quite right when he notes that military command "enables the army to carry out its *proper* mission"—command should facilitate operations that are proper within the scope of war. Concomitant with this responsibility to enable, however, is the responsibility to disable the army from carrying out improper missions—those that are violations of *jus in bello*, for example. This is, in large part, the moral responsibility of command.

I argue, then, that an organization comprised of legitimate combatants must have at least the rudiments of a military command structure. The reasons for this are several. One practical one is that commanders in a military command structure can ensure (imperfectly, but with some acceptable amount of success) the cessation of hostilities during periods of truce or armistice. Loosely affiliated groups without commanders will typically lack such an ability. If a group does not possess the ability to control the violence it propagates well enough to cease fighting when its leader has agreed to stand down, then it lacks a requisite aspect of legitimate combatancy.

The same principle determines a fighting organization's commitment to fighting according to the war convention; without commanders that enforce the rules of war, the frenzy of battle can overcome

---

[15] Martin van Creveld, *Command in War* (Cambridge, MA: Harvard University Press, 1985), 6.

soldiers, resulting in war crimes. In order to guarantee the rights of both combatants and noncombatants in their proximity, military units require the strong discipline that can result from a military command structure. A unit devoid of command structure will remain unable to secure others' rights, and to exercise violence without such an assurance is a moral wrong: it is to invite its members to be criminals, and the organization is akin to a band of brigands rather than a military unit.

The military command structure also lends itself (or at least may lend itself) to a transition to diplomacy. At the halt of armed conflict, the commander can order his unit to defer to political leaders. The commander, then, leads his unit in standing down under the leadership of the diplomat (who might well be the commander himself: examples abound, from George Washington to Fidel Castro to Laurent Kabila). The key point here is that the military struggle has, as its end, a superior peace. A centralized military control allows a fighting force to narrowly attain that goal, or abort it with restraint.

Although the existence of a military command structure does concern the size of a force (there can be no command structure in a single actor, for example), I will postpone the subject of how large a military force must be in order for its members to qualify as legitimate combatants. The issue is a significant one, though, for my criterion of representativeness, and I will discuss it there.

Observance of the War Convention

Groups of legitimate combatants fight fundamentally in accordance with the *jus in bello* confines of the war convention. My purpose in this criterion is to determine whether a fighting group commits itself to fighting war both fairly (that is, mindful of legal restrictions with respect to its competitors) and humanely (with respect to the human lives, both combatant and noncombatant, it will risk). The criterion is vague, perhaps necessarily so. There are wartime actions that are morally ambiguous (how can a commander *prove* that the doctrine of double effect justifies the deaths of *these* civilians?), and we should enter into such discourse with moral humility—perhaps the answers to some questions simply are unknowable for finite minds. But there are also wartime actions that possess unequaled moral clarity, and fighting groups that adopt the violation of human rights as standard procedure deserve moral condemnation. They also surrender their legitimate combatancy—that seems appropriate for fighting organizations that, for example, target noncombatants as a matter of course. At the outset, I would like to consider some reasons to be reluctant about attaching the legitimate combatancy of a group to the group's conformity with the war convention—to be sure, the path is heavily mined.

First, ascertaining a military's commitment to the war convention might be incredibly difficult for many reasons. In the absence of a strong senior commander, different subordinate commanders could demonstrate widely divergent degrees of commitment to the war convention. Whether the violations of the one subordinate unit impinge on the legitimate combatancy of the other I am not prepared to say, although I would think it odd to deny POW status to the latter solely because of the former's infractions.

Too, there seem to be degrees of infraction. I refer not to the number of incidents, although that may be an obfuscating factor as well. We cannot limit legitimate combatancy to morally perfect militaries. I question whether we would find one, yet that should not disqualify all military units from the practice of legitimate war. Many fighting organizations committed to the war convention have suffered from the tragedies that can result from a morally misguided subordinate leader; that fact should not disqualify them from legitimate combatancy, as subordinate groups may remain morally untainted. A more perplexing question might be whether some infractions are worse than others: does a fighting organization lose its legitimate combatancy when it stockpiles biological weapons? When it uses them on enemy troops? Or when it uses them on the enemy's civilian population? Each of these actions constitutes an unambiguous violation of the war convention,[16] and so they are equal in a simple infraction/non-infraction dichotomy. There is, of course, more to say about the

---

[16] In the Biological and Toxin Weapons Convention of 1972, "Each State Party to this Convention undertakes never in any circumstances to develop, produce, stockpile or otherwise acquire or retain: (1) Microbial or other biological agents, or toxins whatever their origin or method of production, of types and in quantities that have no justification for prophylactic, protective or other peaceful purposes; (2) Weapons, equipment or means of delivery designed to use such agents or toxins for hostile purposes or in armed conflict" (Convention on the Prohibition of the Development, Production and Stockpiling of Bacteriological [Biological] and Toxin Weapons and on Their Destruction, April 10, 1972; available from the Avalon Project at Yale Law School, http://www.yale.edu/lawweb/avalon/un/bact.htm). We find the prohibition on using such weapons against troops in both the 1899 Hague Convention's Declaration on the Use of Projectiles the Object of Which is the Diffusion of Asphyxiating or Deleterious Gases, July 29, 1899; available from the Avalon Project at Yale

infractions, and it would seem a strange moral judgment that the use of such weapons was not more morally repugnant than the mere possession. This intuition indicates the need for careful consideration in more closely delineating this criterion.

More troubling, though, is that an insistence on war convention observance threatens to undermine the *jus ad bellum/jus in bello* distinction just war theory holds as basic. Allowing legitimate combatancy to hinge on a military's (or, by extension, the state's) attitude to such issues may involve conflating the two separate aspects. The Serbian army, under Slobodan Milosovic, supplies an example: the state military's policy of ethnic cleansing might have constituted both a *jus ad bellum* reason for humanitarian intervention and a *jus in bello* reason for disallowing potential POW status for Serbian soldiers because of the same Serb policy of ethnic cleansing. In this circumstance, then, one could cogently argue that the Serb soldiers (even the morally upright who were not complicit in ethnic cleansing) would not be insulated from the injustice of their cause by POW status.

Although the criterion presents risks, I think it can be useful. I intend for the criterion to exclude those who target noncombatants as matter of course, for example, from potential POW status. Organizations of this kind do not argue publicly for their inclusion in the realm of legitimate combatants, but they quite often place their struggles in the realm of war. Take, for example, the Hamas Covenant of 1988, in which the group casts its endeavor as a "struggle against the Jews": "The [Islamic Resistance] Movement is but one squadron that should be supported by more and more squadrons from this vast Arab and Islamic world, until the enemy is vanquished and Allah's victory is realised."[17] Osama bin Laden has used similar war talk, and so have other terrorists, including the Aum Shinrikyo cult in Japan and American white supremacist groups such as Christian Identity.[18] Despite seeming assertions to the contrary, actors of this kind (as

---

Law School, http://www.yale.edu/lawweb/avalon/lawofwar/dec99-02.htm; and the Geneva Convention's Protocol for the Prohibition of the Use in War of Asphyxiating Gas, and of Bacteriological Methods of Warfare, 8 February, 1928; available from the Avalon Project at Yale Law School, http://www.yale.edu/lawweb/avalon/lawofwar/geneva01.htm.

[17] The Covenant of the Islamic Resistance Movement, Introduction, 1988; available from the Avalon Project at Yale Law School, http://www.yale.edu/lawweb/avalon/mideast/hamas.htm.

[18] See Mark Juergensmeyer's "Cosmic War," in *Terror in the Mind of God: the Global Rise of Religious Violence* (Berkeley: University of California Press, 2000), chap. 8.

individuals or in groups) are not legitimate combatants, and the reason is not their lack of state sponsorship (I shall cover that momentarily) or their small size. The reason, I think, is rooted in their rejection of the war convention (and specifically in their practice of targeting noncombatants).

To what extent an organization's infraction disqualifies it for legitimate combatancy remains, as I have already admitted, a live question. Shannon French, for example, has developed a theory that takes target, not tactics, as its single criterion.[19] To adopt her idea for my purposes, a combatant organization uses violent force legitimately if and only if it targets only combatants. If this single criterion is met, then it takes on for itself the mantle of legitimate combatancy; if it is not (i.e., if it targets noncombatants), then the organization loses legitimate combatancy, and with it, potential POW status. French's concept allows an organization to retain legitimate combatancy even while violating other *jus in bello* strictures.

While French's concept is helpful, I think it does not go far enough. It is true that organizations that target noncombatants are not organizations of legitimate combatants—in their disregard for the combatant-noncombatant distinction, they place themselves outside the category of groups that have special dispensation to kill, and they are properly regarded as murderers rather than warriors. There are things, however, that organizations can do, apart from targeting noncombatants, that should exclude them from legitimate combatancy, as well. Perhaps the use of biological agents in warfare is a good example. A militant group might intend to narrowly target a military objective with a biological agent, and it might launch the attack in a way that does, in fact, direct the agent exclusively against the military target. Despite the legitimacy of both intent and execution, the attack is illegitimate because it endangers the surrounding noncombatants. The indiscriminate nature of biological weapons has led the international community to ban their use in war. Narrowly targeting a military objective does little to corral the effects of the attack, which might be devastating to many surrounding noncombatants. In this instance, at least, failure to attend to the war convention invalidates the group's legitimate combatancy.

---

[19] Shannon E. French, "Murderers, Not Warriors: The Moral Distinction Between Terrorists and Legitimate Fighters in Assymetric Conflicts," Joint Services Conference on Professional Ethics, Springfield, VA, January 30, 2003.

Although I intend to limn some criteria narrowly applicable to nonstate actors, I wonder whether this condition should be applied to state soldiers, as well. It seems odd to me that state sponsorship should afford POW status to an army that adopts *jus in bello* infractions as a way of doing business. An insurrection that meticulously avoids noncombatant deaths seems much more worthy of potential POW status than does a state army that encourages or orders the rape or torture of civilians as a means of keeping discipline among the populace. Such a question is beyond the scope of this paper, but it is one of crucial importance.

Representativeness

To begin a discussion of my third criterion, I will consider a class that might seem easily dismissible from the category of legitimate combatant: those who conduct violence individually for personal gain—those who harm or threaten harm for money, power, or similar end: bank robbers, serial killers, petty thieves, extortionists. These people violate important rights, and they are unambiguously criminals, and (regardless of what we determine the proper treatment of criminals to be) they are undeserving of POW status. They have committed crimes, and they have no reason to expect immunity from the consequences. Larger groups with similar motives and tactics fall into a similar category, for the mere accumulation of members does not grant the groups special rights that the individuals lacked. The moral distinctness with which we regard such groups manifests itself in our condemnation of criminal gangs and organized crime. That we do not extend to them POW rights when they are captured by state law enforcement agents indicates our unwillingness to call them legitimate combatants. In fact, even when rival gangs attack each other, we view the deaths on both sides not as legitimate wartime killing, but as murder, even when innocents are protected from the violence.

What places these criminals outside the realm of potential POWs? One possible answer is self-interest: perhaps acting singly or as a group for one's own direct personal benefit disqualifies him from potential POW status. This does seem to conform to some held beliefs—drafted soldiers very often do not choose war and they do not fight for their own benefit, and so deserve POW status as sympathetic "'poor sods, just like me,' trapped in a war they didn't make."[20] Sidney Axinn makes a similar distinction between criminals and soldiers involved in legitimate military action: "Robbers act for their own personal goals; the military acts for the goals of someone or something else."[21] This point does not get the distinction quite right, though. Robbers do usually act for personal benefit, but personal benefit is not a necessary component of robbery. And while we think that the criminal might be exculpated if his fillip is utterly devoid of self-interest (e.g., Robin Hood), we do not always exculpate him. The Oklahoma City bombing was such an ideologically motivated (and in that way, selfless) attack, yet I think few would have granted Timothy McVeigh the immunity from his actions that POW status confers.

McVeigh does not qualify for potential POW status primarily due to his nonconformity with the war convention, but a second reason he does not qualify is that he is not representative of a viable political grouping of people.[22] The representativeness of a fighting organization is essential to its members' legitimacy as combatants: it identifies the fighters as wartime proxies for the populace for which they fight. The war rights they take on—the dispensation the war convention accords—rely on the status of the fighters as surrogates. Because this is not the soldiers' war (at least not in its entirety, and oftentimes not at all), the war convention separates them from the legal ramifications of killing. When the soldiers do not act as representatives of (at least some body of) the people, however, they lose their moral immunity from the killing they do in war.

This is a step forward from the oversimple delineation limned by A. J. Barker: "A soldier, serving in the army of a country which is recognized as being at war with his captors' nation, who is taken prisoner in the course of a military operation is a clear case of a person entitled to POW status . . . [i]rregular combatants, fighting on their own initiative, are outside the shelter of the Geneva Convention's umbrella. And if they are caught they are likely to be dubbed war criminals and shot."[23] Although he recognizes the middle ground that limited war, Cold War, and low-intensity conflict reflect, Barker does

---

[20] Walzer, *Just and Unjust Wars*, 36.

[21] Sidney Axinn, *A Moral Military* (Philadelphia: Temple University Press, 1989), 88.

[22] I admit here the inadequacy of the word *viable*—the term requires expansion, but I think must at a minimum include a capacity and willingness of the people for self-determination and self-police.

[23] A. J. Barker, *Prisoners of War* (New York: Universe Books, 1975), 20.

not underscore (as I think he should) the soldiers' representativeness of their people. He disallows (or paints the GC as disallowing) legitimate fighters outside formal government control. It does seem, after all, that all legitimate fighters deserve the same war rights; if Barker seeks to strip irregulars of theirs, he must base his position on the illegitimacy of their status, for there seems to be nothing else on which to base it. History has, it seems, given examples of justified uprising (if we reject Mao Zedong's, perhaps we will consider George Washington's as appropriate), and if some would deny this, they should at least admit that justified uprising is more than merely logically conceivable.

The representativeness that I think is important involves more than simply representing something or someone other than oneself. The military group must directly represent a (segment of) people who exhibit a measure of geographical contiguity. Definitional precision for the term is elusive, but the general idea is straightforward: the people must be bound not only by ideology, but also by an attachment to the land. If the fighters are to claim status as legitimate combatants, those they represent must have a claim to land; perhaps they live there, or perhaps they have an alleged legal or moral right to it. Such a move is, I think, intuitive. War entails the occurrence of invasion into enemy territory, even in revolution. War threatens a government's hold on land. A warring party seeks to occupy and control a land—to impose a rule over the group of people who live within its borders. A military organization that seeks a similar goal on behalf of a people that is connected by territory is one whose members are legitimate combatants and prima facie deserving of POW status when captured.

The territory-connectedness requirement disqualifies at least some potential combatants from POW status. Those nonstate fighters whose impetus is purely ideological fall outside the boundaries if they are not affiliated with the people in an identified geographical region. Some have predicted the withering away of the state and a concomitant rise of the international organization as the next power structure. If the future is a virtual one wherein the strongest interpersonal bonds are neither familial nor proximal, such collectives might very well be the the tie between fighters—international criminal groups might well be harbingers of a new era of (illegitimate) combatant in which battles over resources are fought by belligerent parties that are linked by ideology or common interest rather than a national identity that correlates strongly with geographical continuity. But that world is not yet the one in which we live.

The Import in an Age of Terrorism

What is terrorism? The term has assumed prominence in the past fifty years, but it lacks specificity. The definition of the Northern Ireland [Emergency Provisions] Act 1973, and Part [IV] Miscellaneous and General might suffice: "Terrorism means the use of violence for political ends and includes any use of violence for the purpose of putting the public or any section of the public in fear." But this would seem to invalidate all war, since all war includes necessarily the use of violence for political ends (i.e., the terms "nonviolent war" and "nonpolitical war" are both oxymoronic[24]). Carl von Clausewitz's famous definition provides the relevant counterpoint: "War is not merely an act of policy but a true political instrument, a continuation of political intercourse, carried on with other means. What remains peculiar to war is simply the peculiar nature of its means."[25] If some wars are just—if some groups of fighters inflict violence legitimately—then the Irish provisions are inadequate.

Still, some definitions are better than others. It is not as if, to corrupt a Hobbesian line, one calleth terrorism what another calleth national liberation, although many current thinkers have accepted the improbability of agreeing on a common use for the term.[26] I offer my three criteria as a help to determine legitimate combatancy and establish potential POW status. There are, I admit, points to elaborate and questions to answer, and I would like to suggest one possible objection to my criteria before I conclude.

The Geneva Convention specifies that members of nonstate military organizations must brandish "a fixed distinctive sign recognizable at a distance,"[27] and some lawyers have even affirmed these criteria for legitimate combatants who operate under the aegis of a state.[28] In contrast, my criteria for legitimate combatancy make

---

[24] This is not to say, of course, that there is no such thing as nonviolent struggle. Gandhi's struggle would easily prove that point wrong. To speak of a nonviolent war, however, is to use *war* in its metaphorical, rather than literal, sense.

[25] Carl von Clausewitz, *On War*, ed. and trans. Michael Howard and Peter Paret (New York: Alfred A. Knopf, 1993), 99.

[26] The point is well made in Grant Wardlaw, *Political Terrorism* (New York: Cambridge University Press, 1989), 3–17. See also Sami G. Hajjar, *Hizballah: Terrorism, National Liberation, or Menace?* (Carlisle Barracks, PA: Strategic Studies Institute, 2002), 28–29.

[27] Geneva Convention III, art. 4.

[28] See, for example, David B. Rivkin, Jr., "Treatment of Al Qaeda and Taliban Detainees Under International Law," National Press Club, Washington, D.C., February 27, 2002;

no mention of the appearance of the individuals. Although distinguishing garb is preferable to ambiguous dress on the battlefield, I do not think the reasons are compelling enough to warrant the addition of a separate criterion to my list of three. I think some of our intuitions about historical asymmetrical combat will justify uneasiness with making a distinctive uniform another criterion for legitimate combatancy.

An illustrated history of American uniforms describes the clothing of American rifleman, who was "just as distinctive as the frontier from which he came. . . . Like the ranger of the Old French War before him, he was ever the irregular, hard to manage . . . but deadly when properly employed." His uniform? A linen or deerskin hunting shirt—a "familiar frontier garment,"[29] but hardly a uniform that distinguished him from mere noncombatant hunters. Another example: the recent U.S.-led war in Afghanistan included variously accoutered soldiers of different factions. Troops of the Taliban govern ment were indiscernible from troops of the Northern Alliance, or from the American Special Forces soldiers offering assistance to the latter. If we would extend legitimate combatancy and POW rights to the Revolutionary rifleman or to *any* of those soldiers in Afghanistan, then (in accordance with the *jus in bello/jus ad bellum* distinction), we should consider extending them to other irregulars who, while in civilian clothes, fulfill the three conditions I have offered.

Michael Walzer's correction to the GC gets significantly closer to the right answer for the use of civilian clothes as combat garments. According to him, the key issue is "the use of civilian clothing as a ruse and a disguise,"[30] so that when plainclothes are not deliberately chosen as moral camouflage, the combatant is not turned illegitimate by the wearing. If the American rifleman did not use his frontier clothing in this way, it is not clear that the U.S.'s recent allies or opponents in Afghanistan have used their civilian clothes as a moral camouflage, either. This, of course, does not proclaim all nonuniformed opponents potential POWs, but it does admit that their lack of uniforms does not by itself rid them of legitimate combatancy. Despite my truncated treatment here, I believe Walzer's approach

---

available at the Federalist Society for Law and Public Policy Studies Website, http://www.fed-soc.org/Publications/Transcripts/Belligerents1. PDF.

[29] Frederick P. Todd, *Soldiers of the American Army: 1775–1954* (Chicago: Henry Regnery Company, 1954), plate 2.

[30] Walzer, *Just and Unjust Wars*, 183.

will be useful in another, more complete exploration of the military uniform's moral role in war.

In the end, we must understand that the word *terrorist* as a label is (often) deleterious to a clear understanding of modern conflict. Victim nations routinely identify perpetrator organizations as terrorist without regard to consistency within the moral world of conflict. My aspiration is to further the project to clarify the terms of discourse: when the groups fight in accordance with my criteria, they fight as legitimate organizations, and their members are, by that fact, legitimate combatants. When they fight in accordance with *jus in bello* rules, they do so with moral impunity. They should do so with legal impunity, as well, claiming status as POWs and not criminals when they are captured in the course of conflict.

Nothing New Under the Sun at Guantanamo Bay: Precedent and Prisoners of War

PAULINE KAURIN

Introduction

In early 2002 the Bush administration announced that Taliban and Al Qaeda detainees at Guantanamo Bay, Cuba were not to be regarded as prisoners of war and, therefore, were not able to claim protections under international law—notably the Geneva Conventions relating to treatment of prisoners of war. In subsequent months, there was a great deal of controversy surrounding this decision, both at home and abroad. While much of the debate has centered on what the international statutes (in particular the Geneva Convention and other rules of war) actually say and under what circumstances they apply, I will focus on the aspect of law largely ignored in this debate: precedent. This paper will show that precedent (in relation to treatment of prisoners in times of armed conflict) in American history raises serious questions with the Bush administration position since, even in cases where there was no international statute or the statute was unclear, it has been the practice of the United States to accord prisoner of war status to such detainees. Examples from the American Revolutionary War, the Civil War, and the Vietnam conflict will demonstrate cases where the United States was not required by statute or international custom to accord prisoner of war status, but accorded it anyway. These examples will also support the argument that precedent ought to be considered in the case of the detainees at Guantanamo Bay. Furthermore, if this precedent is to be rejected, a clear and unequivocal rationale must be given as to why such a long tradition of according prisoner of war status no longer applies, what the new precedent will be, and why.

I. The Bush Administration's Case

To start, it will be helpful to outline the problem of the detainees at Guantanamo Bay, discuss the Bush administration policy on these detainees, and briefly examine the aspects of international law most relevant to the issue. Who are these prisoners? As of April 2002, there were between 400 and 600 detainees associated with either the Taliban or Al Qaeda forces who were captured in the course of hostilities resulting from the September 11, 2001, attack on United States targets.[1] Photographs showed the detainees kneeling, manacled, and with various head coverings to shield all or part of their faces from view, ostensibly necessary for security reasons. These photographs and what they showed raised immediate concerns about whether the U.S. government was treating the detainees in accordance with international humanitarian conventions and standards (not to mention the laws of war) among human rights groups in the United States and abroad.

In response to these criticisms, the Bush administration asserted that the detainees were "enemy combatants," not prisoners of war (POW), and that accordingly, the Geneva Conventions did not apply. At the same time, they did go to a considerable effort to publicly demonstrate that the detainees were being treated in a similar fashion (with a few exceptions) to how POWs would be treated. However, the *treatment* was only part of the issue; another equally pressing issue was the legal status of such detainees, which would affect their future access to counsel and their rights: to be tried in a certain manner, not to be tortured, and to be released at the end of the hostilities. What exactly was their status under Article 4 of the Third Geneva Convention (1949)? Where was the support for the administration assertion that the above conventions did not apply to these detainees?

According to the U.S. Army Operational Law Handbook, U.S. Armed Forces "will comply with the [Law of War] regardless of how the conflict is characterized. Judge Advocates, therefore, should advise commanders that, regardless of the nature of the conflict, all enemy personnel should initially be accorded the protections of the Third Geneva Convention, at least until their status be determined."[2] When doubt exists about the status of combatants, then POW/Article

---

[1] Sean D. Murphy, "Decision Not to Regard Persons Detained in Afghanistan as POWs," *American Journal of International Law* 96, no. 2 (April 2002): 475.

[2] Murphy, "Decision," 476.

5 Tribunals must be established to make the determination of status, as was done during the Vietnam conflict.

What exactly is required for an "enemy combatant" to be considered a POW? According to Article 4, the combatants must belong to one of the following categories (of a party to a conflict):

A. Members of armed forces, militias, or volunteer corps forming part of such armed forces
B. Members of other groups who meet all of the following criteria:

   1. are commanded by a person responsible for subordinates
   2. wear a fixed, distinctive sign recognizable at a distance
   3. carry arms openly
   4. obey the laws and customs of war

C. Regular armed forces who profess allegiance to a government or authority not recognized by the detaining power[3]

What was the rationale for the Bush administration to reject the POW status of the detainees without convening Article 5 tribunals? Their initial position was as follows: (1) international law does not apply to members of a nonstate organization; (2) the conflict was not an internal one (such that Al Qaeda might be a protected group under category C above); (3) Al Qaeda members failed to meet four criteria for protection listed in B above; and (4) Afghanistan was not a functioning state, and therefore the Taliban was not recognized as the legitimate government (despite being recognized by the United Nations and some nations as such).[4] In a statement on Feb 7, 2002, the Bush administration suggested that while members of the Taliban might meet the Article 4 criteria *in principle*, Al Qaeda did not and, further, "that the Taliban's actions in violating the laws of war and closely associating itself with Al-Qaeda had the effect of stripping Taliban members of their rights to POW status."[5] The administration went on to insist that while the detainees were not entitled to POW status, they would be given many (though not all) of the same privileges as a matter of policy, but not certain legal protections. (They would not have a canteen, pay, personal financial accounts, and access to scientific equipment, musical instruments, or sports outfits.)

---

[3] Murphy, "Decision," 476.
[4] Murphy, "Decision," 477.
[5] Murphy, "Decision," 477–78.

Beyond these pronouncements, it was unclear what customary legal protections the detainees *would* have under other international law or other conventions (assuming that Article 4 protections did not apply). What is the rationale for not extending certain customary legal protections to these detainees? The administration emphasized again that the Taliban failed to meet all four of the criteria in Article 4 (see B above) by virtue of their association with Al Qaeda. According to the administration, both were guilty of "promoting barbaric philosophies," did not adhere to the Geneva Conventions, and should not be entitled to either those protections or an Article 5 tribunal hearing to determine if those protections were warranted.[6] The determination had already been made; it was obvious, the administration alleged, that these detainees were not entitled to such protections.

What are we to make of these claims? If we look only at the technical letter of the statute (what Article 4 of the Third Geneva Convention actually says), we could cede that the Bush administration has a point. On *their* interpretation of the statute (which was by no means uncontroversial), the United States may not be *required* to accord POW status to such detainees, although one might argue that a tribunal ought to be convened to make that determination rather than the administration making what appeared to be an ad hoc decision. Despite the considerable debate about what the statute says and under what circumstances tribunals ought to be convened, for the sake of argument let us grant that the administration is right on the *letter of the statute*. However, any first-year law student knows that there is much more to law than what the letter of the statute says; law also includes precedent and how judges have interpreted and applied that statute. The controversy to date has been largely concerned with Article 4 as a statute and what it says or with that other international statutes might say, but what about *precedent*? What about how the United States has considered similar cases of enemy combatants in the past?

II. Legal Precedent and Its Application

To get at legal precedent and the role it might play in the case of the detainees at Guantanamo Bay, consider an objection the Bush administration might raise against the consideration of precedent: this war on terror is a totally new, "unprecedented" situation with no analogies in

---

[6] Murphy, "Decision," 479–80.

history or law and therefore, there are either (1) no prior situations or experiences that we might look to for guidance or (2) any that exist do not have enough parallels to apply effectively. In either case, they might argue, looking to precedent is impossible and/or impractical in dealing with this situation. Such an objection is useful since it reveals several misconceptions about legal precedent and its uses. First, this objection assumes that there are certain situations that are entirely new and without relevant parallels to what has come before. Second, it assumes that for precedent to work there must be a very clear (nearly perfect) parallel and that in the absence of such a parallel, one is justified in ignoring prior precedent and/or making new rules. Third, it assumes that precedent is fairly rigid and inflexible and cannot be made to be adapted to a slightly different, but analogous situation.

To address these misconceptions, we need to look at what precedent is and how it works in the law. Precedent is not about acquiring certainty or applying some kind of objective formula that will give one the right (and same) answer each time. Rather we ought to think of it in the same way as our own life experiences: they might give us a guide to follow in many situations, but the tricky part is trying to decide which past experiences are relevant guides when confronting what seems to be a new situation.[7]

Imagine that I go to a party for which the host and hostess have chosen a North African theme. Here is a social situation that seems entirely novel and "unprecedented": when I arrive my host greets me wearing unfamiliar attire and in an unfamiliar language; the décor of the house consists not of couches and tables and chairs, but of draperies, low tables, and cushions on the floor; the drinks that I am offered are unfamiliar and served in unfamiliar vessels; when time comes for dinner, we gather around low tables, the food is piled onto several common dishes, and there are no utensils or individual plates anywhere in sight. What do I do? After I get over the shock of it all, I would likely consider how I have handled other social situations that have been unfamiliar (even if they have not been *this* unfamiliar). So I think about the time I went to another theme party where there was unusual food and décor. What did I do? In that situation, let us say that I watched the other guests and my hostess for cues and followed their lead. Is there any good reason that following such a precedent

---

[7] For this discussion of precedent, I am drawing on C. Gordon Post's discussion in *"Stare Decisis*: The Use of Precedent" in *Readings in the Philosophy of Law*, 2nd ed., ed. John Arthur and William Shaw (Englewood Cliffs, NJ: Prentice Hall, 1993), 19ff.

seems not to be indicated here (e.g., the strategy utterly failed and the host kicked me out of the party and never invited me to another)? If not, I am likely to follow that precedent unless I can think of another case that seems more analogous and would be more helpful in navigating this "new" situation.

Similarly, legal or judicial precedent is a decision or procedure that serves as a guide in the determination of future, analogous cases; it is sometimes referred to as *stare decisis* ("let the decision stand") and has been a central element in the development of common law. Why has this idea been so important? The use of precedent has been a force for stability, rationality, and internal coherence in the law—if one can generally count on courts to look at past decisions as a basis for future decisions, this generates a certain kind of predictability in the law, which one might see as important in providing a coherent system and in influencing the actions of persons who must live by that law. On this view of precedent (where the predictability and rationality of the law are primary considerations), judges and others look for the closest analogous decision or case and then apply that decision to the new case in a straightforward manner.

However, such a strict view of precedent has its own problems.[8] What if the original decision was a flawed one? What if social norms, ethical standards, or public sensibilities have changed? Should one never act in such a way as to ignore or overturn what has gone before? On a less stringent view of precedent, one looks for the closest analogy to the case at hand—not simply in terms of the facts of the case itself—but also considering how the parties are affected, what concepts of equity and justice might require, and what the future impact of the decision might be on the larger society or legal system. Another issue that supports a broader view of precedent is the fact that precedents are often imprecise (it is not clear how the past decision applies to the present case) or there may be situations where more than one precedent might apply. In such cases, judges must try to decide which precedents ought to be followed or how they ought to be applied and interpreted in terms of the present case. This cannot simply be a case of applying a past decision as if it were a strict rule or formula, but must be done taking into account the function of the law and larger considerations of justice.

Furthermore, there may be cases that seem to have no clear precedent or in which the precedent is viewed not to apply. Past precedent

---

[8] Post, "*Stare Decisis*," 21.

can be and is overruled when circumstances seem to warrant, but this is not to be taken lightly since it can unduly undermine the stability, coherence, and predictability of the law. Precedent is to be taken as a guide and absence of a precedent does not bar a decision. C. Gordon Post observes, "The fact that there is no precedent is not conclusive. The law would be an absurd science were it founded on precedent only."[9] Just as in life, past experience is a guide, but we also may have situations where experience is not entirely helpful and we have to rely on other kinds of resources to make a decision—reason, logic, norms, and ideas (e.g., equity and justice). Consequently, we use precedent in the law as a guide about what worked in the past—looking at analogous situations in similar ways for the sake of efficiency, coherence, and predictability, but also recognizing that we may have to overturn past experience or take a new approach if circumstances warrant.

To return to the objection at the beginning of the section, while it is *possible* that there are some situations that are entirely novel, it is unlikely that there is any situation where we cannot find at least *some* analogies with what has happened in the past, with *some* parallels that we might draw from past situations. Clearly there is no such thing as a perfect precedent (because otherwise it would be the exact same situation and we would already know what to do), which is why there are debates about which precedents ought to be applied in a given case and shades of interpretation about the various ways that a particular precedent could be seen to apply to a new case. If we are going to look at the problem of the detainees at Guantanamo Bay as a legal issue, then the first course seems to be to look at analogous cases and see if there are past circumstances that might shed light on the present issue and if there are, to what degree they can apply to the present case. It is certainly possible that the analogies are not close enough to be applicable or that the precedent of the past needs to be overruled, but we would need to make a compelling case for this, rather than simply asserting the necessity for a new rule without any reference to what has been done before.

III. Analogies to Consider: American Revolutionary War, U.S. Civil War, and Vietnam

If we ought to consider analogies in examining the treatment of the detainees at Guantanamo Bay, what might they be? Recall that aside

---

[9] Post, "*Stare Decisis,*" 26.

from members of regular armed forces (either of a recognized or unrecognized state), Article 4 of the Geneva Convention articulates that members of other groups had to (1) be commanded by one responsible for subordinates, (2) wear a fixed, distinctive sign recognizable at a distance, (3) carry arms openly, and (4) obey the laws and customs of war. Where are there analogies for how to treat "terrorists" who do not seem to fit this picture of the enemy soldier, in a conflict that does not seem to bear any resemblance to past "wars," and under circumstances in which the normal rules of engagement (international law, the Geneva and Hague Conventions, and military custom) do not seem to apply?

In this section we will look at three cases that do not seem to meet the usual parameters of conventional warfare waged by conventional soldiers against other soldiers of conventional nation-states: the American Revolutionary War, in which a new and unrecognized nation was at war with its colonial parent; the American Civil War, in which part of the nation seceded and went to war against former compatriots; and the Vietnam conflict, in which regular and guerilla forces fought against their French colonial parents and later, their allies the Americans. In all of these cases, one might raise questions about whether (1) these groups would meet the requirements of international law and custom for prisoners of war; (2) the United States was required to give prisoner of war status to these captured combatants; and (3) if they did, why they did so—on the basis of what law, statute, custom, or precedent.

Consider first the American Revolutionary War. The American forces (mostly militias) were in rebellion against the regular army forces of Great Britain, which had been their colonial parent. While France eventually recognized the autonomy of the new nation (and provided material support), Great Britain (and other nations) did not. While the kind of warfare could generally be seen as conventional, the American militias used strategies that violated eighteenth-century customs of war, such as what in the twentieth century has been termed "guerilla warfare," and that were censured by the British as dishonorable. Much like later guerilla-type groups, they used the geography of the land to their advantage and when possible relied on ambush, strategy, and hit and run tactics to redress the fact that they were out-equipped (including the issue of uniforms) and out-manned. There were battles that would have looked much like the conventional warfare of the time, but conventional battles can and have been a part of other conflicts in which guerilla warfare is used effectively.

How was the issue of captured enemy combatants handled? Apparently, the American states and their militias tried to observe the customary rules of international law in this regard, while the British varied between observing the customs of war and what was considered acceptable in quelling a domestic disturbance (standards lower that the treatment to be accorded to prisoners of war).[10] Both sides apparently observed that the customary rule that prisoners of war cannot be required to perform labor directly harmful to their state of origin (this rule was also observed during the U.S. Civil War). The American Congress permitted captured officers to have their liberty on parole, but not those of inferior rank—as was international custom at the time. Congress provided all officers on parole with freedom (sometimes more freedom than Great Britain allowed captured officers), while Britain allowed American officers the same freedom while in England and more liberal freedom in returning home.[11]

General Washington reported to Congress in 1776 that it was international custom for prisoners of war held by England and France to be maintained by a commissary who contracted for their support and that officers on parole were allowed to negotiate their own bills of exchange.[12] Accordingly, in one of the first Congressional resolutions on the issue, it was provided that British prisoners captured in New York would be maintained at the expense of the Crown. In the same year, it was reported to the American Congress that American prisoners in British hands were allowed insufficient food, so arrangements were made to maintain these prisoners at American expense. Despite this, there was conflict and controversy over the issue since American prisoners continued to be maintained at levels that were lesser than those for contemporary French, Spanish, or Dutch prisoners—including lower rations and no way to supplement the allowances. In addition, when Great Britain did not supply her own prisoners in American hands, Congress resolved to give the same rations to the British prisoners that they British gave to American prisoners, making up for deficiencies when British supplies fell short of these requirements.[13]

---

[10] William S. Flory, *Prisoners of War: A Study in the Development of International Law* (Washington, DC: American Council on Public Affairs, 1942), 17ff.

[11] Flory, *Prisoners of War*, 117.

[12] Flory, *Prisoners of War*, 51ff.

[13] Flory, *Prisoners of War*, 62ff.

In the case of the American Revolutionary War, for the most part, both the Americans and the British followed international customs (since there were few codified statutes at the time). If anything, it was the British who might be accused of not treating American prisoners of war as well as they should have (despite the fact that they generally accorded prisoners customary treatment). The scandal caused by the discovery of the mistreatment of American sailors aboard British prison ships demonstrates the expectation on the part of the public as well as the American government and military personnel that these customs would be followed by both sides. That such treatment was largely accorded by both sides is significant since the British might have taken the position that the Americans were British citizens in rebellion, and therefore guilty of treason, and treated them accordingly. However, they did not and for the most part accorded them prisoner of war status and treatment.

On the American side, leaders might have argued that since Britain did not recognize the United States as a sovereign nation, the Americans were not required to adhere to international customs of war in dealing with British prisoners. However, very early in the war it *was* made clear that prisoner of war status and treatment would be accorded to the British. Further, the Americans went beyond the custom of the day (that each nation pay for the maintenance of their own prisoners of war) and provided support for British prisoners of war when the support given by Britain was insufficient to meet international customary treatment—a fact made all the more significant by noting that this was a new and financially struggling nation.

By the time of the U.S. Civil War, many of the practices that were merely customary in the Revolutionary War were in the process of being codified and made into international statutes. The Treaty of 1785 between the United States and Prussia was one of the earliest codifications of these customs and became important in making specific these practices. Another major innovation was the Lieber Code, which was the first comprehensive codification of customs of war, especially in regards to the treatment of prisoners of war.[14] This code and its principles of military necessity were applied in 1868 to the ban of explosive bullets on the grounds of causing unnecessary suffering, adopted in 1870 as policy for the Prussian government during the Franco-Prussian war, and formed the basis of the Brussels Declaration in 1874 which in turn influenced the Hague Conventions of 1899 and 1907 (the basis for

---

[14] Flory, *Prisoners of War*, 18.

contemporary rules of war).[15] In addition, it was Lieber himself, an abolitionist and Union backer, who gave the U.S. Army guidance on the treatment of Confederate prisoners and the handling of guerilla and other irregular forces. He argued that the federal government could, according to the laws of war, accord Confederate soldiers prisoner of war status on humanitarian grounds (belligerency status) without recognizing the legitimacy of their government.[16]

The Lieber Code specified standards of confinement that were humane, but also compatible with safety, and forbade the subjection of prisoners to conditions not necessary to their maintenance (such as torture).[17] While the rule on rations (that rations given prisoners of war should be similar to military rations of the "detaining state") was endorsed in principle by both sides, in practice the Union did not provide the same rations as the Confederate side (who generally observed by the rule and supplied the same rations to Union prisoners as they did to their soldiers). Despite these problems, one of the most extensive uses of parole may have been during the U.S. Civil War; Union and Confederate prisoners of war were regularly discharged on parole ten days after capture.

However, both sides found problems with the other side's treatment of prisoners of war, and their criticisms led to changes in the Geneva Convention (1864) and to what might be considered the first war crimes trial: Andersonville. At Andersonville in Georgia, Union prisoners of war were held in conditions that were a terrible blot on the Confederacy; there was an unsurpassed record of depravity, disease, and atrocities and an unparalleled mortality rate.[18] Union officials accused the Confederacy of violating the laws of war, namely, of impairing and injuring the health and destroying the lives of about 45,000 Union prisoners of war at Andersonville, Georgia by subjecting them to torture and great suffering, confining them in unhealthy and unwholesome quarters, exposing them to the inclemency of winter and the burning suns of summer, compelling them to use impure water, and furnishing insufficient and unwholesome food.[19] In the

---

[15] Burrus M. Carnahan, "Lincoln, Lieber and the Laws of War: The Origins and Limits of the Principle of Military Necessity," *American Journal of International Law* 92, no. 2 (April 1998): 215.

[16] Carnahan, "Lincoln, Lieber and the Laws," 214.

[17] Flory, *Prisoners of War*, 57.

[18] John McElroy, *This Was Andersonville*, edited by Roy Meredith (New York: McDowell Obolersky Inc., 1957), xx–xxi.

[19] McElroy, *This Was Andersonville*, 339.

trial it became clear that this horrendous situation was not merely due to neglect or negligence, but also was the calculated design of two men, Werz and Winder. Moreover, there was no military reason for this kind of treatment—no military advantage that could be said to accrue to subjecting Union soldiers to such conditions.

The scandal and outcry raised in the wake of Andersonville, like that following the mistreatment of American sailors during the Revolutionary War, indicates the extent to which the customs of war, especially in the codified form of the Lieber Code (1863), were expected to be followed. If we look at the letter of the law (or a strict interpretation of custom), the Union side might have argued that to treat the Confederate prisoners of war well would be to legitimize the rebellion and secession of the Southern states. After all, these citizens were in rebellion and ought to be treated as those who had committed treason. However, as noted above, the Union (at least in principle and to a lesser degree in practice) did accord the Confederate soldiers prisoner of war status and treatment. Even more interestingly, the Confederate side, like the Americans during the Revolutionary War, could have argued that since the Union did not recognize them as a legitimate state, they were not obliged to respect the Lieber Code (which was Union policy) or other rules of war. The blot of Andersonville notwithstanding, the Confederate side did not take this tack and accorded prisoner of war status and treatment to the Union combatants they captured.

What about more contemporary examples? One could argue that the above two examples do not tell us much because both sides generally accepted the customs of war, codified or not. In addition, much of the warfare in both of these conflicts was what we might consider "conventional," as opposed to the sustained guerilla warfare (with a few "conventional" engagements) of Vietnam. Vietnam seems to be a closer analogy to the so-called War on Terrorism than the Revolutionary War or the Civil War are, since the Vietnamese were explicit about their use of nonconventional means of warfare and their rejection of the traditional laws and customs of war. It was alleged by those in both U.S. military and civilian circles who wanted to abandon or modify the Geneva convention that the Vietcong did not wear uniforms (but rather the notorious black pajamas), did not have a standard command structure (being organized into small groups of three to nine men), did not carry arms openly, and did not adhere to the rules and conventions of war. Let us consider in detail the U.S. military treatment of Vietcong soldiers, especially the irregular forces.

First, some definitions and distinctions will be helpful in clarifying the nature of the different Vietnamese groups that were involved in the conflict. The term Vietcong was used to delineate Communist forces operating in South Vietnam and included all of the following: National Liberation Front of South Vietnam, People's Liberation Armed Force (PLAF), Communist Party of South Vietnam (People's Revolutionary Party), and People's Army of Vietnam (PAVN).[20] The National Liberation Front of South Vietnam was a communist front organization headed by a central committee with elements down to the village level; there were twenty "independent" organizations with a total membership estimated between 200,000 and 300,000. The People's Liberation Armed Force (National Liberation Front Army) included a main force (the "hard hats," which comprised a full military force) and various paramilitary forces, which were guerilla in nature. The Regional and Territorial units were bands of guerillas that operated full time as guerillas, while there were also local guerilla groups who farmed in the day and operated as guerillas near their homes at night.

According to Annex A of Directive Number 381-46 (December 27, 1967), which laid out the Criteria for Classification and Disposition of Detainees, detainees whose status has yet to be determined are ". . . entitled to humane treatment in according with the provisions of the Geneva Conventions."[21] In several places this document states that such detainees are entitled to Article 4 (Relative to the Treatment of Prisoners of War) Geneva Convention protections until their status has been determined by a competent tribunal. It is also made clear that the U.S. views the Vietnam conflict as international in character, and, accordingly, the Geneva Conventions do apply. It further indicates that the United States bears responsibility for making these determinations and that detainees are not to be transferred (to the Government of South Vietnam [GVN], for instance) until such a determination has been made.

Further, detainees will be referred to a tribunal when (1) they have committed a belligerent act and (2) either there is doubt as to their status, or a determination has been made of non–prisoner of war status (NPW) and the detainee or his advocate claims he is entitled to

---

[20] Douglas Pike, *The Viet Cong Strategy of Terror* (Saigon: U.S. Information Agency, 1970), 1970), 121.

[21] Charles Berans and Jerome Silber, "Contemporary Practice of the United States Relating to International Law," *The American Journal of International Law* 62, no. 3 (July 1968): 766ff.

prisoner of war status.[22] The document also lays out the rights of detainees, which include right to counsel and an interpreter and most importantly, that ". . . no person may be deprived of his status as a prisoner of war without having had an opportunity to present his case with the assistance of a qualified advocate or counsel."[23]

Prisoners of war were defined as those belonging to one of the following categories: the Vietcong (Main Force and Local Force), North Vietnamese Army regulars (NVA), and irregulars including full-time guerilla units that operate outside their home area, self-defense forces that operate in their home area, and secret self-defense forces that operated in Government of Vietnam–controlled areas.[24] VC and NVA soldiers were accorded this status by their membership in these organizations, and irregulars were accorded this status if they were captured engaging in combat or other belligerent acts or could have been proved to have done so (excluding acts of terrorism, sabotage or spying). Non–prisoner of war status was accorded to the those who were entitled to PW status, but were subject to trial by GVN for offenses against the law; those who were members of irregular guerilla units detained while not actively engaging in combat or belligerent actions or where it could not be proved that they had done so; those suspected of spying, sabotage, or terrorism; those who voluntarily submitted to GVN control; and innocent civilians.

Despite the fairly clear policies in this document, in addition to the Geneva Conventions and other U.S. policies, questions were raised about whether (and to what extent) American troops should follow the laws of war, and whether doing so would put them at a combat disadvantage. It was alleged that the VC irregulars (and sometimes others) did not wear uniforms regularly or in the sense required by the rules of war; sometimes they wore NVA uniforms or, more often, the "black pajamas," and at times they dressed as peasants—with nothing to distinguish them from civilian noncombatants in the area. It was also alleged that, on a regular basis, the VC did not follow the rules of war—engaging instead in guerilla tactics, sabotage, terrorism, and misinformation, and preferring to avoid the larger "conventional" engagements.[25] Finally, a great deal was made (espe-

---

[22] Berans and Silber, "Contemporary Practice," 769.

[23] Berans and Silber, "Contemporary Practice," 771.

[24] Berans and Silber, "Contemporary Practice," 767.

[25] George K. Tanham, *Communist Revolutionary Warfare: From the Vietminh to the Vietcong* (New York: Praeger, 1967), 136ff.

cially in the American press) of the treatment, or rather mistreatment, of U.S. prisoners of war, claiming that they were subjected to conditions (notably torture) prohibited by the Geneva Conventions.

What happened in practice? While the official policy was to accord prisoner of war (POW) status to captured VC (even irregulars), clearly the results in the field were mixed—largely because of the practical and logistical issues involved in fighting a guerilla enemy and the sense that "the other side isn't playing by the rules, so why should we?" It was this second issue that came into conflict with a long precedent of at least attempting to uphold international law and the customs of war when news of the so-called My Lai massacre hit the American press.[26] What should be made of the reaction to what happened at My Lai? For one thing, it did show the public and policy makers the practical difficulties inherent in upholding such standards in "unconventional" warfare, but it also showed the moral, legal, and political consequences of not doing so. At the time, the argument was not so much that these standards did not apply (that the Geneva Convention was not relevant or applicable, in a legal sense, to this conflict), but rather that it was practically impossible, unrealistic, or militarily disadvantageous to carry out what these laws and conventions required given the field conditions faced in the Vietnam conflict.

In spite of the controversy, one of the major results of the trials in the wake of My Lai was a revolution in how the U.S. military trained its soldiers (especially the enlisted); their training now included clear, specific instructions in the Geneva Conventions that concerns the treatment of captured POWs and enemy combatants.

IV. Conclusions

What conclusions can we draw from the above discussions? In all of the above situations, despite the fact that the U.S. could have argued that it was not required by the letter of international law or the customs of war to accord POW status to captured enemy combatants, it did so. Further, it did so in cases where it was not convenient or advantageous (financially, politically, or militarily) and where not doing so could have provided a clear advantage—notably in the case of Vietnam.

---

[26] For a fuller discussion of what happened at My Lai, the impact on those soldiers involved, on American society and the Vietnam conflict, see Michael Bilton and Kevin Sim, *Four Hours in My Lai* (New York: Penguin, 1993).

Given the fact that the U.S. was not required by *statute* or *custom* to accord prisoner of war status and treatment to these enemy combatants, what accounts for the fact that they followed this course? It is my claim that it is precedent that accounts for this consistency, even in cases that did not seem to fit the conventional model of war and thus may not seem to be directly analogous to cases where POW status was automatically accorded. In all of the cases it is clear that the public, critics, and policy makers (both military and civilian) raised questions and that policy determinations had to be made; this suggests that it was not automatically clear what should be done about prisoners of war who did not fit the usual conventions and traditions. There was a public discourse of sorts (admittedly quite limited) about how the American military would treat these persons.

Even if one were to reject the examples and arguments from the American Revolutionary War and the U.S. Civil War as following antiquated ideas of chivalry and customs of war (that the precedent appealed to in those cases can no long be seen to apply), the example of Vietnam presents a clear and specific precedent as to how enemy combatants who do not meet the four criteria of Article 4 should be treated. However, this precedent was not followed (or even mentioned) in the present case. Why not?

First, if one wants to argue that the precedent (even of Vietnam) does not apply in this case, one needs (as judges who overturn a prior precedent must) to provide an argument and compelling reasons as to why the precedent ought to be rejected; this can also mean "rejected," not just for this case, but for future cases—in effect generating a new precedent. Why should this precedent be overturned? What is the argument for the new precedent? Failing to address this issue risks a great deal—treating the law as a function of power and whim rather than of reason, predictability, and coherence. Second, the wording or the application of the *statute,* while not irrelevant, does not get at this issue—precedent is also part of the law.

In looking at precedent we need to look for analogous situations (just as we did in the case of the North African dinner party described above) and see what was done and why. While there are some analogous elements to all of the cases discussed above, Vietnam seems to have the most analogous points since it was a conflict in which there were both regular (NVA, some VC) and irregular (VC) troops. In the case of the Guantanamo Bay detainees, the regular forces might be the Taliban, and the irregular forces, some of the Taliban and the Al Qaeda members. The same issues that the Bush administration raised with regard to the Taliban and Al Qaeda were also raised during the Vietnam conflict. And yet, POW status was extended during Vietnam to even irregular VC as a matter of policy, and to some degree in practice.

Given these similarities and the clarity of the precedent from Vietnam, I would argue—in the absence of a clear case as to why the precedent does not apply or should not be followed—that a similar policy can and should be followed here. This means that POW status could and should be accorded to all categories of enemy combatants (regular and irregular) with the one exception that was allowed in Vietnam—sabotage, terrorism, or spying—which would clearly exclude many of the detainees with whom the Bush administration seems most concerned. Bringing this exception to bear on the present case also undermines the Bush administration's claim that there is no precedent for dealing with terrorists—at least in the case of Vietnam, there is a clear and specific one. In addition, the status of all the detainees must be determined in accordance with the procedures set up during Vietnam (Article 5 tribunals).

Why? What is the argument for following that precedent? To address this question, I want to echo a line of argument quoted by Kenneth Anderson in his article "What To Do With Bin Laden and Al Qaeda Terrorists: A Qualified Defense of Military Commissions and United States Policy On Detainees at Guantanamo Bay Naval Base": "The United States government could have pursued terrorist suspects by traditional law enforcement means, in which case the Geneva Conventions would not apply. . . . But since the United States government engaged in armed conflict in Afghanistan—by bombing and undertaking other military operations—the Geneva Conventions clearly do apply to that conflict."[27]

To this point, I would add that if the United States chooses, as it has, to use the tools of war in dealing with terrorists, then international law and the rules of war (not just the Geneva Conventions) must be followed; this includes not just following the particular statutes involved, but also means following legal precedent unless a case can be made for a new precedent.

---

[27] Kenneth Anderson, "What To Do With Bin Laden and Al Qaeda Terrorists: A Qualified Defense of Military Commissions and United States Policy On Detainees at Guantanamo Bay Naval Base," *Harvard Journal of Law and Public Policy* 25 (Spring 2002): 628.

We (I say we because the Bush administration does and says what it does on my behalf as a U.S. citizen) cannot abandon the laws of war (either statute or precedent) simply because (1) the letter of the statute might be seen not to apply—on a very narrow reading of that statute—though the spirit of the statute and precedent clearly do, and (2) we find it inconvenient or inhibiting to our conception of the war effort. If you live by the rules of war, you die by the rules of war. Any attempt to circumvent this raises disturbing questions about the extent to which and under what circumstances each nation gets to be its own arbiter of when and how international statute and precedent apply to them. It is hardly necessary to point out the very serious and wide-ranging consequences of such a view, especially when the United States is fond of appealing to international law, the rules of war, and moral norms in making its claims against groups like the Taliban and Al Qaeda, not to mention legitimate nation-states.

*   *   *

This chapter has attempted to address a lacuna in the discussion of whether prisoner of war (POW) status and treatment will be accorded to the Taliban and Al Qaeda detainees at Guantanamo Bay: precedent. I have argued that three cases, the American Revolutionary War, the U.S. Civil War, and the Vietnam conflict, all provide analogous points that we should look at in thinking about the present case. While the Vietnam case has the closest analogy (and several policy suggestions were made on the basis of the precedent from that conflict), all of the examples demonstrate that the United States has, even in cases where it was not required by the customs of war or international statute to do so, accorded prisoner of war status and treatment to enemy combatants captured in the course of hostilities. In formulating present and future policies regarding these detainees, the Bush administration needs to take into account not just what the letter of the international conventions and statutes say, but also what precedent indicates. If they determine that past precedent is not applicable and/or a new precedent is indicated, (like judges) they must give a clear and compelling argument and rationale for the change in precedent—as opposed to just asserting that it does not apply.

Counterterrorism: Torture

| 13 |
Terrorism and Torture

FRITZ ALLHOFF

1. Introduction

After the events of 9/11, the concept of torture has emerged as one that is both pertinent and provocative. National polls have shown that some Americans support torture in some situations, though the majority still stands opposed. Torture has not received a tremendous amount of discussion in the philosophical literature, though I suspect that the leftward slant of academia would, for the most part, ensure scant support for torture. In this paper, I would like to first discuss why torture is an important issue and then advance an argument that supports torture in limited cases.

The *Encyclopedia of Ethics* defines torture as "the deliberate infliction of violence, and through violence, severe mental and/or physical suffering upon individuals. It may be inflicted by individuals or groups and for diverse ends, ranging from extracting information, confession, admission of culpability or liability, and self-incrimination to general persuasion, intimidation, and amusement."[1] I think that this is a good definition. Notably, torture is not necessarily a form of punishment, though it could be—both deterrence and retribution theorists could advance arguments in its support. Rather, torture can also be used instrumentally in order to achieve important aims, such as the acquisition of important information.

This essay was previously published in the *International Journal of Applied Philosophy* 17, no. 1 (2003): 105–18. Reprinted by permission.
[1] L. C. Becker and C. B. Becker, eds., *Encyclopedia of Ethics* (New York: Routledge, 2001), 1719–20.

It is of course worth noting that torture is illegal in the United States and that no United States agency can legally engage in torture abroad.[2] As absolute as this policy stance seems, there are important questions regarding its implications. For example, if an American intelligence officer is standing quietly in the corner of a room while a foreign government official subjugates a terrorist suspect to torture, has the American government violated its mandate? Less hypothetically, American officials have admitted that the United States has transferred prisoners to the intelligence agencies of Jordan, Egypt, and/or Morocco, all of which are known for using torture as a method of interrogation. Reportedly, some of these prisoners have even been handed over along with lists of questions to which they might know the answers and whose answers would be valuable to the United States.[3] While the transfer might not always be accompanied by a list of questions, it would be very naïve to think that the United States would not welcome and has not accepted the information that resulted from interrogations by hostile interrogators, whether that information has been actively solicited by our government or not.

A related concern has to do with the definition of "torture"; while some practices might clearly violate our antitorture stance, there are others whose standing is less clear. A recent *Washington Post* article detailed American interrogation methods and quoted American officials who admit to the beating of prisoners, the withholding of medical treatment, and "stress and duress" techniques, such as sleep deprivation, hooding, and forcing prisoners to hold awkward positions for hours. Prisoners may be placed in environments which resemble those of hostile countries (e.g., Arabs may be distraught to observe an Israeli flag flying overhead), or they may be subjugated to interrogations to female agents—this is psychologically traumatic for men raised in conservative Muslim cultures. The officials have maintained that these practices, while certainly unpleasant, have neverthe-

---

[2] This is due in no small part to interpretations of the Eighth Amendment and its prohibition against "cruel and unusual punishment." I certainly have little to contribute to the legal interpretations, but it is worth noting from the outset that the forms of torture that I will end up endorsing are *not* ones that involve torture as punishment. Thus we may be able to quickly slide past this (legal) hurdle.

[3] "Ends, Means, and Barbarity," *The Economist*, January 11, 2003. While officials have claimed that fewer than one hundred prisoners have been involved in such transfers, thousands have been held with "American assistance" in countries which are known for brutal treatment of prisoners.

less fallen short of torture; they maintain that all treatments of prisoners is consistent with the Third Geneva Convention of 1949 which delineated acceptable practices of confinement and interrogation.[4] Despite the interesting legal and policy questions inherent in a debate regarding torture, I am more concerned with the morality of torture than with the legality of it but, insofar as legality tracks morality, if torture could be shown to be morally permissible then there might be cause for legal reform.[5]

2. The Conflict between Utilitarian and Deontological Approaches

One reason that questions about the moral permissibility of torture are so interesting is that the two leading schools of moral thought, utilitarianism and deontology, seem to disagree as to the moral status of torture. For all of the talk about the great differences between these programs, at the end of the day they seem to agree on most substantive moral questions. Torture is an interesting dilemma because the two groups not only would give different answers to the problem, but would *obviously* give different answers.

First, consider utilitarianism. The utilitarian argues that the right action is the one, out of those available to the agent, that maximizes total aggregate happiness. We could quite easily imagine a scenario wherein the disutility of torturing a captive (his pain, the discomfort of the torturer, expense, permanent negative effects to both, chance of negative events causally connected to torture, etc.) is outweighed, or even dramatically outweighed, by the utility of torture (information is provided that saves many lives and therefore garners all of the associative utilities). This utilitarian approach is most conspicuously displayed in the so-called ticking time-bomb cases that have been discussed by Michael Levin and Alan Dershowitz; they have both

---

[4] Dana Priest and Barton Gellman, "U.S. Decries Abuse but Defends Interrogations: 'Stress and Duress' Tactics Used on Terrorism Suspects Held in Secret Overseas Facilities," *Washington Post*, December 26, 2002.

[5] For example, Alan Dershowitz has argued for the legal sanctions of torture though "torture warrants" that would be issued by judges. See his "Is There a Torturous Road to Justice?" *Los Angeles Times*, November 8, 2001. There may, however, be reasons to think that even if torture were morally permissible, it should not be legally sanctioned. See, for example, Tibor Machan's "Exploring Extreme Violence (Torture)," *Journal of Social Philosophy* 21 (Spring 1991): 92–97.

argued that torture is *obviously* justified when it is the only way to prevent a serious and imminent threat.[6]

The utilitarian might not welcome this consequence and might argue that, as an empirical fact, such conditions as would be required to ensure these utility forecasts will never transpire (and thus his theory is not actually committed to torture). This is irrelevant since the point is merely that utilitarianism would, in some cases, support torture. It makes no difference whether cases are real or imagined; all that matters is the theory's commitment to the moral obligation to torture in some cases. The cautious utilitarian could also argue that I have presupposed act-utilitarianism when in actuality we should be rule-utilitarians (the right action is the one, out of those available to the agent, that accords with a rule that, when generally followed, maximizes happiness). Perhaps the general adherence to the rule "torture is wrong" is more likely than its negation to maximize happiness. Unfortunately, the problems with rule-utilitarianism are well documented; one only needs to ask whether rules have exceptions. Then, if the answer is yes, rule-utilitarianism collapses into act-utilitarianism and, if the answer is no, rule-utilitarianism really is not very utilitarian at all. I therefore find neither of these responses very effective and take it to be fairly straightforward that utilitarianism is, in some cases, committed to the moral permissibility and even moral obligation to torture.

On the other hand, deontology would seem to prohibit torture in all cases. Invoking Kant as the traditional torchbearer of this approach, we can see that torture would fail the categorical imperative test (whether applying the first or second formulation). Perhaps the easiest way to see this is by applying the second form, which states that we may only treat humanity, whether ourselves or others, as an end and never as a means only. By torturing a captive, we are treating him as a means *only* (e.g., towards the acquisition of information); he is certainly not being treated in a manner to which he would consent. Torture fails to respect him as an autonomous agent and constitutes an attack on his dignity.[7,8]

---

[6] See Levin's "The Case for Torture," *Newsweek*, June 7, 1982, which is a nice (albeit nontechnical) article the presents this view in somewhat more detail. See also Dershowitz, "Torturous Road."

[7] We could also see that torture would fail the law form of the categorical imperative. The maxim "I torture the captive" would yield a contradiction in will when universalized and compared with my standing intention, which would entail the desire that I, the torturer, not be tortured.

I think that because utilitarianism would, in some cases, support torture and because Kantian deontologists would, in all cases, reject it, torture has the position of being a very interesting concept for ethical inquiry. People no doubt have their allegiances to utilitarianism or deontology but, given the conflict, there is at least something to talk about and some forum within which to advance arguments to support one conclusion or the other.

3. What about Rights?

One way to try to quickly end the debate is to assert that people have rights and that torturing them violates their rights.[9] Insofar as these two claims are true, torture could be argued to be morally impermissible. Are they true? As a descriptive claim, people certainly do have

---

[8] Stephen Kershnar has argued that this appeal to Kant's second formulation is not enough to "override" the warrant to torture on the grounds of desert. If this is true, it would not affect my conclusion. However, the true Kantian would see dignity as an incommensurable value, and not one that merely provides a value that can be outweighed by competing considerations. Therefore I do not think that Kershnar's argument is likely to convince a Kantian; thus the tension with which I am concerned still remains. See his "Objections to the Systematic Imposition of Punitive Torture," *International Journal of Applied Philosophy* 13, no. 1 (1999): 47–56.

[9] Following Wesley Hohfeld's classic distinction, rights are typically broken down into four categories: claim-rights, liberties, powers, and immunities. A claim-right imposes duties on others. For example, if someone has a right not to be killed, then everyone else has a duty not to kill him. Someone has a liberty to do *x* if nobody has a claim-right against him doing *x*. But, unlike claim-rights, liberties do not confer duties on others. For example, I have the liberty to win a footrace; nobody has a claim-right against me winning the race but, at the same time, nobody (particularly the other racers) has a duty to let me win the race. Powers are abilities to change someone's rights status. Ministers, for example, can change the rights of a couple by marrying them—once married, their legal rights have changed. Immunities exempt one from certain powers. Thus someone may be given an immunity such that a judge (who has powers) cannot change that person's rights, such as through restrictions of liberties. Torture, if it violates rights, would violate claim-rights; the most sensible interpretation of torture would be that people have a right not to be tortured, which means that others have duties not to torture them. I suppose that torture could, in some senses, restrict liberties in that, while someone is being tortured, they lack the ability to pursue some ends that they would otherwise be able to. But violation of liberties seems to me to be a nonessential part of torture. We could, for example, imagine torturing someone in such a way that they were still free to exercise their liberties (or at least the majority), such as torturing while, at the same time, allowing the recipient the ability to walk around, talk to his friends, etc. Thus I take the substantial purported rights violation in torture to involve violation of claim-rights.

rights; in the United States these are most overtly delineated in the Bill of Rights. Even as a normative claim, most everyone agrees that people have rights, though the justifications for rights are certainly debatable.[10] Even John Stuart Mill recognized that utilitarianism needed to be able to accommodate a system of rights,[11] though many rights theorists would be unhappy with the derivative value that utilitarianism would assign to rights.

But does torture actually violate any right? Some people might think not. It could be argued that we forfeit whatever rights might protect us against torture once we engage in certain activities, such as terrorism.[12] The suggestion might be that through our complicity in terrorist activities, we give up certain protections (both legal and moral) that we might otherwise have had and, consequently, there exist no remaining rights which torture could be said to violate.[13] If this is true, that rights are the kinds of things that can be forfeited through certain circumstances, then torture would be substantially easier to defend since, given those circumstances, there would be no rights violations. Absent rights violations, appeals to the greater good could easily justify torture. There are, of course, questions as to what kinds of circumstances lead to forfeiture of rights, whether such forfeiture is partial or absolute (i.e., consists in forfeiture in some or all rights) and, if partial, which rights are the ones that are forfeited. These would be substantive questions that are certainly worth pursuing. But it is unnecessary to answer any of these questions if torture can be justified *even if* it violates rights—then the conditions and details of rights forfeiture are largely irrelevant.

So let us now presume that torture does, in fact, violate some right. I am not sure that this is always true (especially given complic-

---

[10] See, for example, Jeremy Waldron, ed., *Theories of Rights* (Oxford: Oxford University Press, 1984).

[11] John Stuart Mill, *Utilitarianism* (Indianapolis: Hackett, 1979), chap. 5.

[12] I will consider fighting terrorism (whether domestic or international) as the prototypical application of torture. The reason for this is that terrorist activity frequently consists in broad networks and derives from advance planning. The situations where I shall argue that torture is most appropriate involve these sorts of features. There are certainly nonterrorist situations wherein I would also support torture, and the choice to discuss terrorism should not be viewed as evidencing any ideological bent; I choose it merely for convenience and simplicity.

[13] There could be also be a more moderate position, one that I see instantiated in our legal system, that complicity leads to forfeiture of some, but not all, rights (such as the right to freedom, but not the rights to legal representation and due process).

ity in terrorist activities) but, if torture can be defended given its violation of rights, then it can certainly be defended when it does not violate rights. Thus it seems to me that this is the position that one wishing to argue for torture must consider; if successful in this endeavor then everyone should be persuaded, but if torture can only be successfully defended by supposing that it does not violate rights, then those who suppose that it does violate rights will not be convinced. The question then to answer is, supposing that rights are inalienable and are therefore never forfeited, regardless of the atrocities committed, can torture be justified?

I think that the answer is yes. The existence of a right, particularly a claim-right, provides a reason for someone not to commit a certain act against the possessor of the right. For example, if Smith has a right to life, then this right provides a reason for Jones not to kill him. For him to do so would be wrong because it would constitute a violation of Smith's right to life. But this reason is stronger than, or even incommensurable with, other reasons. For example, Jones could not justifiably say that, though he recognized that Smith had a right to life, he elected to kill Smith because of the tremendous pleasure that he would derive from the murder. The fact that Smith's death would bring Jones pleasure no doubt gives Jones a reason to pursue Smith's death, but this reason is rendered inoperative in virtue of Smith's having a right to life. To deny this would be to completely misunderstand the notion of a right.[14] In this sense, Ronald Dworkin has argued that rights are trumps because, regardless of what end Jones could realize from Smith's death, the fact that Smith has a right to life will always ensure that Jones cannot justifiably kill Smith.[15] Thus when the interests of one person come into conflict with the rights of another, the adjudication must always be decided in favor of the possessor of rights.

But what happens when rights come into conflict with each other? In this case, some right will necessarily be violated (recall that, for the sake of argument, that we are now assuming rights to be inalienable, so it will not do to suggest that, dependent upon circumstances, one of the two conflicting rights goes away). Imagine that a policeman comes across a gangster who is preparing to execute five people who

---

[14] Unless, of course, one were a utilitarian. Given that torture can easily be defended on utilitarian grounds, let us consider instead the (more traditional) nonutilitarian notion of rights.

[15] Ronald Dworkin, *Taking Rights Seriously* (Cambridge: Harvard University Press, 1977), ix.

witnessed the gangster's latest crime. The five victims are about to have their rights violated and the policeman can prevent these rights violations by shooting the gangster, though doing so would violate the gangster's rights. This situation yields a rights conflict: either the gangster will have his rights violated or else the five witnesses will have their rights violated. I take it to be fairly obvious that, in this situation, the policeman is morally justified in shooting the gangster (and moreover that he is morally blameworthy if he does not).[16]

What this shows is that there can be cases involving rights conflicts where one right has to be violated in order to prevent further rights from being violated. Now the application to torture should be apparent. Assume that a captive has knowledge that could prevent the deaths of innocent lives. Further assume that he is unwilling to divulge his information but could be coerced through torture. By violating his right not to be tortured, we can therefore ensure that the innocents' rights to not be killed unjustly are not violated. Even if all rights violations were equally undesirable (which is most likely not true) it certainly seems appropriate to torture the captive to obtain the information; not only are the innocents' lives saved, but rights violations are minimized. Even if you are not a utilitarian, this minimization of rights violations should seem attractive.[17]

Some people, most notably Robert Nozick, have nevertheless objected to this "utilitarianism of rights." Nozick has argued that rights violations are always unjustifiable, even if they are necessary to prevent further rights violations. Nozick thus conceives of rights as "side constraints," which is to say that rights are absolute and inviolable; no considerations or circumstances can warrant intentional assault on anyone's rights, regardless of the end being pursued (including minimization of rights violations overall).[18] This is cer-

---

[16] It would be very hard to argue with someone who wanted to dispute this conclusion, which I think that very few people would. Perhaps some deontologists would still maintain the wrongness of this act; I make some comments on the plausibility of this position below.

[17] Appealing to a minimizing of rights violations is not utilitarian, but is probably still consequentialist (though I do think that deontologists could find some merit to this approach, or even that it could be directly accommodated by their theories). This idea is worked out nicely in Amartya Sen's "Rights and Agency," in *Consequentialism and its Critics*, ed. Samuel Scheffler (Oxford: Oxford University Press, 1988), 187–223.

[18] Robert Nozick, *Anarchy, State, Utopia* (New York: Basic Books, 1974), 28–35. Alan Gewirth argues for a similar position in "Are There Any Absolute Rights?" *Philosophical Quarterly* 31 (1981): 1–16.

tainly a controversial thesis—many people think that if we really value rights, then the minimization of rights violations is more attractive than rights fetishism.

Nevertheless, two points can be made in response to Nozick's position. First, Dworkin has suggested that, in cases of rights conflict, we should look not at the explicit formulation of the right but rather to the values that suggested the right in the first place.[19] So, if individuals have a right to life, it is because life itself is something that is valuable and worth preserving. Given a conflict then, where the violation of one person's right (to life, let's say), could prevent the violation of five other persons' right to life, the values that led to the creation of the right to life would suggest violating the one in order to prevent violation of the five.[20] By considering why we would endorse rights in the first place (because we value the objects of those rights), it seems permissible to act such that the underlying values (and their associative objects) are preserved to the highest degree possible.

The second response that could be made to Nozick is more on his own terms. He asks, "Why . . . hold that some persons have to bear some costs that benefit other persons more, for the sake of the overall social good?"[21] This question is indicative of a concern about certain theories of rights, including utilitarianism, that would advocate violating the rights of certain (innocent) people so that others may benefit. I think that Nozick is certainly right in that this conclusion, if drawn, is at least prima facie undesirable. But, insofar as we are discussing whether or not to torture terrorists (among others), we do not have innocent people! I think that we can allay Nozick's concern by agreeing that we should not torture innocent people such that others may benefit, but by saying that complicity in terrorist activities con-

---

[19] Dworkin, *Taking Rights Seriously*, 191.

[20] This is, of course, much different from assuming that we should kill innocent people in order to harvest their organs to save the dying. Those that are already dying are not having any rights violated and therefore we could not violate the rights of the innocent "donor" in order to minimize overall rights violations (we would end up with one rather than zero). The case I discuss above closely approximates Bernard Williams famous Jim and the Indians case wherein the journalist is given the option of executing one Indian so that all of the Indians are not executed. (Williams even agrees that Jim should accept the offer, though uses this thought experiment as evidence against utilitarianism since he thinks the decision is not obvious, even though choosing to execute obviously maximizes utility). See J. J. C. Smart and Bernard Williams, *Utilitarianism: For and Against* (Cambridge: Cambridge University Press, 1973).

[21] Nozick, *Anarchy, State, Utopia*, 33.

stitutes a forfeiture of innocence. We certainly must admit that there is an important moral difference between torturing an innocent girl so that the sadist frees his hostage and torturing a terrorist who, through his own actions, has created a situation wherein someone's rights are being or will be violated. I think that this distinction is enough to allow torture of terrorists while still being responsive to the spirit of Nozick's concern.

As a final remark, it should also be noted that even Nozick, in a footnote, admits that it is an open question whether these side constraints are "absolute or may be violated in order to avoid catastrophic moral horror."[22] While it certainly seems to me that this admission compromises Nozick's stance, I could nevertheless grant that rights, in normal situations, could (or should) be understood as side constraints. However, many of the cases that I am interested in are precisely those in which rights would be violated in order to prevent catastrophic moral horror! So, while either of the two above responses might allay Nozick's concern, it is not altogether clear that his opposition would be very strong in the cases that I am considering.

Therefore, I think that a strong case can therefore be made for the idea that torture can be justified, even if it entails rights violations, so long as we find ourselves in such a quandary that rights will end up being broken whether torture occurs or not. In these situations, because some rights violation is bound to occur regardless, we might as well either serve the greater good or else aim to minimize the overall violation of rights (even in a way sensitive to Nozick's concern). Either goal suggests the permissibility of torture.

4. Under What Conditions Is Torture Morally Permissible?

In this section, I would like to try to lay out specific guidelines for when I think that torture is warranted. I propose four conditions, all of which must be satisfied to justify torture. Before listing these, I take it to be obvious that the captive should be allowed the opportunity to voluntarily disclose information (perhaps after worrying about the possibility of torture for a while) before torture is initiated.

First, I think that torture should only be used to retrieve information that could be used to prevent future threats from occurring. This

---

[22] Nozick, *Anarchy, State, Utopia*, 30. I would like to thank Michael Levin for directing me to this point.

restricts the scope of torture by eliminating two other commonly suggested potential usages: to force confessions and to deter crime.[23] There are, I think, good reasons to object to these usages. Forced confessions are highly unreliable; under severe duress people will often give false confessions (e.g., during the Spanish Inquisition). So there are not good reasons to believe that forced confessions are true. If the authorities are highly confident about the involvement, then a conviction in court should be easy and the confession would almost be superfluous (though perhaps expedient).[24] So it seems tortured confessions are, at worst, likely untrue and, at best, unnecessary.

Another option would be to torture criminals for the deterrent value—if prospective criminals knew that they might be tortured, then they might abstain from crime. First, it seems quite unfair to torture one person so that another may not commit a crime. But, second, it is unnecessary. If deterrence was all that mattered, then we could accomplish the same effect by creating a myth that criminals are tortured without actually torturing any of them. The results would be the same and nobody would have to endure the hardship. Assuming that the myth could be sustained and that there would not be risks for leakage (which I think to be reasonable assumptions), there is no need to actually torture anybody to accomplish a deterrent effect.

Information, however, seems to be an appropriate aim. The acquisition of information differs from both forced confessions and deterrence in a relevant way: torture may well be the only way to realize the goal. Forced confessions are unnecessary insofar as we have a judicial system that should be able to render the appropriate convictions. Deterrence merely requires the perception of torture, not actual torture. So the torture, in either of those cases, is unnecessary. But, it is very plausible that the only way to obtain the information that

---

[23] The *Encyclopedia of Ethics* also listed intimidation and amusement as purposes of torture. I take these to be obviously impermissible. A less common suggestion is that torture should be used for retribution. I do not really have any comments on this idea other than to point out that it hinges upon the plausibility of retributive theories of punishment, which I find to be lacking. However, if retribution can be defended, then torture on retributivist grounds would readily follow.

[24] If the evidence from which the authorities derive their certainty of the involvement is inadmissible in court, then perhaps the confession really is needed. Even in these cases, I think that forced confessions should be disallowed and, minus this alternative, I think that the authorities would work more diligently and prudently in obtaining the incriminating evidence.

would lead to the prevention of some future crime would be through torture; there exists no redundancy program in the sense that we have in the other cases. Perhaps the suggestion could be made that intelligence should pursue leads and might be able to thwart the crimes without anyone ever needing to be tortured. But empirically, especially once time constraints are considered, this reliance on intelligence is unwarranted and imprudent. Thus torture may, in fact, be the only way to acquire the important information, which is a reason to endorse its practice.

Second, there needs to be a reasonable expectation that the captive has knowledge of the relevant information. Torture cannot be permissibly used to "fish" for information. If, for example, we know that the captive worked in a building where terrorists were known to conspire, but that he was only a janitor and was therefore highly unlikely to have had access to any information that might be used to thwart terrorist activities, it would not be permissible to torture him. But if, on the other hand, reliable intelligence reveals the captive to have been intimately associated with those who likely planned a threat, torture would be appropriate. If the association is unclear or dubious, then torture should not be exercised (at least until further intelligence is forthcoming). Furthermore, there are pragmatic reasons for not torturing someone who is not thought to have the information—he may produce misinformation.

Third, there must be a reasonable expectation that the information that the captive has knowledge of corresponds to an imminent and significant threat. If the threat is temporally distant, there is no reason to pursue torture now. Between the present and the time that the threat becomes imminent, developments might take place that would render torture (in the present) unnecessary. For example, it is possible that the captive will have an ideological shift and no longer wishes to contribute to the terrorist act. If this is the case, he may voluntarily provide the information needed to stop the act. Also, it is possible that the threat is revealed through some other means (e.g., intelligence, the confession of someone else). It would certainly be better to wait for these further developments than to needlessly engage in torture. Similarly, the threat must be significant. A "terrorist act" that involves the destruction of an unidentified dog house certainly does not warrant a torture-laden inquiry to discern the location of the bomb. But, if we can reasonably assume that the captive knows the location of a bomb that is going to explode in some building at noon tomorrow, thus killing thousands of people, there would be both an imminent and significant threat and, given satisfaction of the other criteria, torture would be acceptable.

Fourth, there needs to be a reasonable expectation that acquisition of the information can lead to prevention of the terrorist act. If it is thought that the situation cannot be disarmed, even if the details are forthcoming, there is no reason to torture. For example, imagine that we know the captive has details concerning a bomb that will detonate an unoccupied building tomorrow but all of our bomb squads are already assigned to important projects (expensive, occupied buildings, let's say), then there is no reason to pursue the information. Similarly, if we know that the bomb will detonate in thirty minutes but we do not know where, there is no reason to start torture that will give us the answer too late.

So, I think that the conditions necessary to justify torture are: the use of torture aims at acquisition of information; the captive is reasonably thought to have the relevant information; the information corresponds to a significant and imminent threat; and the information could likely lead to the prevention of the threat. If all four of these conditions are satisfied, then torture would be morally permissible. For example, imagine that we have just captured a high-ranking official with an internationally known terrorist group and that our intelligence has revealed that this group has planted a bomb in a crowded office building that will likely explode tomorrow. This explosion will generate excessive civilian casualties and economic expense. We have a bomb squad prepared to move on the location when it is given, and there is plenty of time for them to disarm the bomb before its explosion tomorrow. We have asked this official for the location of the bomb, and he has refused to give it. Given these circumstances (which satisfy all four of my criteria), I think that it would be justifiable to torture the official in order to obtain the location of the bomb.

5. What Forms of Torture Are Permissible?

After arguing for the permissibility of torture under certain circumstances, something should be said as to which forms of torture should be allowed. There are certainly a wide range of (historically) practiced techniques, which can range from the mundane (e.g., food deprivation) to the creative (e.g., removal of fingernails). Perhaps some forms of torture are more permissible than others? Or maybe there are some that should be avoided altogether? The first obvious remark is that the inflicted torture should never inflict more than the minimum trauma necessary to obtain the desired compliance. For example, if someone would be willing to divulge important information after being deprived of his lunch, there is no reason to remove all his fingernails. So torture programs would necessarily be tailored to both the physical and psychological constitutions of the captives. These assessments no doubt present some epistemic burdens, but psychological profiling should reveal to within a reasonable margin what would be the minimum necessary.

Generally, I think that torture can be broken down into three categories: physical, psychological, and other-directed.[25] Physical torture involves an infliction of physical pain (or discomfort) with the intention of surpassing the threshold of the captive. Examples of this form would be electrical shock or drowning/suffocating. There is no doubt a psychological element to these forms (e.g., it is incredibly disconcerting to find oneself in the process of being drowned), but the primary assault here is on the physical constitution of the captive—the physical elements *lead* to the psychological elements. Psychological torture consists in assaulting the psychology of the captive. Bright lights, sleep deprivation, and harassment are all examples of this form. These techniques inflict a tremendous amount of psychological pressure without attempting to harm the body in any way; the psyche is targeted directly. I think that both physical and psychological torture, in all their forms, should be allowed, though I reiterate that only the minimum necessary to extract the information is allowed. This rejoinder, for all intents and purposes, effectively eliminates *any* uses of many of the so-called inhumane and brutal forms of torture.

The third category of torture, other-directed, occurs when someone other than the (primary) captive is tortured in order to coerce his cooperation. In the aforementioned discussions of both physical and psychological torture, it was assumed that the recipient of the torture would be the same person in whose compliance we were

---

[25] There are surely other useful ways to categorize forms of torture, but I find these to be intuitive and helpful for future discussion. We could also discuss tortures as acts (e.g., electrical shock) versus omissions (e.g., food deprivations), but I think that most of the interesting questions fall under which acts are permissible, so this distinction would be unilluminating. If one thought that the problem with torture was that it violated a sphere of independence that all rational beings have, we might want to talk of tortures as being invasive (e.g., sodium pentothal and other "truth drugs") versus noninvasive (e.g., bright lights). There is nothing wrong with any of these approaches, I just choose mine for ease and intuitive appeal.

interested. We could certainly imagine cases, however, where an effective way to reach the desired goal would be to torture someone close to the captive, most likely in plain view. Examples of this would be raping a terrorist's daughter or burning his mother. It is possible that such techniques would be highly effective, and that they might also be supported by considerations of prudence—if the bomb will explode soon, it would not do to go through a physical torture process wherein the captive continuously loses consciousness because of the pain.

I do not think that other-directed torture is morally permissible for two reasons. First, we return to Nozick's question: why should some people bear the costs so that others may receive the benefits? I argued earlier that the complicity of the former would be a good reason—they *created* the risk (or were party to its creation) and therefore are obviously not innocent bystanders. This complicity is certainly morally relevant. There are good reasons to think, however, that the innocent bystander should not have to endure torture so that we can coerce the terrorist. This bystander has not done anything to deserve the treatment, whereas the terrorist has.[26]

Secondly, and more satisfyingly, I think that it is highly unlikely that other-directed torture will ever be necessary. Given the availability of other forms of torture, and given the proviso that we should never torture more than the minimum necessary, other-directed forms will not need to be used. If the options are psychological torture by other-directed torture or direct psychological torture, the latter is certainly more desirable (why involve the extra person?), and I see no reason to think that it would be any less efficacious. Insofar as other-directed torture targets the psyche of the terrorist, and therein presupposes some likelihood of loss of resistance, I think that there must be some other path to this goal through some other form of psychological torture through less controversial practices.[27]

---

[26] The utilitarian, of course, might not care at all who is tortured, so long as the ends justify the means. I think this attitude is problematic, though I do not propose here to launch into a critique of utilitarianism. At a minimum, such a response would fail to respect the "separateness of persons" (in John Rawls's famous phrase) by treating people as utility containers rather than as distinct beings worthy of respect. See John Rawls, *A Theory of Justice* (Cambridge: Harvard University Press, 1971).

[27] We could, of course, lie to the terrorist and tell him that his daughter will be or is being raped in an attempt to gain disclosure.

6. Final Remarks

Although I have argued that, in some carefully delineated cases, torture would be appropriate, there are several reasons for caution. The only aim for which I have endorsed torture, retrieval of information, presupposes that torture could be employed to successfully retrieve information. As a matter of empirical concern, is this true? I have found no indication to think that it is not. Some people, particularly terrorist operatives, are trained to withstand torture, particularly as pertains to information extraction. Nevertheless, there is no evidence that anyone can resist torture-laden interrogations indefinitely; the psychological trauma and the degree of confusion are simply too severe. Two of the more famous torture cases, those of Guy Fawkes during the Gunpowder Plot of 1605 and of Abdul Hakim Murad, a Pakistani terrorist suspect captured in the Philippines in 1995, are illustrative. Fawkes endured many treatments, ranging from hanging by his wrists to the rack, and, within four days, gave up the names of his conspirators. Murad, however, lasted longer; despite having cigarettes extinguished on his genitals, sitting on ice cubes, and being nearly drowned, he remained mostly silent. But, when interrogators told him that he was being sent to Israel, he started talking out of fear of even worse treatments from Israeli interrogators.[28] Everyone has a limit and, given time, any information can be extracted. Experience seems to show that not even that much time is required—many prisoners disclose quickly. Obviously the interrogators need to know what the most effective techniques would be; this would allow them to extract the information more quickly and allow them to minimize the suffering of the prisoner—psychological profiling can go a long way toward addressing these concerns.

But there is a more substantial problem: misinformation. While we might be confident that there are ways to extract the necessary information, a greater concern has to do with the relevant information being masked by irrelevant, or false, information, some of which the terrorists have been trained to weave into their disclosures. This undoubtedly presents a serious problem, particularly as terrorists from the same cells might have the same misinformation which could serve to corroborate itself. Nevertheless, I do not think that this is a reason not to torture, just that there will be higher demands placed

---

[28] Peter Maass, "If a Terror Suspect Won't Talk, Should He Be Made To?" *New York Times*, March 9, 2003.

upon the intelligence community to filter through the acquired information. By checking interviews against other facts, they can hopefully go a long way toward figuring out what to trust and what to reject. However, the prospect of misinformation does complicate the situation.

In this paper, I have argued that torture is, under some circumstances, morally permissible. In doing so, I have not presupposed utilitarianism to be correct, but have argued that even other normative approaches would be able to accommodate this conclusion. The conditions that I have suggested must be met in order to allow torture are: pursuit of information, reasonable expectation that captive has the information, reasonable expectation that the information corresponds to an imminent and significant threat, and reasonable expectation that the information can be used to disarm the threat. There are, of course, substantive issues as to what constitutes reasonable expectation, but I think that we could settle these ostensively, or else be confident that we have made progress on the formal account. I have also stressed that, although I would support torture if these conditions were met, we should still be prudent to administer the minimum amount of torture necessary (measured both in terms of intensity and quality) that is necessary to achieve the desired goal. Hopefully this moderate position has both intuitive appeal and is theoretically attractive.

| 14 |

Torture Interrogation of Terrorists: A Theory of Exceptions (With Notes, Cautions, and Warnings)

WILLIAM D. CASEBEER

Introduction

Since September 11, there has been a groundswell of support among the general population (and even among some professional ethicists) regarding the need to permit torture interrogation of terrorists and suspected terrorists in certain cases. The arguments in *favor* of torture interrogation are usually consequential; they rely on the horrific outcomes of failing to torture certain kinds of terrorists (such as those who possess information about the planned use of weapons of mass destruction) for their moral force. The arguments *against* torture interrogation are sometimes consequentialist, but most often deontological; they usually rely on some conception of inviolable human rights and the duties that correspond to those rights for their persuasiveness.

Conflicts between consequentialist and rights-based moral theories are not new. Here, I use insights from previous attempts to meld utilitarian and deontic moral approaches into a coherent system to formulate a "theory of exceptions" that tells us just when it is morally permissible to engage in torture interrogation; such a theory will provide us with *principled exceptions* to absolute rights.[1] It closely resembles Michael Walzer's doctrine of "Supreme Emergency" in terms of structure and has four critical upshots. First, there are van-

---

[1] Nicholas Fotion calls this attempt to articulate just when we are permitted to do otherwise morally impermissible things a "theory of exceptions" (see his keynote address to the 2003 Joint Service Conference on Professional Ethics). I use his language here.

ishingly few circumstances wherein torture interrogation of terrorists would actually be justified; while they exist *in principle*, meeting the requirements of the exceptions theory proves very hard to do *in practice*. Second, owing to the extraordinary prima facie pressure exerted by the basic human right not to be used as a mere means, most exceptions (while morally permissible) nonetheless leave those involved in the decision to torture with moral "dirty hands." Third, owing to the epistemic difficulty of removing one's self from the exigencies of the circumstance, exceptions require dramatic oversight, and such oversight might have to be international in nature to be effective. Finally, most consequentialist justifications for the permissibility of torture neglect to consider the institutional and character-based harm that we do to ourselves when we actually attempt to build a system for torture interrogation that the utilitarian would find praiseworthy. Perversely, consequentialist justifications for torture interrogation require well-trained torturers who know where and when to apply pain, but establishing the institutions required in order to sustain such well-honed practice is fraught with perils that the utilitarian would condemn, all things considered.

I conclude that torture interrogation *is* permissible in tightly constrained circumstances, and that we should not rule it out *tout court*; nevertheless, in practice it will be practically impossible to justify any particular decision to act on an exception to the prohibition of torture interrogation of terrorists. Moreover, our decisions to act will require an oversight apparatus that is not presently in place and that may not be possible to create. Grappling with these issues may very well force us to articulate yet more clearly just what the common bond of *humanity* requires of us, morally speaking.

Preview

First, I'll briefly motivate an examination of torture interrogation before discussing its definition and previewing my methodology. I then examine (at a high level of granularity) utilitarian, deontic, and virtue theoretic aspects of the practice. I reconcile the viewpoints offered by the three major moral theories in a doctrine that parallels "supreme emergency." After laying out torture techniques along a spectrum of objectionability, I conclude that while, in theory, the requirements can be met, meeting them in practice is very difficult, and that we should keep in mind sundry "notes, cautions, and warnings" before condoning torture interrogation in real-world circumstances.

A word on terminology: when you first learn to fly an Air Force airplane, you are given a document called a "Dash One." This document contains all the procedures you need to study in order to safely fly the aircraft. It also contains: notes—important information to keep in mind as you operate the airplane; cautions—telling you what equipment could be damaged by following inappropriate procedure; and warnings—discussing an item that you ignore at the peril of serious injury or death. This paper constitutes a "Dash One" for torture interrogation, with notes, cautions, and warnings stringent enough such that we should think twice before we declare the practice airworthy at all.

Motivating the Issue

Since the tragedy of September 11, calls for torture interrogation of terrorists have come from unlikely places. According to one online poll conducted by About.com, 71% of those taking the poll approve of torture interrogation of a suspected terrorist (58% in all circumstances, 6% to prevent acts of terror and gain information about other terrorists, and 7% just to prevent upcoming terrorist action; n = 2514 as of February 2005).[2] When otherwise staunch defenders of civil liberties, such as Alan Dershowitz, argue that torture might be permissible and that courts should be allowed to issue torture warrants, we should take note.[3] There are indications that these sentiments resonate with government officials. For example, Cofer Black, the former head of the State Department's Counterterrorism Center, says, "There was a before 9/11, and there was an after 9/11. . . . After 9/11 the gloves come off."[4] A recent *Washington Post* article quotes a government official supervising the transfer of Camp X-Ray (Guantanamo Bay, Cuba) detainees as saying, "If you don't violate someone's human rights some of the time, you probably aren't doing your job. . . ."[5] The cover story for the January 9, 2003 issue

---

[2] About.com, Crime/Punishment Poll Results, http://crime.about.com/gi/pages/poll .htm?poll_id=2149603124&linkback=http://crime.about.com/library/blfiles/ blpoll-torturingterrorists.htm, accessed February 10, 2005.

[3] Alan Dershowitz, *Why Terrorism Works* (New Haven, CT: Yale University Press, 2002).

[4] Cofer Black, quoted in Dana Priest and Barton Gellman, "U.S. Decries Abuse but Defends Interrogations," *Washington Post*, December 26, 2002, A01.

[5] Priest and Gellman, "U.S. Decries Abuse."

of *The Economist* was about torture interrogation, as was that of the October 2003 issue of *The Atlantic Monthly*.[6] Given the positions of public intellectuals, government officials, and public interest in the issue, it is time for a serious reexamination of the moral issues surrounding torture interrogation.

Preliminaries and Methodology

What do we mean by torture interrogation? According to two major international treaties governing the practice, torture interrogation has a certain nature (severe physical or mental pain and suffering inflicted upon its victim), is accomplished by certain perpetrators (public officials), and has a certain aim (obtaining information or confessions).[7] In this paper, I limit myself to consideration of whether a government official should intentionally inflict pain upon a terrorist or suspected terrorist in order to gain information. I will not consider torture as a form of punishment, revenge, or character development—my focus is on torture *interrogation*.

In order to answer the question of whether there can be circumstances in which such a practice is justified, I draw upon three traditional tools of moral analysis (the "big three" moral theories of utilitarianism, deontology, and virtue theory)—I throw everything and the kitchen sink at this problem. This, then, is an exercise in moral casuistry (in the nonpejorative sense): "A resolving of specific cases of conscience, duty, or conduct through interpretation of ethical principles."[8] My analysis will not necessarily satisfy partisans of any of the major moral theories; my hope is that it is a reasonable attempt to accommodate our considered moral judgments about the permissibility of torture.

---

[6] Mark Bowden, "The Dark Art of Interrogation: A Survey of the Landscape of Persuasion," *The Atlantic Monthly* 292, no. 3 (October 2003).

[7] See the UN Declaration of Human Rights of 1948, or the UN Convention Against Torture of 1984, both of which the United States has signed (for a much more thorough review of the relevant international treaties and legal documents, see Love Kellberg, "Torture: International Rules and Procedures," *Occasional Papers*, no. 15 (Stockholm: Swedish Institute of International Affairs, 1998). In this essay, I am concerned more so with the morality of torture interrogation, less so with its legality.

[8] *Webster's Ninth New Collegiate Dictionary* (Springfield, MA: Merriam-Webster, 1987), 213. I hope I am not engaging in casuistry in the second sense of the term: "specious argument."

Substantive Issues

Utilitarian approaches to torture consider it in light of John Stuart Mill's "Greatest Happiness Principle," which states that right actions are those which produce the greatest amount of happiness (or prevent the greatest amount of unhappiness) for all sentient creatures, where by happiness Mill means the presence of pleasure or the absence of pain.[9] Famously, utilitarians come in two flavors. Act utilitarians think that the pertinent level of analysis for consideration of consequences is the individual action: with each action that you take, maximize happiness. Rule utilitarians, on the other hand, think that act utility is short-sighted; instead, we should find that set of rules or laws that, if followed, would produce the greatest amount of happiness, and follow them. Rule utility is the more popular form of utilitarianism among ethicists of that bent.[10]

An act utilitarian would license torture in certain circumstances. When an act of torture would, all things considered, maximize happiness or minimize unhappiness, then it should be done. The rule utilitarian would be more circumspect, as, on some readings, respect for "the rules" amounts to a de facto respect for the rights of individuals ("rights as rules," for example: your right to free speech is a reflection of the fact that in my hypothetical rule utilitarian rule set, I would have a rule that said, "Allow people to speak their mind, for all will be better off if we do so.") Even all but the most hardcore of rule utilitarians, however, would admit that the rules have exceptions and that they can conflict (as Mill himself believed).[11]

Some of the utilitarian considerations that would enter the picture include the short and long-term harm done to the prisoner, and the benefits of obtaining the information the prisoner is thought to hold (modulated by the likelihood of actually obtaining it). The scenario that is normally offered to support a utilitarian justification for torture interrogation is the (infamous) "ticking bomb" scenario: a terrorist has planted a bomb beneath a football stadium. There's not enough time to search the stadium to find it. If we torture the terrorist, he will tell us where the bomb is and we can defuse it before it explodes and

---

[9] See chapter two of John Stuart Mill, *On Liberty and Utilitarianism* (New York: Bantam Books, 1863/1993).

[10] See Brad Hooker's *Ideal Code, Real World: A Rule-Consequentialist Theory of Morality* (New York: Oxford University Press, 2003). Exemplars for each school include Peter Singer, an act utilitarian, and Richard Brandt, a rule utilitarian.

[11] See the last two pages of chapter two of Mill, *On Liberty and Utilitarianism*.

kills thousands of innocent people. In popular treatments, however, the utilitarian analysis usually stops after considering harm to the prisoner and benefits of gaining information.

This is an incomplete analysis, though, as we should also consider the costs and benefits of establishing the *institutions* necessary to enable effective torture. This includes the training and equipping of a professional torture force (sloppy torturers are not as effective at getting suspects to divulge the information necessary to realize the benefits of the interrogation), accomplishing the basic scientific research necessary to support effective torture practice, and oversight and review (so that the torturers really do torture only in the justifiable cases).[12] In addition, there are character-development issues that even the utilitarian should be concerned about: what of those involved in the professional torture interrogation unit? Will they lead healthy and complete human lives? What will the long-term psychological consequences of being a torturer do to their chances at achieving some measure of human happiness? Even when taking these consequences into account, though, it is conceivable that a utilitarian, particularly an act utilitarian, would permit torture interrogation in certain instances. I'll discuss this in more depth in a moment.

The second major moral theory, deontology, does not focus on consequences to ascertain the morality of an action; rather, it focuses on the nature of an action to judge its worth: does the action's very structure respect the rights of human being? Do we have a duty not to engage in torture interrogation, and do individuals have a right not to be tortured? Deontological approaches are concerned with respecting the existence of those things that make morality possible at all—the transcendental preconditions for there to be morality—namely, the existence of human free will and reasonability. Our agency gives us a dignity, Immanuel Kant would say, that is beyond price. Kant captures the demands of duty in one formulation of his "categorical imperative" (that thing which commands free and reasonable creatures unconditionally, at all times and places): "Never treat humanity, either in your own person or in the person of others, merely as a means, but always also as an end." [13] We avoid treating other humans

---

[12] For a thorough discussion of these issues, see Jean Maria Arrigo's paper "A Consequentialist Argument against Torture Interrogation of Terrorists," Joint Service Conference on Professional Ethics, 2003, United States Air Force Academy, http://www.usafa.af.mil/jscope/JSCOPE03/Arrigo03.html.

[13] See Immanuel Kant, *Grounding for the Metaphysics of Morals*, trans. James W. Ellington (Indianapolis, IN:. Hackett Publishing Company, 1785/1993), 36.

as mere means by getting their consent, either implicit or explicit, but in the best of cases explicitly, to involve them in our plan, project, or practice. Questions of consent are thus paramount.

Kant's theory of justice allows you to treat people as they, with their own maxims and principles, ask to be treated. In this way, Kant would say that the death of a combatant in a war, so long as such a combatant was willingly involved in the process required to wage war, is not necessarily a violation of the demands of the categorical imperative. But the consent we give in such ways is not unbounded; when I cease to be a combatant, I am no longer consenting to give up my life for the cause that I am defending.

The rights-based focus of a deontological perspective means that those looking to license torture must obtain the consent of those being tortured. Needless to say, it is implausible to think that terrorists have given such consent. They would not give it explicitly, and the implicit consent also seems to evaporate once they have been captured, as the terrorists are no longer combatants at that point.[14]

Setting aside issues of justice (recall that we are torturing in order to obtain information, not to punish), then, the tone of the Kantian corpus is difficult to reconcile with the practice of torture interrogation. Deontic approaches give us a prima facie argument against torture interrogation: it is a violation of human rights.

The third major approach to morality—virtue theory—is usually left out of discussions about torture interrogation.[15] In part, this may be because it is sometimes difficult to wring out public policy–related guidance to a particular moral issue using the virtue theoretic critical infrastructure. Virtue theorists such as Aristotle or Plato focus on *eudaimonia*, variously translated as flourishing or proper functioning.[16] What kind of person must I be if I am to live a fruitful human life wherein I fulfill the human telos or end—my function? Virtues are those states of being that enable us to be excellent human beings,

---

[14] Arguably, in any case. Much more philosophic work needs to be done here, and it may very well be that certain kinds of terrorists do not cease to be combatants in the logical and causal chain required to do harm to another when they are captured. For more discussion of this issue, see Jeffrie G. Murphy's seminal article, "The Killing of the Innocent," *The Monist* 57, no. 4 (1973): 527–50.

[15] See, for example, Henry Shue's excellent article "Torture" in *Philosophy and Public Affairs* 7, no. 2 (1978): 124–43, which does not discuss in any detail the virtue theoretic aspects of the practice.

[16] Consult, for instance, Aristotle's *Nichomachean Ethics* or Plato's *Republic*.

while the vices are those states which cause us to be dysfunctional human beings. What habits must I have if I am to flourish, and what kind of person, in the ultimate sense, do I want to become? While virtue theory might not have as a direct entailment that virtuous persons would *never* be involved in torture interrogation, that is at least a plausible first pass of its indirect entailment. Virtuous people are probably not involved in the intentional and coerced causation of pain and suffering in other human beings, at least not in ordinary circumstances. And if they are, they probably face a "dirty hands" problem (that is, even if torture interrogation is justified in certain exceptional circumstances, torturers may nonetheless be "damaged goods," so to speak, from a moral psychological point of view) in much the same way that (some would argue) those involved in warfare where innocents are killed may have dirty hands.

Virtue theoretic considerations speak most strongly against the maintenance of a professional torture force. To be the kind of person whose *techne* just is to skillfully apply pain to others for the purpose of forcing information from them is not a prescription for a complete and fulfilled human life. This is problematic, as the utilitarian would demand that the torturer be well-trained, skilled in the "profession," and precise in the application of pain—the utilitarian would not want excess pain to be generated, nor would torture that fails to cause the victim to reveal the information be praiseworthy. But these very skills require time and experience to develop, and it is exactly this aspect of the practice of torture interrogation to which the virtue theorist would have the strongest objection.

To summarize our "first draft" analysis, then: if there are reasons to torture, they will almost certainly be act utilitarian in nature. Act utilitarian considerations are important, but they should probably be "side constrained" (as Robert Nozick would argue) by deontic or rule utilitarian considerations. Nonetheless, what of exceptional circumstances? Is it really the case that I must respect a right though the heavens may fall? Other rights-based theorists have attempted to accommodate this intuitive objection from the utilitarian camp. In the case of war, Michael Walzer argues that while the innocent noncombatant has a right not to be killed, in certain exceptional circumstances we can justifiably violate that right. Walzer calls those exceptional circumstances cases of "supreme emergency." Can we articulate a parallel set of standards for torture interrogation?

Supreme Emergency for Torture Interrogation

In his book *Just and Unjust Wars*, Walzer argues that when a danger threatening a nation-state is of a certain nature, we can justifiably, but with regret, violate the rights of innocent people not to be killed in order to prevent it. The danger threatened must not merely be the loss of my life, or even that of a few hundred combatants or innocents; rather, it must be a grave danger that threatens the very existence of a nation-state, a political community, or a culture. The danger must be "supreme," and not merely run-of-the-mill. Moreover, this danger must be imminent, both spatially and temporally; if the danger is distant, then the likelihood that we can avert it without violating someone's rights increases dramatically. The "imminence" and "nature of danger" tests are framed against a backdrop of last resort, of course; if there is a way we can prevent the danger from occurring without violating human rights, then we are morally obligated to do so. In other words, respect rights until the heavens really are about to fall; but when they *are* about to fall, you may justifiably, but with regret, intentionally kill an innocent person or otherwise violate someone's rights. This bit of casuistry is designed to nod respectfully in the act utilitarian direction in those most extreme of circumstances.[17]

We can formulate a parallel doctrine for torture interrogation. It may help to think of a spectrum of torture interventions. At one end, we have as anchor torture interrogation methods that leave no lasting physical or mental damage and only minimally disable the human agency that deontic approaches remind us to respect.[18] At the other endpoint are methods that are catastrophic, leaving lasting physical or mental damage, and causing such severe pain that human dignity is crushed. Methods at the "no lasting damage" end might include such approaches as putting a hood over a suspect, bombarding them with noise, depriving them of sleep or of food (only minimally), or forcing them to stand before interrogation. These methods, for example, were used by Great Britain in the 1970s when questioning suspected Irish

---

[17] For a thorough discussion of supreme emergency, with enlightening historical examples, see Michael Walzer, *Just and Unjust Wars: A Moral Argument with Historical Illustrations*, 2nd ed. (New York: Basic Books, 1992), chap. 16.

[18] The hardcore Kantian may insist that agency is an all or nothing affair. I don't intend to engage in heavy deontic exegesis here; I rely on the commonsense intuition that some rights violations are much less serious than others, and that my free will can be disrespected in minimally disruptive ways and in maximally disruptive ways.

Republican Army members, and were called "the five techniques."[19] The threat of the use of force, or a lie told to encourage the divulgence of information, might also fall towards the "no lasting harm to agency" end of the spectrum. Of course, even these methods, when applied continuously over time, can become extremely cruel, at which point they would move towards the other end of the spectrum. Methods which fall on that end from the get-go include such things as catastrophic damage to the brain or to the sexual organs, the breaking of bones, or similar tactics that cause prolonged and intense suffering.

The "easy cases," then, will be those where the minimally threatening methods are used so as to prevent a catastrophic danger. Extremely mild "torture" interrogation might be morally required in those circumstances. But if the consequence to be prevented is mild, even they would be morally *prohibited*. On the extreme end of the spectrum, if the consequence prevented is mild, the tactics are again obviously morally prohibited. The truly hard case regards the use of torture interrogation techniques that drift away from the "no harm done" end of the spectrum but which nonetheless seem to be required to prevent a "supreme emergency"–style catastrophic danger from materializing. In those cases, I would argue, torture interrogation may be a morally justifiable tactic. Figures 1 and 2 make this clearer.

Figure 1. *Easy cases on the torture spectrum*

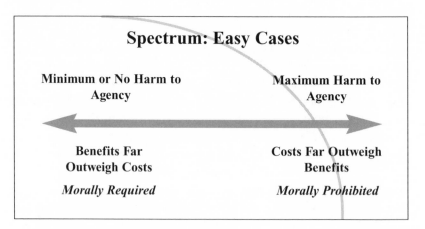

Spectrum: Easy Cases

Minimum or No Harm to Agency   Maximum Harm to Agency

Benefits Far Outweigh Costs   Costs Far Outweigh Benefits

Morally Required   *Morally Prohibited*

---

[19] See Gisli Gudjonsson, "Custodial Confinement, Interrogation, and Coerced Confessions," in *A Glimpse of Hell: Reports on Torture Worldwide,* ed. Duncan Forrest (New York: New York University Press, 1996), 206–10. The Forrest volume is a useful reference for facts about many aspects of torture interrogation.

Figure 2. *The hard case on the torture spectrum*

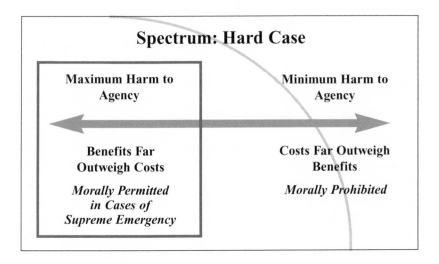

The Difficulty of Meeting the Requirements
in Practice

But note that meeting the requirements similar to those for "supreme emergency" is exceedingly difficult in practice. While we can envisage such scenarios arising theoretically, practically speaking we will almost never be confronted with them. First, note that usually it is only a *toy* ticking-bomb-style scenario that leads to a favorable cost-benefit analysis; when the oft-neglected institutional and character-based harms are included, it becomes more difficult to see when the practice could be warranted. Moreover, it will hardly ever be the case that a single act of terrorism will threaten the very existence of a nation-state or political community; the supreme emergency requirement will be difficult to meet. The imminence of the danger requirement will probably only be met in radically underspecified thought experiments like the ticking bomb scenario (indeed, the very intelligence that will enable us to know we are facing an imminent danger will also likely serve to give us means to discover the source of the danger without having to resort to torture interrogation). Finally, we will rarely be in a case of last resort. Other methods of intelligence collection will usually be available, and the efficacy of torture is doubtful in many circumstances (keep in mind that we are allowed to violate rights only if that will be an *efficacious means* to prevent the danger).

Notes, Cautions, and Warnings for a Theory of Exceptions

As we grapple with this attempt to articulate a theory of exceptions telling us when torture interrogation is permissible, we would do well to keep in mind the notes, cautions, and warnings implicit in our substantive analysis. *Note* that even when the exceptional circumstance is present, we have a "dirty hands" problem—we have violated human rights, and this makes even the exceptional circumstances problematic, morally speaking. Be *cautioned* that in order to prevent self-deception about whether we are in supreme emergency from occurring, and in order to jump the epistemic hurdles presented by these cases, torture interrogation will require oversight; such oversight will at the very least require the intervention of our judiciary and perhaps the Congress, and it may even have to be international in order to be truly effective. Finally, keep in mind this *warning*: if we are not careful, our attempt to train and equip for these exceptional circumstances can create a culture that permits the worst degradations to dignity know to humanity to be licensed by our political institutions and carried out by our fellow human beings. We should take a deep breath before creating such a culture.

Conclusion

Our attempt at reasonable casuistry about the problem of torture interrogation has brought us full circle. I have argued that it is possible to formulate a theory of exceptions for torture interrogation. This theory can be patterned after another attempt to reach a reasonable compromise between utilitarian and deontic demands: Walzer's doctrine of supreme emergency. However, the requirements for this test are stringent enough that while severe forms of torture interrogation might be permissible in certain circumstances, those circumstances will almost never present themselves in actual practice. For all practical purposes, the requirements will never actually be met. Our common bonds of humanity demand certain things of us, and while those bonds can be broken in certain extremes, there are practical and epistemic hurdles to be cleared before we can do so justifiably. Our "Dash One" for torture interrogation gives us reason to doubt whether our torture interrogation airplane can get enough altitude to clear those hurdles in all but theoretical circumstances.

Contributors

Fritz Allhoff earned an M.A. degree in philosophy in at the University of California at Santa Barbara, where he is currently a Ph.D. candidate. He is currently a postdoctoral fellow in the Ethics Institute of the American Medical Association. His areas of specialization include normative ethics, bioethics, and philosophy of law.

Richard C. Anderson served as an Assistant Professor of Philosophy at the United States Military Academy at West Point from 2001 through 2004. He earned an M.A. degree in philosophy from the University of Connecticut. His areas of interest include aesthetics, philosophy of science, Asian philosophy, and ethics and the use of force.

Michael Baur is Associate Professor of Philosophy at Fordham University. He earned M.A. and Ph.D. degrees in philosophy from the University of Toronto, and a J.D., *cum laude*, from Harvard Law School. He is the editor of nine books, and has published over twenty-five articles in scholarly journals and books.

Lorraine Besser-Jones is a postdoctoral fellow at Stanford University. She earned an M.A. from Claremont Graduate School, and M.A. and Ph.D. degrees from the University of North Carolina at Chapel Hill. She is a specialist in the areas of ethics and the history of ethics (especially Hume), as well as moral psychology.

Michael W. Brough is a Major in the United States Army and has taught at the United States Military Academy at West Point, where he was Assistant Professor of Philosophy. He holds a Master of Science degree from the University of Missouri, and an M.A. degree in philosophy from the University of Texas. His areas of specialization include normative ethics and the ethics of the use of force.

William D. Casebeer is a Major in the United States Air Force and Associate Professor of Philosophy at the United States Air Force Academy. He is currently stationed at the Naval Postgraduate School. He holds an M.A. in Philosophy from the University of Arizona and a Ph.D. in Cognitive Science and Philosophy from the University of California at San Diego. He is the author of a dozen papers on topics ranging from moral cognition to military ethics to arms control and virtual reality. His book *Natural Ethical Facts: Evolution, Connectionism, and Moral Cognition* was published by MIT Press in 2003.

Andrew Fiala is Associate Professor of Philosophy and Humanistic Studies at the University of Wisconsin, Green Bay. He earned an M.A. in philosophy from California State University, Long Beach, and a Ph.D. in philosophy from Vanderbilt University. He is the author of *The Philosopher's Voice* (SUNY Press, 2002), *Practical Pacifism* (Algora Publishing, 2004), and *Tolerance and the Ethical Life* (Continuum, 2005). He has written on Pragmatism, toleration, and just war theory, as well as on Hegel and nineteenth-century philosophy.

Trudy Govier is a philosopher, author, and public speaker who lives and works in Calgary, Alberta, Canada. She earned an M.A. in Philosophy from the University of Calgary and a Ph.D. in Philosophy from the University of Waterloo (1971). She has taught at Trent University in Peterborough, Ontario, at Simon Fraser University, and at the Universities of Amsterdam, Calgary, and Lethbridge. She is the author of ten books, including most recently *A Delicate Balance: What Philosophy Can Tell Us About Terrorism* (Westview Press, 2002), *Forgiveness and Revenge* (Routledge, 2002), *Dilemmas of Reconciliation* (edited with Carol A. L. Prager, Wilfrid Laurier University Press, 2003), and *A Practical Study of Argument*, 6th ed. (Wadsworth, 2005).

Liam Harte is Assistant Professor in Philosophy at Westfield State College in Massachusetts. He earned a Master of Philosophy degree from the University of St. Andrews, Scotland, and a Ph.D. from Loyola University of Chicago. A specialist in social-political philosophy, he has lectured extensively on globalization, terrorism, and social change.

Pauline M. Kaurin is Visiting Assistant Professor of Philosophy at Pacific Lutheran University. She holds an M.A. degree in philosophy from the University of Manitoba, and a Ph.D. in philosophy from Temple University. Her areas of specialty include philosophy of war, eighteenth- and nineteenth-century philosophy, and ethics.

Simon Keller is Assistant Professor of Philosophy at Boston University. He earned M.A. and Ph.D. degrees from Princeton University. His publications range from Plato to distributive justice to time-travel.

Brett Kessler is a Major in the United States Army and an Instructor in Philosophy at the United States Military Academy at West Point. He earned an M.A. degree in philosophy from the University of Colorado at Boulder. The title of his M.A. thesis was: "Justice and Terror: The Just War Tradition, Terrorism, and a Moral Response to 9/11."

Phillip McReynolds is Adjunct Assistant Professor of Philosophy at the Pennsylvania State University. He earned M.A. and Ph.D. degrees from Vanderbilt University. He has published on Pragmatism, the moral standing of nonhuman animals, and technological culture.

Timothy Shanahan is Professor of Philosophy and Chair of the Department of Philosophy at Loyola Marymount University. He earned an M.A degree in the history and philosophy of science and a Ph.D. degree in philosophy at the University of Notre Dame. He is the author of *Reason and Insight* (Wadsworth, 2003) and *The Evolution of Darwinism* (Cambridge University Press, 2004). He organized the conference "Understanding Terrorism: Philosophical Issues," September 11–13, 2003, at Loyola Marymount University, Los Angeles.

Daniel Statman is Professor of Philosophy at the University of Haifa, Israel. He earned a Ph.D. degree from Bar-Ilan University. He has authored or edited six books on such topics as moral dilemmas, virtue ethics, and moral luck. He is also the author of some forty articles on ethics, moral psychology, and the philosophy of law.

Index